TRADING BASES

TRADING BASES

---◆---

A STORY ABOUT WALL STREET,

GAMBLING, AND BASEBALL

(Not Necessarily in That Order)

JOE PETA

DUTTON

DUTTON
Published by Penguin Group (USA) Inc.
375 Hudson Street, New York, New York 10014, U.S.A.
Penguin Group (Canada), 90 Eglinton Avenue East, Suite 700, Toronto, Ontario M4P
2Y3, Canada (a division of Pearson Penguin Canada Inc.); Penguin Books Ltd, 80 Strand,
London WC2R 0RL, England; Penguin Ireland, 25 St Stephen's Green, Dublin 2, Ireland
(a division of Penguin Books Ltd); Penguin Group (Australia), 250 Camberwell Road,
Camberwell, Victoria 3124, Australia (a division of Pearson Australia Group Pty Ltd);
Penguin Books India Pvt Ltd, 11 Community Centre, Panchsheel Park, New Delhi – 110
017, India; Penguin Group (NZ), 67 Apollo Drive, Rosedale, Auckland 0632, New
Zealand (a division of Pearson New Zealand Ltd); Penguin Books (South Africa),
Rosebank Office Park, 181 Jan Smuts Avenue, Parktown North 2193, South Africa;
Penguin China, B7 Jiaming Center, 27 East Third Ring Road North, Chaoyang District,
Beijing 100020, China

Penguin Books Ltd, Registered Offices: 80 Strand, London WC2R 0RL, England

Published by Dutton, a member of Penguin Group (USA) Inc.

First printing, March 2013
10   9   8   7   6   5   4   3   2   1

REGISTERED TRADEMARK—MARCA REGISTRADA

LIBRARY OF CONGRESS CATALOGING-IN-PUBLICATION DATA

Peta, Joe.
    Trading bases : a story about Wall Street, gambling, and baseball (not necessarily in
that order) / Joe Peta.
        p. cm.
    Includes index.
    ISBN 978-0-525-95364-7
    1. Baseball. 2. Gambling. 3. Wall Street (New York, N.Y.) I. Title.
    GV867.3.P—dc23   2012043509

Printed in the United States of America
Set in Janson MT Std
Designed by Alissa Amell

While the author has made every effort to provide accurate telephone numbers, Internet
addresses, and other contact information at the time of publication, neither the publisher
nor the author assumes any responsibility for errors, or for changes that occur after
publication. Further, the publisher does not have any control over and does not assume
any responsibility for author or third-party websites or their content.

ALWAYS LEARNING   PEARSON

To Caitlin,

an 8 WAR wife, with a replacement-level husband

Contents

◆

Contents

PART THREE • SUCCESS

TRADING BASES

PART ONE

◆

THE MODEL

1

Manny Sanguillén Couldn't Find His Car Keys

It's the middle of the afternoon on March 31, 2011, Major League Baseball's Opening Day, and I have bets riding on four baseball games being played simultaneously. It's a Thursday, so the stock market is open, but I have no idea what the S&P 500 is doing. What I do know is that the Cincinnati Reds just scored four runs in the bottom of the ninth inning, making my first bet of the season a winner. This sets off a flurry of incoming texts and e-mails and causes me to wheel about with joy.

Opening Day marks the culmination of a month of writing baseball-related essays for my friends, but contrary to the stereotype of the statistics-obsessed, stay-at-home, male baseball blogger, I am neither clad in my boxers nor sitting in my mother's basement. In fact, when the year began, I occupied a seat on a Wall Street trading desk, just as I had for the previous fourteen years. I had signed a lucrative contract in the past year to trade technology stocks for a multi-billion-dollar Japanese investment bank.

While not a basement-dwelling blogger, neither am I the consummate Wall Street–trading, carefree Manhattan bachelor. I have a wonderful family. Eight years prior, I married a beautiful California girl and moved to San Francisco, where we chased our two tutu-clad daughters around a house overlooking the Pacific Ocean and the Golden Gate Bridge. So why am I sitting in a wheelchair 2,500 miles away, alone in a New York City apartment, unemployed and risking not only my money but my friends' as well?

Born in 1965, I grew up a sports-crazed child, like so many post–Baby Boomer boys. I devoured every word of the *Philadelphia Inquirer* sports section, collected baseball cards, treated the arrival of a new issue of *Sports Illustrated* like a weekly holiday, and played hours and hours of APBA baseball and Strat-O-Matic basketball simulation games, all of which eventually led my brain to become stuffed with random facts and trivia.

In some of those stories from *Sports Illustrated, Inside Sports,* and *Baseball Digest,* a fact referred to in passing often came to mean as much or more to me than the article's overall theme. I know I'm not alone. Gather a dozen or so forty-something guys and throw phrases at them like "Todd Marinovich never had a Big Mac" or "Wade Boggs ate chicken before every game" or "Sidd Finch could have joined the New York Philharmonic" and if they are sports-obsessed, they will know what you're talking about and can identify the complete story.*

Here's another: "Manny Sanguillén couldn't find his car keys."

Whenever I hear the name Roberto Clemente, the first thing I think is "Manny Sanguillén couldn't find his car keys."† On December 31, 1972, Roberto Clemente, of the Pittsburgh Pirates, one of the greatest right fielders of all time and the first ballplayer of Latin-American descent to be inducted into the Baseball Hall of Fame, boarded a plane in his native Puerto Rico to take relief supplies to victims of a devastating earthquake in Nicaragua. He invited his best friend, Manny San-

---

*In order, the primary theme of each story was actually: Marv Marinovich raised his son from birth with the sole purpose of developing an NFL quarterback. Wade Boggs may have been one of the best hitters of his era, but he also had some strange habits (see also: Adams, Margo). Finally, Sidd Finch, a multi-talented renaissance man, was the most promising pitching prospect ever to report to a major league spring-training camp. Opinion on the 1985 *Sports Illustrated* story, "The Curious Case of Sidd Finch" is split into two camps. Most consider it a George Plimpton masterpiece, but Mets fans rue it as a horrible hoax.

†Actually, another image, regrettably, also comes to mind when I hear the name Roberto Clemente. During college, my roommate Mike confided in me that when he needed to delay orgasm, he'd think about Roberto Clemente. Horrified by this overshare, I exacted my revenge by telling people Mike couldn't *have* an orgasm without thinking about Roberto Clemente. This became a running joke, and we trotted out this comedy routine in bars and at parties. Usually men laughed and women fled. Once, however, after Mike unveiled his punch line amid peals of drunken laughter, there was one guy who never changed his expression. Mike and I didn't know who he was (and would never find out), and for a moment I was uncomfortable. As the laughter ended, he simply gazed a bit over Mike's head as if deep in thought and asked, "Hitting or fielding?" I sure hope he's enjoying a career as a sitcom writer somewhere.

guillén, the Pirates' catcher, to join him. Reportedly, Manny instantly agreed. The plane, later determined to have been a death-trap-in-waiting due to poor maintenance and an excessive payload, crashed shortly after takeoff, killing all aboard. But Manny Sanguillén wasn't aboard. He couldn't find his car keys and missed the flight. Forty years later, that's the part of the story I remember. I was only seven years old when Roberto Clemente died, but the Manny Sanguillén angle has stuck with me forever.

Manny Sanguillén has spent the years since knowing that a random incident saved his life. But what about all of the times your life would have changed immeasurably and you *don't* know it? How many times do you take yourself out of harm's way and never feel the relief that you averted disaster? It's what made the Gwyneth Paltrow movie *Sliding Doors* so fun to watch, and it's the basis of the home-security industry's sales pitch. You'll never know if that ADT sign on your front lawn discourages burglars or not, but ADT sure tries to convince you it does.

On January 2, 2011, a quiet, overcast, and brisk Sunday morning in New York City, I couldn't have been more excited to begin the year. I had just spent Christmas in California with my wife and two daughters, who were finishing the school year before moving cross-country to join me. The previous summer, I had taken a job with Nomura Securities, a Japanese investment bank attempting to penetrate the U.S. broker-dealer market, helping to launch an equities-trading desk in New York. Not only had Nomura given me a one-year, seven-figure guarantee but I was also working for a close friend, a thirty-year-old whiz kid named Pascal. At the end of 2010, our trading desk had been up and running for three months, essentially an exhibition season. A new trading year began the next day, and I couldn't wait to get started. Our trajectory had been straight up since the launch, but now it was time to really focus on results, continue to take market share, and fulfill the mandate to make money that senior management had given us. My overdeveloped sense of competition had gripped me all Christmas break, and I had one goal for 2011: to be the most profitable trader on my desk, a mantle I wore at Lehman Brothers from 2001 to 2003, the last time I filled a similar role. Pascal, not only my boss but a fellow technology stock trader on the Nomura desk, knew this and wasn't about to cede *his* distinction as not only the most profitable trader at Barclays Capital (formerly Lehman Brothers) but possibly on the entire Street since 2007. The culture and energy of trading desks have always suited me, and be it 7 A.M. in New York or 4 A.M. in San Francisco, I've never dreaded coming to work. The dynamic on this desk, even in my mid-forties, had me leaping out of bed each morning to get to work, Red Bull– and coffee-free, unlike many of my twenty-something colleagues.

7

Coming back to New York City after the holidays on the morning of January 2 and sporting a very happy disposition, I approached the intersection of West Broadway and Park Place in downtown Manhattan, just a block from my apartment. That block is known for two things: Nationally, it gained notoriety in 2010 as the site of a controversial proposed mosque near Ground Zero. Locally, the controversy felt a little overblown. It's hard to equate the word *hallowed* with a building that housed a Burlington Coat Factory and still has COATS AND MORE . . . FOR LESS branded into the façade. Residents knew the block better for the best bar promotion in the neighborhood. During a Yankees game, the Dakota Roadhouse gives every customer a free beer each time the Yankees hit a home run. The promotion is ingeniously titled, "They Slug, You Chug!" It's no wonder a seemingly endless supply of freshly minted twenty-something graduates are drawn to New York City every year.*

The light turned green before I reached the corner and I never broke stride as I started across the street. As I crossed, I caught a glimpse of two police officers standing in the doorway of 49 Park Place, part of the site of the proposed mosque. I was contemplating the contrast between the quiet Sunday morning and the security patrol when my field of vision filled with the

*Another great NYC bar promotion: the mid-nineties Yahtzee Challenge at the Gramercy Watering Hole. On each visit to the bar, you could plunk a dollar down and receive five dice. If you rolled Yahtzee (five of a kind) in one roll, you got the massive glass jug of dollar bills behind the jar. Lose and your dollar ended up in the jug. I swear by the time that thing was won, they could have filled a Mini with all those dollar bills. Come to think of it, I probably could have bought a Mini with the amount of money I put in that jug.

red and white paint of an oncoming FDNY ambulance, turning left onto Park Place from West Broadway. As I reached the middle of the intersection, the center of the grille of the nearly four-ton truck struck me in the left hip. Knocking me forward and spinning me sideways, the truck continued forward as I started to rotate and fall.

CRACK!

CRACK!

The driver-side front tire ran over my right foot as I fell, and my leg wrenched sideways, instantly fracturing both bones between my knee and ankle. When the ambulance finally stopped I lay crumpled beneath the base of the driver's side door. As I screamed in agony, behind my head and out of my sight line, I heard the driver's door open. Details jumbled together in the ensuing minute—the policemen at my side almost instantly, the sound of a second ambulance arriving, the presence of onlookers on the curb, the paramedics refusing to give me morphine—but the first words after the driver's door opened I can still hear clearly. He stepped out, looked down at the situation, and said, "Oh, no. Oh, no. Oh, no."

Of course, this caused me to look down at the source of my agony. Bent at a nearly 45-degree angle in the middle of the shin, my right leg was nearly flat at what was obviously a clean break of the bone. My jeans looked like they were on an ironing board in the middle of where my shin should have been. While I never lost consciousness, I also never stopped scream-

9

ing. Through the screams, though, one 1980s-era sports memory popped into my head: We have a Joe Theismann situation here.*

Two hospitals, four days, a dozen screws, and a butter dish–size plate in my leg later, I awoke from an eight-hour surgery with the first reduction in pain since the accident. The days that followed were far from pain-free, though, and in the narcotic haze of the ensuing weeks, I was stuck in a wheelchair and stranded the width of the country away from my family. I was fired from that seven-figure job six weeks after retuning to work in a wheelchair. I kid you not. They literally rolled me off the trading floor. A former colleague told me that even a woman who worked in the pantry off of the trading floor later exclaimed, "They fired the guy in the wheelchair?"†

(That last paragraph is factually correct. I was fired from my job just weeks after suffering a massive leg injury and still

---

*No one who saw Lawrence Taylor's sack of Joe Theismann on a mid-eighties episode of *Monday Night Football* could ever forget the graphic nature of the resulting leg injury. Nor ABC's insisting on showing it over and over and over. Michael Lewis immortalized the play in an entire chapter of *The Blind Side*.

†If I were to present, in the style of *The MTV Movie Awards*, the winner of the Worst-Acting Organization in a Time of Crisis, you would think Nomura would wrap up the award. Not quite. Ladies and gentlemen, for your voting consideration, I present to you the City of New York. Not only did the driver not check on my condition or offer an apology (he wasn't on a run, didn't have a patient, and simply had to have been looking away from the road), despite nearly killing me; the City of New York didn't even follow up until mid-February. At that point I received a letter that—wait for it—was actually a bill, charging me nearly $900 for taking me to the hospital. That's right: After running me down in the street, the city billed me for the subsequent ride to the hospital. I don't know if the city has provided ambulance drivers with some bizarre incentive system to drum up business, but this is tantamount to someone from the water company setting your house on fire and then charging you to put out the blaze.

confined to a wheelchair. However, I am not implying, nor should any reader infer, that Nomura fired me *because* I was in a wheelchair. Nomura fired others on the desk during that time period, all of whom were able to walk off the trading floor under their own power.)

Jobless, unable to travel, and largely confined to my apartment, I inhabited an unfamiliarly dark place. I couldn't focus long enough to read a book or even watch an entire movie. I didn't watch a single NFL playoff game start to finish, including the Super Bowl, because I didn't have the mental stamina to do so. My iPad came to bed with me each night, since I needed it by my side for the inevitable 1 A.M. wake-up from nightmares. And that's when the *Sliding Doors*/Manny Sanguillén tangents took hold in my mind.

On that fateful January morning, I had woken up in West Chester, Pennsylvania, after spending New Year's Day with my parents. I took Amtrak to New York but transferred in Newark, New Jersey, to a PATH train to lower Manhattan. The train pulled in, I got off, and I joined a procession of weekend travelers heading from the train to the escalators leading to street level. Whether there were mechanical issues or a reduced capacity due to the holiday weekend I'll never know, but that morning only one escalator was running upward. The PATH station is forty feet below street level, and when you stand at the bottom of the escalators and look up at the steepness, you realize how far underground you are. As I stood in the slow-moving line, I noticed escalators open for climbing, even though they weren't running. Grumbling at this delay, my impatience kicked in, and I took action. Despite lugging an overnight bag weighing about twenty pounds, I slipped over to a nonmoving escalator and began jogging up it. Less than thirty seconds later, I was at the top, winded, but happy to know I'd probably saved about three minutes.

Of course, as I realized over and over during my post-nightmare episodes of insomnia, it also got me to the intersection of West Broadway and Park Place three minutes sooner.

That kind of thinking—that obsession with "What if I had just waited in line?"—can drive you nuts. While my leg was certainly going to take a significant amount of time to heal, it became apparent to me that some mental scars had formed as well.

My weakened state had left me vulnerable to negative thinking. I needed something to focus my mind and occupy my thoughts during the long recovery. I turned to baseball-preview publications, various data-packed baseball-analysis websites, and the spreadsheets I began to build myself. Bringing together my love of trading and markets, models and sports betting, I decided to use the findings of baseball's "sabermetric" community to build a model that would beat the Las Vegas baseball line.

In March, as spring training rolled along, I sent summaries for all thirty teams to my friends, previewing the 2011 season. As the model began to take shape, the betting began, I became consumed with the start of the baseball season, and my mental state rapidly improved. At first, I thought that my focus on the model building, constant critical reasoning, and the need for analytics accounted for the return of my upbeat outlook. But another factor was an even bigger catalyst: my love of baseball.

At the end of *Ball Four,* his candid account of his days as a major league baseball player, Jim Bouton penned one of the greatest concluding lines ever written.[*] He wrote, "You see, you spend a good piece of your life gripping a baseball and in the end it turns out that it was the other way around all the time."

My own baseball career ended in high school, and since the ultra-competitive softball leagues that consumed the Virginia Tech campus in the mid-eighties, I haven't spent much time on a diamond. Yet, on a sunny day in May, at AT&T Park, in San Francisco, still on crutches and accompanied by my four-year-old daughter, it became as clear to me as it was to Jim Bouton. It wasn't just the model, the gambling, or the daily puzzle to be solved in the form of the Vegas line that had lifted my spirits, buoyed my recovery, and returned me to the world of sleep-filled nights. It was baseball. Baseball, which I'd fallen in love with at age six, still had a grip on me.

---

[*]Great last lines, other media. Film: "I'm having an old friend for dinner." —Hannibal Lecter, *The Silence of the Lambs.* Television: "Have a good life." —Sam Malone, quietly, to an out-of-earshot Diane Chambers, from the vastly underrated *Cheers* episode "I Do, Adieu." And, finally, music: "Yes, I wish that for just one time, you could stand inside my shoes. You'd know what a drag it is to see you." —Bob Dylan, in the devastating parting shot ending "Positively 4th Street."

2

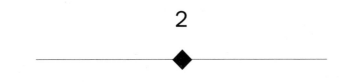

How I Discovered Cluster Luck

Unlike the boxes filled with APBA or Strat-O-Matic player cards that didn't quite fit on the doorstep between the screen door and front door of my childhood home, mail today doesn't arrive on the doorstep with a thud. UPS or FedEx drivers ring the doorbell, or in the case of New York City apartment living, deliveries are often left with the doorman.

However, if your postman *did* drop off a box at your front door containing *Baseball Prospectus 2011: The Essential Guide to the 2011 Baseball Season,* at nearly six hundred pages it *would* land with a thud. Its arrival in mid-February generally coincides with the arrival of pitchers and catchers at spring training, making it, in my household, another harbinger of spring. There are lots of baseball-preview publications; what has always attracted me to the *BP* annual is its witty writing and incisive commentary. The analysis is unique, and *BP*'s thought-provoking, sometimes groundbreaking studies not only raised many fans' standard for preview publications; it deepened their understanding of the game. Its alumni have gone on to work in major league teams' front offices and, in the case of Nate Silver, of FiveThirtyEight fame, even elevated data analysis in other fields. In fact, since I started reading *BP* over a decade ago, it has become the most stimulating and anticipated material I pore over each year.*

I read *BP* differently every year. Sometimes, I read it front to back for an alphabetical review of all thirty major league teams. Other times, I start with the Phillies, my hometown team and still my favorite. This year, I decided to do a more thorough preview of the upcoming season on a division-by-division basis, starting with the American League East. And since confinement to my apartment during recuperation from my surgery meant I had plenty of time to perform my own analysis, I kept a calculator, pencil, and paper handy.

I started with the Baltimore Orioles and decided, based on the data, that last year's season-ending optimism was misplaced. I jotted down my conclusion: "Strong 2010 finish resulted from a mirage of one-run victories, unlikely to be

---

*R.I.P., *Sports Illustrated*'s Swimsuit Issue, which held that distinction from 1977 to 1998.

repeated." By the time I'd gotten through the Red Sox ("in-credible 2010 production given their injuries; off-season acqui-sitions suggest league's best offense in 2011"), the Yankees ("as dominant on offense as ever thanks to their usual blend of power and patience"), and the Toronto Blue Jays ("home run power in excess of the league average not seen since steroid testing began"), something was bothering me about the Tampa Bay Rays, the winners of the division in 2010. How could they have scored runs on a par with the Red Sox and, to a slightly lesser degree, the Yankees, the highest-scoring team in base-ball? I pulled out the calculator and started jotting down some figures.

The Tampa Bay Rays of 2008–10 had become the latest un-derdog success story in baseball, supplanting the Oakland A's from a decade ago as the darlings of the crowd who root for third-party candidates, the Jamaican bobsled team, and mid-major colleges during March Madness. Like those A's, the Rays have succeeded over multiple seasons despite revenue con-straints. Making the Rays' achievements even more impressive is that Tampa is a small-market franchise in the same division as the two foremost economic powerhouses, the Boston Red Sox and the New York Yankees. Both the Red Sox and Yankees generate and spend (on player salaries) far more money than every other team in baseball. Despite this persistent disadvan-tage, the Rays managed to win the division twice (2008 and 2010) in a three-year period and captured the American

League pennant in 2008, a feat the early-2000s Oakland A's could not accomplish.*

As I read through the section on the Rays and examined their statistical performance, I couldn't figure out how they not only won their ultra-competitive division but had the best record in the entire American League. Wondering if I was digesting the data correctly, I started by examining their offense. The 2010 Rays didn't hit for average, posting a batting average of .247, which was not only materially below the American League average of .260 but solidly below the National League average of .255. (Owing to the designated hitter, American League teams, on average, post better numbers in every offensive category than National League teams.) The Rays' batting average of .247 ranked 26th (out of thirty) in all of baseball in 2010. Of course, that doesn't tell the whole

---

*Here's a great sports-bar question: Which team's accomplishments were more impressive, the 2000–03 Oakland A's or the 2008–11 Rays? The initial reaction of many is probably that the Rays' run was more impressive, given that they actually made it to a World Series while the four consecutive A's teams failed to win a playoff series. I don't think that's right. Those A's teams made the playoffs four straight years, three of them as a division winner. The one time they were the wild card they won one hundred and two games and still lost the division by fourteen games! They didn't lack for competition. The A's averaged ninety-eight wins over four years while the Rays averaged just ninety-two. Now, the fact that the A's went 0-4 in the playoffs is their supposed black mark, but it's more accurate and illuminating to state that they went 0-4 in the deciding fifth game of four straight best-of-five division series—the roulette round of baseball. I think the A's success is more impressive by a solid margin. Still, I don't really have a comeback for the inevitable steroids retort. It has to be acknowledged that, while the early 2000s were the apex of the steroids era in all of baseball, the contributions of Jason Giambi and Miguel Tejada—both American League MVPs—were essential to the A's success. As much as I love *Moneyball*, and consider it one of the best *business* books ever written, that has to be considered. Then again, Brad Pitt was the A's GM in the movie—Rays' backers have no comeback for that, as their wives nod knowingly.

story of a team's hitting prowess, as the calculation for batting average (hits/at-bats) treats all hits exactly the same. A .247-hitting team with a lot of home runs and other extra-base hits will score a lot more runs than a .247 team that hits a lot of singles. The Rays, however, didn't compensate for that low batting average with power, posting a slugging percentage (total bases/at-bats) of .403 for the year, exactly the league average. That slugging percentage ranked 14th out of all thirty teams. Slugging percentage still gives credit to singles, though, so it's not a perfect measure of raw power. When singles are stripped out of their slugging percentage, the Rays posted an above-average extra base hit per at-bat performance, finishing eighth in baseball with a .156 isolated-power reading.* Finally, the evaluation of any offense must factor in walks, which generate additional base runners who frequently score on subsequent base hits. To their credit, the Rays did walk more often than any other team in baseball, which boosted their on-base percentage to tenth in the majors, an impressive achievement given their 26th-ranked batting average.

So in 2010 the Rays hit singles at a rate that placed them in the bottom quartile of baseball. Their league-leading walks

---

*Isolated Power, or ISO, is a measure of extra bases per at-bat. It's essentially slugging percentage with singles stripped out. Do a little algebra and you find that you can derive ISO as simply slugging percentage minus batting average. In Tampa's case, because its batting average of .247 was below league average and it posted a league-average slugging percentage of .403, its ISO of .156 had to be above the league average.

still only got them to the second quartile in terms of producing base runners. Their slugging percentage was league-average, but they had just enough pop in their bats to slip into the first quartile of isolated slugging. Reading that paragraph over and over, I saw a team that should be above average, but not by a lot, in runs scored for 2010. So how to explain this:

The Tampa Bay Rays scored 802 runs in 2010, the third-most in all of baseball.

This just didn't look right as I started looking at other teams' run production and their ranking in those same offensive categories. For example, the Red Sox were materially better in every one of the above-mentioned categories and only scored sixteen more runs than the Rays. The Cincinnati Reds and Milwaukee Brewers scored twelve and fifty-two *fewer* runs, respectively, than the Rays, despite outperforming Tampa in each category. And these aren't just rounding errors, either. Take a look:

Team	Batting Avg.	On-Base Percentage	Slugging Percentage	ISO	Runs Scored
Tampa Bay Rays	.247	.333	.403	.156	802
Boston Red Sox	.268	.339	.451	.183	818
Cincinnati Reds	.272	.338	.436	.164	790
Milwaukee Brewers	.262	.335	.421	.161	750

While Tampa's run-scoring didn't seem to pass the "eye test," I needed to examine more precisely what kind of relationship historically existed between a team's ability to get on base (on-base percentage, or OBP), hit for power (slugging percentage, or SLG), collect extra base hits (isolated power, or ISO), and score runs. This was going to take more than a calculator, so I turned to my computer and started entering data into a spreadsheet. I learned that over an extended period of time, there is a very stable relationship when a team is on offense. Across all of baseball, teams will score (a bit more than) one run for every two hits they get. It's close enough, though, to say that, on average, two hits equals one run.

MLB Ratio of Hits per Run, 2008–10	
2010	2 hits for every run
2009	1.94 hits for every run
2008	1.95 hits for every run

Of course, that's league average, and in this case, being above or below league average is almost always a function of a team's collective skills in getting on base, hitting, and hitting for power. Comparing two 2010 teams from the National League highlights the interplay between those three factors and scoring runs.

Atlanta Braves	1,411 hits and 740 runs scored
Chicago Cubs	1,414 hits and 685 runs scored

While Cubs fans are probably nodding knowingly and saying, "No surprise here. Once again, we're the cautionary tale,"* the cause for the difference in hits needed per run is pinpointed by looking at the three different offensive factors that turn hits into runs. First, walks aren't accounted for. The Braves walked a whopping 151 more times than the Cubs, or 32 percent more often. A summary of this difference is evident by looking at OBP.

Braves 2010 OBP	.339
Cubs 2010 OBP	.320

Also, looking at the raw hit totals doesn't tell you what kind of hits they were. In creating runs, obviously, all hits are not equal. Singles are worth less than doubles, and so on. This is where slugging percentage comes in, capturing total bases per at-bat, instead of just hits.

Braves 2010 SLG	.401
Cubs 2010 SLG	.401

Finally, digging a little deeper into slugging percentage and stripping out the effect of singles yields ISO.

---

*I absolutely love Cubs fans. Normally, negative people are no fun to be around, but that's not the case with Cubs fans. Make no mistake about it, they are pessimists, they expect the worst, and on the surface they're filled with hate. Hate for the Cardinals, hate for the White Sox, and hate for their ill-fated existence as a Cubs fan. But they are hilarious, even charming, in their wallowing. More than any fan base I've encountered, they deserve a World Series championship in their lifetime or, at the very least, a National League pennant.

Braves 2010 ISO	.143
Cubs 2010 ISO	.145

So although the Braves had slightly fewer hits (just three) of almost the exact same kind (matching SLG with just a slightly *lower* ISO), compared with the Cubs they scored more runs. Why? The Braves created many more baserunners via walks than Chicago and, as a result, had a much higher OBP.

The point of using the Cubs and Braves to look at these three factors is that almost all of a team's hits-per-run performance can be predicted by looking at these three factors. I concluded: Given a league-average OBP (.325), SLG (.403), and ISO (.145), a team should be expected to score one run for every two hits they produce.

Now let's go back and apply these factors to Tampa's run-scoring abilities in 2010:

OBP	.333 (10th in the league)
SLG	.403 (14th in the league)
ISO	.156 (8th in the league)

As a team, Tampa was mildly above average in getting on base with exactly league-average slugging, complemented by above-average but in no way league-leading or elite power. (They were 12th overall in home runs, the largest determinant of ISO.) Looking at the distribution (and it's a bell curve, or "normal" distribution) of hits per run across all thirty teams last year, you'd expect Tampa to fall in the second quartile, which begins at 1.915 (eighth) and finishes at 1.978 (15th). To be as conservative as possible, Tampa could be assumed an eighth-place standing in hits per run, or a ratio of 1.915.

Back-of-the-Envelope Conclusion: Based on their 1,343 hits, accompanied by an OBP of .333, league-average slugging of .403, and solid but not top-tier ISO of .156, Tampa would be expected to have scored 701 runs (1,343/1.915).

However, as noted, Tampa actually scored 802 runs last year. In fact, Tampa's hit-to-run ratio of 1.675 was by far the best of any team over the last *five* years. (The Yankees' 2007 rate of 1.711 was second, and Boston's 2009 rate of 1.714 was third. Both of those teams crushed the ball and had hitting stats far superior to Tampa's.) Honestly, it's not even close. No team this decade created so much (runs) out of so little (hits).

This anomaly called for an even more exact statistical examination. In trying to determine the effect that OBP, SLG, and ISO had on hits needed per run scored, I had constructed a problem common in the study of statistics that can be solved via regression analysis. A regression analysis measures the effect independent variables have on a separate or dependent variable. In this case, I proposed the dependent variable, hits per run, is dependent on a team's OBP, SLG, and ISO. (Because there is more than one variable, this is known as a multiple regression analysis.) A regression analysis can confirm a relationship between the variables and in doing so determine how much weight to put on each variable. It can also disprove any effect between the variables. (For instance, adding the age of a team's manager as an independent variable would produce no effect on a team's hits per run, and a regression analysis would reveal this fact.)

Using data from 2008–10 for all ninety team-seasons (thirty teams over three years), I regressed OBP, SLG, and ISO against hits per run. The regression analysis determined Tampa should have needed 1.855 hits for every run scored. Instead, as noted, they scored a run for every 1.675 hits. Had they performed to expectations, they would have scored seventy-eight fewer runs. Stated another way, based on their hitting and base-reaching abilities, Tampa scored an incredible seventy-eight runs above expectations.

I began to seriously wonder if Tampa's 2010 success really deserved all the praise it got or if I could attribute this amazing efficiency in converting hits into runs, and ultimately their overall record, to luck. What is luck? To determine the existence of luck, random occurrences, as opposed to predictable skill-based factors, must be identified and defined.

In 1978, Bruce Springsteen released a song called "Prove It All Night," the first single off of the *Darkness on the Edge of Town* album. I was thirteen in 1978, a walking collection of raging hormones wrapped in a package of awkwardness inside a shell of social ineptitude. So of course I figured "Prove It All Night" was some sort of rock-and-roll paean to sexual prowess. More than twenty years later I changed my mind after hearing Bruce perform the song live on a number of different bootleg concert recordings. In introducing the song during the *Darkness* tour, Bruce says,* "It's not enough to do it once. In this world you've got to do it again and again and again. You gotta prove it all night." Maybe that *is* some sexual boast from his youth, but to me, now, it sounds exactly like my standard for distinguishing luck from skill.

When evaluating baseball results, skill-based performance is repeatable; results based on luck are not. For example, hitting home runs is a skill. Before a season begins, you can make a very accurate guess as to which player will lead the league in home runs. In fact, you're essentially on even footing with anyone else making the same guess, just by choosing from any of the top ten home run hitters from the year before. Same with pitchers and strikeouts. What about doubles? Now that's a little more interesting. The league leader changes virtually every year, with Brian Roberts the only player to lead his league in doubles twice in the last ten years (all statistics through 2010). By contrast, Alex Rodriguez (five titles), Albert Pujols (two), and Ryan Howard (two) have accounted for nearly half of the league home run titles over the last ten years. Hitting doubles

---

*There is some paraphrasing here. Every concert recording is a bit different.

requires skill but is also heavily influenced year to year by luck (stadium bounces, fluctuations in home runs per fly balls hit, etc.).

So those are examples of skill-based and partially skill-based accomplishments. What accomplishments are not skill-based and completely the result of randomness? The team that leads the league in Most Wild Pitches Committed by the Opponent. A team's performance on Tuesdays compared with other days. Similarly and sometimes controversially, it's been shown repeatedly that "clutch performance"—that is, performance in high-leverage or "clutch" situations—varies widely from year to year among both pitchers and hitters. Commentators, talk-radio hosts, and fans love to equate a player's success with his intestinal fortitude or mental toughness, seeing those as the factors that allow him to outperform his peers when a game is on the line.

Over and over, however, studies show there is no such thing as a "clutch" player. Albert Pujols may be the best eighth- or ninth-inning hitter in baseball when the game is tied or his team is down one run, but he's also the best hitter in baseball overall, so one shouldn't conclude that he possesses a magical power to perform in clutch situations. The degree to which a player exceeds (or falls short of) his overall performance in clutch situations each year is random. Good luck, for the purposes of this book, means being on the happy side of random occurrences; bad luck is the opposite. The existence of either in one year is not predictive of future performance in the next year and is therefore not skill-based.

In turning hits into runs in 2010, it turns out Tampa was the beneficiary of a special kind of luck that I call *cluster luck*.* Tampa's hits happened to occur disproportionately when runners were on base. In other words, in the highest-leverage and smallest-sample-size situations, Tampa's hitters performed way above their previously demonstrated abilities. That may seem like an example of players raising their game in the clutch, but I can demonstrate that it was simply good luck.

Players *do* hit better with runners on base. As any baseball fan knows, though, this isn't because the hitters are trying harder; it's because pitchers perform differently in two ways with runners on base, and both benefit the hitter: Physically, pitchers throw differently (they work from "the stretch," as opposed to "a windup," generating slightly less momentum when releasing the ball), and strategically they execute differently (sometimes, with no place to put additional runners, they must challenge batters with strikes). We can see this by examining the batting average (BA), OBP, and SLG—known as splits, or as *BP* dubbed it, "triple-slash splits"—of batters in different situations.

---

*Oh, how I wish this would catch on. Vörös McCracken gets credit for DIPS, Keith Woolner has VORP, Bill James coined "sabermetrics," and I'd love to be associated with a catch-phrase of my own. Few things would be more satisfying than hearing Vin Scully intone, "For the Dodgers this year, it's been a constant story of misfortune. They've persistently found themselves on the wrong side of cluster luck all season long."

2010 MLB Splits (BA/OBP/SLG)	
Bases Empty	.252/.315/.396
Runners On	.264/.339/.411
Improvement	+12/+24/+15

2010 Tampa Splits	
Bases Empty	.230/.313/.386
Runners On	.269/.358/.425
Improvement	+39/+45/+39

That's an incredible difference between the improvement lines for Tampa and all major league teams. Even more striking are the differences for the player who was most responsible for this disparity, Carl Crawford:

Bases Empty	.273/.321/.448
Runners On	.350/.399/.555
Improvement	+77/+78/+107

Some will still want to say Carl Crawford, an All-Star, is a clutch performer and raises his game when it matters, but if that's so, why didn't it show up in the first seven years of his career? Carl Crawford has always been a very good player. From 2002–09, across nearly ten times more ABs than he had in 2010, his improvement splits were as follows: +20/+27/+44.

All three of those numbers are above average (from above, +12/+24/+15), but Carl Crawford is an above-average player, so this isn't surprising. Rather than assuming Carl Crawford acquired an ability to perform in the clutch last year, I'm more inclined to conclude this: In small-sample-size, high-leverage situations in 2010, Carl Crawford turned into Alex Rodriguez,* despite the fact that he's never demonstrated Rodriguez-type skills before. Even more supportive of the "cluster luck" theory, Crawford's overall 2010 numbers were in line with his whole career. That's a one-time fluke of distribution, and therefore Tampa's 2010 run creation overall is not repeatable. (Jason Bartlett, with improvement splits of +80/+37/+163, was also a large contributor to this phenomenon in 2010, but with fewer runner-on-base ABs than Crawford, he didn't have quite as large an effect.)

Thus my conclusion was that Tampa's overall offensive performance was based on a random spike in hitting with runners on base, or cluster luck, and was therefore unlikely to be repeated in 2011. In other words:

If the 2011 Tampa Bay Rays got exactly the same overall offensive production from exactly the same players as they did in 2010, they'd score somewhere in the neighborhood of eighty fewer runs.

But Tampa Bay wasn't bringing back the same players on offense in 2010. In fact, the biggest free-agent hitter to change

---

*Crawford's 2010 on-base percentage plus slugging, or OPS, with runners on base totaled .954. A-Rod's career OPS is .958.

teams in the winter of 2011 was the aforementioned Carl Crawford. Taking all these factors into account, I came to the conclusion that the changes in Tampa's lineup from 2010 would
cost them more than twenty runs of overall production during
the 2011 season, in addition to the drop from cluster-luck re-
version.

By the time I'd saved the spreadsheet, I had a deep conviction that the 2011 edition of the Tampa Bay Rays would score
about one hundred runs less than the team scored in 2010, and
I didn't think that was necessarily a consensus opinion. So now
the questions in my mind were: What does this mean for their
season win total—and how can I make money off this view?

3

Cluster Luck Quantified

After the Lehman bankruptcy, in 2008, which ended my thirteen-year tenure with the firm, I took a job at UBS, an enormous investment bank headquartered in Switzerland. My job was to support UBS's institutional customers, such as mutual funds, college endowments, hedge funds, etc., which traded stock electronically. Traditionally, stock trades occurred over phone lines in a person-to-person manner, especially on the NASDAQ, a broker-to-broker stock market where I spent my formative years on Wall Street as a market maker. That description doesn't really paint a complete picture, though; during the 1990s, hotel accommodations, mail-order-catalog purchases, and rental car reservations were also conducted over the phone, but when it came to trading NASDAQ stocks, there was a lot of screaming, phone-throwing, and smashed equipment that made it unique among phone-based businesses. However, by 2008, electronic trading had gained market share across all of Wall Street, and trading became a much more dispassionate discipline.

The eighteen months I spent at UBS was the only stretch of my fifteen-year career on Wall Street that I wasn't a trader, in the sense that I didn't have my employer's capital at my disposal to trade, and therefore risk, on a daily basis. Technically, my job fell into the category of "sales," but since I didn't relish "asking for the trade,"* which is absolutely necessary to be a successful salesperson, I focused on data analysis as a way to help customers.

In 2005, Charles Schwab, one of the largest retail stock brokers in America, had gotten out of the stock-execution business and outsourced the trading of all its customers' orders to UBS. Big investment banks like UBS don't usually have retail customers. Instead, the customers responsible for the millions of shares of stock that investment banks trade each day are institutions such as hedge funds and behemoth mutual funds like Fidelity, or pension funds like CalPERS, or Harvard's endow-

---

*Stock brokers on Wall Street are an interchangeable lot. On most orders it's impossible for one bank to distinguish itself from another on either price or service. So often the salesperson must ask or, some might say, beg the customer for an order. I found it humiliating and in direct conflict with the sales resistance my father instilled in me from a young age. "Don't buy a Coke with that burger because it costs less bundled together. Look at all the signs in here promoting it. That's what they *want* you to do. We'll get one from the machine at the gas station."

ment. Within days of joining UBS, I discovered I had access to a database that recorded every share of stock traded by Charles Schwab's customers. While lots of firms on Wall Street (Goldman Sachs, Citigroup, Morgan Stanley, et al.) trade vast amounts of stock for their customers each day, none of them had orders anywhere close to UBS at the retail-customer level. Because of Schwab's nationwide presence, these trades collectively contained a wealth of data from which to draw conclusions about individual investor sentiment, a huge short-term variable in valuing the stock market. This meant UBS, with exclusive access to this data, had the ability to distinguish between the actions of its institutional customers, the professional investor, and Schwab's retail customers. For years, this mountain of data had just been sitting there. If interpreted correctly, it could be extremely valuable to portfolio managers and traders all across Wall Street. It is the story of our age across many different industries: The company with the most data has an advantage over its competitors. UBS had something unique but raw. The data needed to be properly analyzed and then distilled into an easy-to-understand format. Looking at the Schwab trades as a proxy for the behavior of all retail investors, I developed statistics, created metrics, and discovered trends, all of which led to the formation of some very predictive market signals. Armed with this analysis, I disseminated my findings in the form of a daily research note. Because of the unique content, the note quickly won a large audience inside as well as outside the firm. I often was asked, "Where do you come up with this stuff?"

The answer was simply Bill James.

Author of the legendary (at least in the world of statistically obsessed baseball fans) *Baseball Abstract* series, which first got national attention in a 1981 *Sports Illustrated* article, Bill James essentially created the entire field of the statistical study of baseball called "sabermetrics."* The *BA* series ended after about a decade, and the last of *The Bill James Historical Baseball Abstract* tomes was published in 2001. But James's influence on the game only increased. Hired by the Boston Red Sox in 2003 as a consultant, he came on board in time to provide counsel to the front office as it made roster decisions that would directly lead to the team's first World Series title in eighty-six years.

His indirect influence has left an even greater stamp on the game. Within baseball, virtually every team now has a director of statistics, or even a GM, who is not only familiar with James's work but has been profoundly influenced by it. Outside the game, there exists a sizable publishing niche, both in print and online, devoted to the study of baseball analytics. Although to my knowledge he never specifically tailored his writings to fantasy baseball, you can bet every league winner employs

---

*You know the old joke about the football player who's so important to his team, so dominant in all facets of the game, that "he even plays in the band at halftime"? Well, Bill James's influence on the sabermetrics community is total; he even invented the term. The Society for American Baseball Research was established in 1971. James took the acronym "SABR" and used it to create the word "sabermetrics."

some sort of predictive analysis that can be traced back to a Bill James theory, whether or not the fantasy player knows it. It's not an overstatement to say that every piece of research conducted or advancement made in the analysis of baseball over the last decade has built on, or was at least inspired by, work originally authored by Bill James.

James developed a following not only because of the data he cited and the statistics he invented but because he wrote well, too. Like Warren Buffett, whose professional accomplishments overshadow his ability to write exceptionally well, James didn't just dump numbers on his readers; he wove them into a story. That's the style I emulated and adopted when I wrote commentary at UBS. By telling stories, James excelled at the difficult task of writing stimulating essays while feeding the reader extra helpings of numbers and data. As one fan of his writing told me, when Bill James wrote, "the reader didn't even know he was eating his vegetables." But what exactly did those devoted readers get out of his work?

It's clear what the general managers and owners of MLB teams eventually found valuable. Broadly, James sought to uncover why teams won baseball games, what skill sets organizations should seek in players, and how to predict a team's performance based on the melding of its players' skill sets. Bill James explained how to construct teams that win more games.

Hard-core baseball fans with an appreciation for statistics saw a new window on their world open. Fantasy baseball players found edges in predicting future player performance. Amidst those groups of readers, I've always felt a bit isolated. I never will own a baseball team, nor will I work in one's front office. I'm less interested in the hours of tedious work required to dominate a fantasy baseball league when the payoff is basically pride and maybe a couple hundred dollars. Nor, when it comes to differences of opinion, am I interested in intellectual arguments, per se.

When Apple came out with the iPhone in 2007, a heated debate developed on the trading desk at my firm's hedge fund as to whether the iPhone was a threat to the BlackBerry's dominance of the smartphone market. One analyst scoffed at Apple entering the phone market. Yet he would not agree to slap down a $100 bet on the stock performance of Apple vs. Research in Motion (the maker of the BlackBerry) for any time period of his choosing. Nor, despite his outspokenness, would he risk other people's money (that's what running an investment fund really is—betting other people's money) by putting on a pairs* trade in support of his opinion. He just smugly insisted, "Apple has no idea what it's doing in the phone business.

---

*A pairs trade is a way of betting on the relative performance of one stock vs. another without any outlay of cash required. In this case, the analyst would have sold short (that is, sold stock he didn't own), say, $1 million worth of Apple (AAPL) and then used the proceeds from the short sale to buy $1 million worth of Research in Motion (RIMM). As the trades are "paired" against each other, this is a market-neutral strategy. If RIMM outperforms AAPL as they both rise, his trade is a winner. But it's also a winner if both stocks fall and RIMM falls less than AAPL. He'd be indifferent to moves in the overall market. (While it doesn't require any cash, it does raise the leverage of the fund, and that's a topic for a later chapter on risk in betting and on Wall Street.)

We'll see in the end." My aggravation manifested itself in speechlessness and probably a red face. It's almost beyond my comprehension how someone could perform research, form a strong opinion, and then not want to express his conviction in that opinion—in other words, back up the work he's done, with money. That's why I traded for a living. Now, to be clear, I'm not talking about an uncontrollable gambling urge. I didn't sit around trading desks saying, "You think it's going to rain tomorrow? I'll give you three-to-two odds it doesn't. Let's bet lunch at the Palm." I'm talking about doing research, believing that work creates an edge over others, and then *investing* in that edge.

That same mind-set sparked the idea that would be the first step out of my post-accident cloud. Why not try to build upon the sabermetric research of Bill James and others and make money by betting on the outcome of baseball games or entire seasons? As I became more and more engrossed in my own research, I set out to take on baseball's oddsmakers, armed with my discovery of cluster luck and established sabermetric principles. As I started to build a dizzying amount of complex spreadsheets, I felt the same urge to jump out of bed and get to my computer that I did as a trader. Stuck alone in a New York City apartment and ingesting painkillers, I had to use a walker to do my figurative "jumping," but the surge of energy, absent in the first couple of months after the accident, felt good.

The first principle I would employ was Bill James's Pythagorean theorem. Ever wonder why baseball standings have evolved to include, on some websites and newspapers, the columns RS (runs scored) and RA (runs allowed)? That's due to the growing influence of James's Pythagorean theorem, the most basic building block of the model I set out to build. James discovered that a team's winning percentage at the end of any year could be estimated, with a great deal of accuracy, by using just two inputs: the team's RS and RA. That simplicity is pretty stunning when all the different ways to measure a particular baseball team's achievements are considered. Regardless of its home runs, strikeouts, batting average, earned-run average (ERA), division, or era, any given team's season can be reduced to this sentence: "Tell me how many runs a team scored and how many it allowed and I'll tell you how many games it won."

James first published the formula in the early 1980s, and it looked like this:

$$RS^2 / (RS^2 + RA^2) = \text{Team Winning Percentage}$$

Owing to the presence of the squared factors, James dubbed his creation "the Pythagorean theorem." Many have further refined James's original Pythagorean theorem.[*] It is widely

---

[*]The formula has been found to work in football and basketball, too, with exponent fiddling. I suppose it might work in hockey, but until a hockey fan who knows how to work a calculator is unearthed, this will remain unproven.

agreed that the most accurate exponent, that little superscript number, is 1.83, not 2, and that is the formula that's used today.*

Take the 2010 Cleveland Indians. They scored 646 runs and allowed 752. Plug those numbers into the formula and the result is:

$$646^{1.83} / (646^{1.83} + 752^{1.83}) = .4309$$

A winning percentage of .4309 over 162 games translates to 69.8 wins. The Indians actually won sixty-nine games in 2010. Why is this useful? The number of runs that a team scores and allows in a season is accumulated over 162 games, a number large enough to remove sampling bias. Therefore it is thought to be a fair representation of the talent of the underlying team. James's Pythagorean theorem can be used to compare a team's expected win total based on its season-long performance to its actual wins. There is, of course, some randomness, or noise, around a team's final win total. However, when a team's actual results deviate by four wins or more from the Pythagorean estimate, a threshold has been passed and nonrepeatable results can be assumed.

Using the insight into teams' performance that this equa-

---

*In fact, Clay Davenport, at Baseball Prospectus, (and others) have refined it even further, making the exponent float based on the run environment a specific team plays in. For my purposes, though, 1.83 is accurate enough.

tion provides, I took the first step in determining which teams had tended to be lucky or unlucky, in terms of the number of games they had won in any given year. This differed from calculating cluster luck, which measured how fortunate a team like the Rays was in amassing its runs scored. The Pythagorean theorem measures how lucky a team was in converting its actual runs scored and runs allowed into wins. Remember, luck represents performance that is not repeatable.

Teams on the Far Ends of the Luck Spectrum in 2010	
Team	2010 Wins vs. Pythagorean Estimate
Houston Astros	+7.97 wins above estimate
Pittsburgh Pirates	+3.66
Baltimore Orioles	+3.02
Chicago Cubs	+2.35
Kansas City Royals	+2.31
Oakland A's	−4.25
Arizona Diamondbacks	−4.29
St. Louis Cardinals	−5.16 wins below estimate

Only six teams out of thirty finished 2010 more than three wins from their Pythagorean estimate, and just four of those deviated by four wins or more. Looking at the two biggest outliers, Houston scored 611 runs and allowed 729, good for 68.03 wins, according to the equation. Houston won seventy-six games. That 7.97 spread was 4.31 wins wider than the Pittsburgh Pirates', 2010's second-"luckiest" team. In fact, only Pittsburgh and Baltimore were above their Pythagorean projection by more than 2.5 wins, so Houston's total of seventy-six wins, given its hitting and pitching talent, was truly unlikely. At the other end of the spectrum, the St. Louis Cardinals scored 736 runs and allowed 641. Projected to win 91.16 games, they only won eighty-six. That made them "unlucky" by -5.16 games. So the Astros were lucky and the Cardinals unlucky; by my definition of luck, neither of their 2010 results (in terms of wins) was likely repeatable, given the performance of their players. Relying on this level of demonstrated talent, I restated the Astros 2010 performance in terms of 2011 expectations:

The Houston Astros could field in 2011 exactly the same players as last year, and if they performed at a level that produced exactly the same amount of runs scored and runs allowed as in 2010, they'd be expected to win sixty-eight games, or eight less than they won in 2010.

But, as noted in the previous chapter, stripping out the effects of cluster luck determines the number of runs a team *should* have scored, given its total offensive performance. It turns out that Houston's offense benefited from cluster luck to the tune of twenty-one runs. Because scoring and allowing runs across all of baseball is a zero-sum game (another team gives up the runs that its opponent scores) it follows that if teams like Tampa (+78 runs due to cluster luck) and Houston (+21 runs) were scoring more runs than their hitting results should have produced, there were pitching staffs that must have been *unlucky* in giving up those runs. Learning which teams were unlucky could be just as valuable as identifying the lucky ones.

I went through this exercise for each team's offensive production, and collectively MLB teams benefited in 2010 from cluster luck to the tune of 130 runs. I then ran the same regression on pitching performance that I used to determine the excess or shortfall of runs scored by offenses and learned that Houston's pitching staff gave up seven more runs than expected, given the level of their opponents' hitting.

I put it all together and made a final conclusion on Houston's 2010 performance. If the season were repeated with the same players, performing at exactly the same level, I'd expect Houston to score 590 runs, not 611, and give up 722, not 729. Plug 590 runs scored and 722 runs allowed into the Pythagorean formula and the resulting winning percentage of .409 equates to sixty-six wins. Suddenly, Houston looked like a far worse team heading into 2011 than the team that won seventy-six games in 2010. When I did this for every team, it appeared that Houston had the second-worst team in baseball in 2010, ahead of only the Pittsburgh Pirates. Worse even than the Seattle Mariners, Baltimore Orioles, and Kansas City Royals. Worse than the Chicago Cubs, Cleveland Indians, and Arizona Diamondbacks. What do these seven teams have in common? All of them actually lost more games than the Houston Astros in 2010. I didn't know it at the time, but all seven would go on to post better, mostly far better, records than the Astros in 2011—exactly as the model predicted.

The 2010 standings, adjusted for cluster luck and Pythagorean theorem under/over performance* (actual wins in parentheses):

AL East		AL Central		AL West	
NY Yankees	97 (95)	Minnesota Twins	89 (94)	Texas Rangers	90 (90)
Boston Red Sox	93 (89)	Detroit Tigers	85 (81)	Oakland A's	84 (81)
Tampa Bay Rays	89 (96)	Chicago White Sox	85 (88)	LA Angels	74 (80)
Toronto Blue Jays	86 (85)	Cleveland Indians	69 (69)	Seattle Mariners	68 (61)
Baltimore Orioles	68 (66)	Kansas City Royals	72 (67)		

NL East		NL Central		NL West	
Philadelphia Phillies	90 (97)	Cincinnati Reds	91 (91)	San Francisco Giants	89 (92)
Atlanta Braves	92 (91)	St. Louis Cardinals	87 (86)	Colorado Rockies	88 (83)
Florida Marlins	79 (80)	Milwaukee Brewers	80 (77)	San Diego Padres	83 (90)

*Besides Houston, there are a few other items to note. St. Louis, unlucky based on the Pythagorean theorem (from page 40), benefited from cluster luck in both hitting and pitching to the point that it swung to the lucky side of the ledger, albeit by just one win. Arizona was the mirror image of Houston, so its 2011 division championship may not have been as surprising as it appeared. Neither Philadelphia nor San Diego led any luck category but finished high enough in all of them that, collectively, they both finished with seven more wins than they "deserved." In Philadelphia's case, the roster changes discussed in Chapter 4 are projected to offset any regression in 2011.

NL East		NL Central		NL West	
NY Mets	74 (79)	Chicago Cubs	76 (75)	LA Dodgers	82 (80)
Washington Nationals	74 (69)	Houston Astros	66 (76)	Arizona Diamondbacks	73 (65)
		Pittsburgh Pirates	57 (57)		

As I studied the adjusted standings for 2010 and noted how much worse the Astros were than their 2010 record suggested, I went to the web to determine team expectations from the perspective of Las Vegas oddsmakers. Bookmakers post a total wins market for each team and allow bettors to wager on whether a team's ultimate win total for the season will be over or under the posted number. For the Houston Astros, the 2011 over-under market for total wins stood at 72½. This total on a team that I strongly believed had sixty-six-win talent. Las Vegas was offering to take the other side of a wager I'd win if the Astros finished 2011 with seventy-two wins or fewer. The trader in me smiled.

When trades with a positive expected value present themselves on the trading floor, you jump in with both feet. Betting on baseball futures (i.e., total season wins) was no different. Relying on just cluster-luck identification and a team's deviation from its expected win total was only the first step in creating final projections, but it was time to see if other trades were suitable investments as well.

4

Players' Performance Projected

Stripping out the effects of cluster luck and identifying teams whose final win total wasn't reflective of its run-scoring and run-prevention talents, and thereby restating the league standings in a given year, is illuminating, but there is a problem in using them to predict the following year's results. Two, in fact. First, players age, and as is true in all performance fields, sometimes the change is for the better, in the case of a someone approaching their prime,* and sometimes, in the case of a player or performer with eroding physical skills and on the downside of a career, for the worse.† Second, team rosters change, some-

---

*Think a topless Janet Jackson on the cover of *Rolling Stone* promoting her 1993 album, *Janet*.

†Think a topless Janet Jackson's infamous "wardrobe malfunction" during the Super Bowl XXXVIII halftime show, in 2004.

times dramatically, between the end of one season and the start of the next one. In each case, an attempt must be made to quantify how much value a player will add, or subtract, from his team. Therefore, before examining how to project differences in a team's performance from one year to the next based on aging, roster changes, and other factors, it's useful to examine the theoretical value one player can have to his team.

Baseball discussions like this have helped sell beer in bars across America since Prohibition ended. If Ted Williams had played for the Yankees and Joe DiMaggio for the Red Sox, thereby playing in stadiums perfectly suited for their respective left- and right-handedness, would their careers have been even better? How many more games would the Orioles have won in recent seasons if they hadn't passed on drafting two-time Cy Young Award winner Tim Lincecum in 2006? If Roy Halladay were on the Pirates, would they contend for a playoff berth? Who really is the most *valuable* player in any given season? While similar debates have raged in bars and around watercoolers for generations, today's baseball fan has a way to quantify some of his views.

Toward the end of the 2011 baseball season, a debate emerged as to whether or not Justin Verlander, a starting pitcher for the Detroit Tigers, deserved consideration for the American League Most Valuable Player Award. His supporters cited not just his superb traditional statistics but two additional facts that underscored Verlander's "value" to the Tigers: the

Tigers' record when Verlander started games, vs. when he didn't, and Verlander's record pitching with the Tigers coming off a loss in their last game. Verlander didn't necessarily have any detractors, but a vocal band of baseball analysts believe, in general, that starting pitchers shouldn't be eligible for the MVP award because, as exemplified by Verlander's thirty-four starts, they play in roughly one-fifth of a team's games only. Instead, they claim, the Cy Young Award honors the best pitcher in each league, and therefore the MVP Award is for everyday position players.

The argument that a pitcher shouldn't be the MVP because he doesn't play every day has always seemed specious to me. While it seems that a position player on the field for every play of every game would have a greater influence on his team's record at the end of the year, that's not really the case. One thing that the field of sabermetrics has taught baseball observers, and tools such as the Pythagorean theorem and the debunking of clutch performance more or less prove, is that a team's success is determined by the sum of all its events during the year. Here's some data to consider while you're drinking beers and talking baseball with another fan: Every team's season essentially comes down to 12,400 plate appearances, 6,200 battles between pitcher and hitter while in the field and 6,200 while at bat. From 2006 to 2010, the ten MVP Award winners from both leagues—all position players—averaged 674 plate appearances. The ten Cy Young Award winners from those same years faced on average, 938 batters a year. Even factoring in defense, except for first basemen, the average Cy Young Award candidate will have his hand in a higher percentage of outcomes for those 12,400 mini-battles than any other MVP candidate. So the idea that a pitcher has less "value" than position players in determining his team's success is unconvincing.

It's the other side of the argument that is more interesting for model-building purposes, however. When Justin Verlander took the mound in 2011, the Tigers went 25-9. When he didn't start, they went 70-58. Until the Tigers got hot in September (they went 20-6, including 16-5 in games Verlander didn't start), there stood a very real chance they could have been under .500 in games Verlander didn't pitch and still have made the playoffs. This was cited repeatedly as an example of Verlander's "value" to the Tigers. That leads to an interesting hypothetical question: If Justin Verlander started all 162 games for the Tigers in 2011, instead of just thirty-four, what would Detroit's record have been at the end of the year? (The underlying assumption—entirely unrealistic, of course—is that the Tigers would get *exactly the same performance* out of Verlander in the extra 128 starts. Or, stated in a slightly less unrealistic way, imagine the Tigers had a starting pitching rotation of five pitchers of the same caliber as the 2011 version of Verlander.) I asked this question to a dozen or so baseball fans toward the end of the 2011 season, and every answer I got had the Tigers breaking the record for most wins in a season (116, by the 2001

Seattle Mariners). Most said at least 120 and, based on the logic that he started in one-fifth of Detroit's games, some, having multiplied twenty-five wins in those he did start by five, answered 125.

I would have taken the under against every one of them. Why?

According to the Pythagorean theorem, a team's winning percentage depends on its runs scored and runs allowed. Half of that equation is already fixed: The 2011 Detroit Tigers scored 787 runs; that number doesn't change regardless of who takes the mound and makes the Tigers a team to be reckoned with no matter who pitches for them. In his thirty-four starts, Justin Verlander allowed seventy-three runs, or 2.15 per game. That comes to 348 runs allowed over an entire 162-game season. However, Verlander isn't pitching every inning in the season in our assumption; he's only *starting* every game and doing so in the same manner over all 162 that he did in the thirty-four games he did pitch. In his thirty-four starts, he averaged just over 7.33 innings per start (an incredible display of stamina in baseball's current era), so over 162 games that still leaves 262 innings for the Tigers bullpen to pitch. Excluding any pitcher who started a game in 2011—because they wouldn't be needed with five Verlanders—the Tigers bullpen allowed .4927 runs per inning pitched. Over 262 innings, that comes to 129 runs. So a pretty good approximation of the Tigers' performance with Justin Verlander starting all 162 games is that they would score

787 runs and allow 477. Plug that into the Pythagorean theorem and you'd expect the Tigers, with an all-Verlander starting pitching staff, to win 115 or 116 games. Not 120 or more.

The Detroit Tigers won ninety-five games in 2011. If they had been able to trade the rest of their starting pitchers for four more Justin Verlanders, I would have expected the 2011 Detroit Tigers to win about twenty more games, a level no better than the 2001 Mariners or the 1998 Yankees. While I suspect that's a lower win total than most would estimate, the point of the exercise is arriving at a value for one player relative to another. On average, Justin Verlander, during his fabulous 2011 season was worth five more wins than another member of the Tigers' five-man rotation. Keep that in mind if you ever hear a fan of a last-place team say, "If we could only trade Brett Myers for Justin Verlander, we'd make the playoffs."

This type of critical reasoning represented a crucial step in developing my model. I could now quantify, in terms of wins, the effects of a team's roster changes from one year to the next. Of course, I was using estimates, but I felt the logic underpinning the calculations was sound. I set about to quantify the effect of roster changes for each team and found the Philadelphia Phillies to be one of the more interesting studies.

The Philadelphia Phillies, four-time defending champions of the National League East, and just one year removed from back-to-back World Series appearances, made the most dramatic move of the 2010 off-season. Looking at my 2010 analysis, it appeared to me as if the team's front office had come to the same conclusion I had. The Phillies were lucky to have won ninety-seven games the year before, and without upgrades they had little chance of duplicating their best-record-in-baseball achievement. But how much improvement was needed and how could they quantify it?

There is additional value to be found in the Pythagorean theorem, thanks to the elegance and simplicity of the equation. Let's look at it again. The 2010 Phillies scored 772 runs and allowed 640. Their expected winning percentage works out to .585 as follows:

$$772^{1.83} / (772^{1.83} + 640^{1.83}) = .585$$

A .585 winning percentage translates to ninety-five wins. The Phillies actually won ninety-seven, but if they were to score 772 runs every year and allow 640, they would, in theory, average closer to ninety-five wins. So what if, thanks to an improving Atlanta Braves squad within their division, the Phillies thought they needed to win one hundred games to win their division or secure home-field advantage, etc.? What would they need to do to improve their team from an expected ninety-five wins to one hundred? Here's the additional value the Pythagorean theorem provides. Some trial-and-error fiddling with the formula reveals that for every ten runs by which the Phillies improve their run differential, they can expect to win one more game. Twenty runs equals two games, etc. This really is an amazing revelation, not just for statistically minded fans but for the front offices of major league teams as well. Management wants to win five more games than last year? Figure out a way to score fifty more runs, allow fifty fewer runs, or some combination of the two totaling fifty and their club can expect to win five more games.

Turning back to the restated 2010 standings from the previous chapter, I found that through a combination of outperforming the Pythagorean estimate by two games and benefiting from cluster luck on offense (nearly three wins) and while pitching (two wins), the restated 2010 standings showed a Phillies team winning ninety-seven games with ninety-win talent. Within the Phillies' league, the San Francisco Giants were the defending World Series champions, and within their division, the Atlanta Braves looked very formidable, while the Washington Nationals had plucked away Jayson Werth, the Phillies' leading offensive contributor in 2010, in free-agency. Without a roster upgrade somewhere, the Phillies reign as the dominant NL team over the last three years looked imperiled.

During the 2010 off-season, the Phillies shocked the baseball world with their signing of Cliff Lee, seemingly assuring their win total would stay in the nineties. Looking at their 2010 performance revealed the Phillies not only added a superstar pitcher; they replaced their weakest contributors from 2010 in the process. Even I, a die-hard Phillies fan, had trouble processing this fact: The 2010 Phillies won ninety-seven games, a fourth-straight division title and came within two games of getting back to their third-straight World Series, and they did so despite the fact that lightly regarded pitchers Jamie Moyer and Kyle Kendrick started fifty regular-season games. Moyer and Kendrick surely started more games for the team with the best record in baseball in 2010 than they started for every fantasy team in America...combined! In 2011, those fifty starts projected to be taken instead by Cliff Lee and Roy Oswalt. (Oswalt, a trade-deadline pick-up in 2010, started only twelve games for the Phillies the rest of the season. At about thirty-two starts each, Lee and Oswalt could be projected to start sixty-four games in 2011, or fifty-two more than they did in 2010, replacing the starts of Moyer and Kendrick.) That should mean considerable run-prevention improvement for the Phillies in 2011.

Like most elite players during their prime seasons (from twenty-eight to thirty-two years old), Lee and Oswalt are remarkably consistent. Year after year, Oswalt has pitched a little over two hundred innings and given up a little more than eighty runs a season. Over that same time, Lee has pitched the same amount of innings and given up just under eighty runs each year. Put them together and, in 2011, the Phillies could very realistically project to get four hundred innings of production out of

Lee and Oswalt while surrendering 160 runs. Here's what they got the previous year from the pitchers they were replacing:

Pitcher	Innings Pitched	Runs Allowed
Moyer	112	64
Kendrick	181	103
Oswalt	83	18
Relievers	44	22
Total	**420**	**207**

That's an improvement of forty-seven runs (160 vs. 207). Applying the every-ten-runs-equals-a-win tenet, the addition of Cliff Lee and a full season of Roy Oswalt meant the Phillies should win five more games in 2011 vs. the 2010 restated standings. Therefore, holding all else constant, my model projected the Phillies would win ninety-five games in 2011 as a result of their improved pitching staff.

Economists love to use the expression "holding all else constant" because it's very useful for isolating a single variable in an experiment. However, in baseball, just as in economics, nothing happens in a vacuum. As such, I saw at least four problems with the conclusion that the Phillies would win ninety-five games in 2011:

1. There is no consideration for aging on the projections for Oswalt and Lee. Consistent as they may have been re-

cently, the aging curve ensures one's level of production must eventually diminish over time.

2. There is no probability assigned to games missed due to injury.

3. There were other changes to the Phillies' roster from 2010 to 2011.

4. Even without other changes, the returning players need adjustments to their 2010 performance for age, injuries, nonrepeatable performance, etc.

For instance, could the incredible Cy Young Award–winning season of Roy Halladay, complete with a perfect game and a post-season no-hitter, really be duplicated in 2011? What, instead, is a realistic projection of his future performance? If it were even possible to objectively answer that question, repeating the same exercise for the effect of every roster change and age effect for every player on every team, as I just did for the Phillies' starting rotation, would take weeks.

Fortunately, Nate Silver automated the process more than a decade ago.

You may know him today as "the FiveThirtyEight blog guy" at *The New York Times,* but next to Bill James, Nate Silver probably has had as much influence on the advancements in sabermetric analysis in the last decade as anyone else. He's at least in the inner circle. As a member of Baseball Prospectus, in 2003 Silver introduced his algorithm for predicting individual player performance, which he whimsically named PECOTA after a fairly obscure late-eighties middle infielder on the Kansas City Royals, Bill Pecota.* Essentially a database of every player in professional baseball history for whom reliable statistics are available, PECOTA identifies past players comparable with each current player based on position played, prior performance, body type, age, etc., to project future performance. For instance, at age thirty-three at the start of the 2011 season, Roy Oswalt most resembles Warren Spahn, Mike Mussina, and Don Sutton when they were thirty-three, and therefore his 2011 projection takes into account their performance arc, including injury risk.

PECOTA represented groundbreaking work in 2003, is absolutely indispensable if you are a fantasy baseball player, and for my money is still the gold standard of projection systems today, in that it provided the framework for many subsequent systems. Silver has moved on to political commentary, which may seem an odd career arc, but I'm sure he saw the same similarities in data analysis between political polling and baseball that I see between trading and baseball.

I use PECOTA to compare projected performance for 2011 vs. actual contribution in 2010 for every player on each team. In 2010 the Phillies starting pitchers performed at a level that

---

*PECOTA officially stands for "player empirical comparison and optimization test algorithm."

was 18.6 wins above replacement, or WAR. WAR is a bedrock of sabermetric analysis, and its calculation is unbelievably complicated.* However, the concept is relatively straightforward: If replaced by a player with the talent level of a typical bench player, minor leaguer, or free agent available during the season on the waiver wire, how many wins would the change cost his team? Additionally, since we know the value of a win is ten runs, we can simplify the WAR concept further by concluding, "In 2010, the Phillies starting pitching held opponents to 186 fewer runs than they would have if they had been replaced with the best of readily available, low-cost free-agent or minor league pitchers." Here's how it broke down by starter:

Starting Pitcher	2010 WAR
Roy Halladay	8.1
Cole Hamels	5.3
Roy Oswalt	2.5
Joe Blanton	1.4
Jamie Moyer	0.6
Vance Worley	0.5
Kyle Kendrick	0.2
Total	**18.6**

*Not only is it complicated but, among the sabermetric community, there is no consensus on how to treat all of the inputs. As such, although the concept is the same everywhere, you can find different WAR calculations for any player on different websites. Since I used Baseball Prospectus's PECOTA projections for 2011, I also used its 2010 WAR calculations to ensure I kept my year-to-year comparisons valid.

According to PECOTA projections, the Phillies would get 25.6 WAR from their starting pitchers in 2011 as follows:

Starting Pitcher	2011 WAR
Roy Halladay	6.8
Cliff Lee	5.8
Roy Oswalt	5.3
Cole Hamels	4.8
Joe Blanton	2.7
Kendrick, Worley, et al.	0.2
Total	**25.6**

That's an improvement of seven wins, or seventy fewer runs allowed than in 2010. Doing the same exercise with the hitters yields an expected drop of 5.1 wins, or fifty-one fewer runs scored. (The projected offensive drop-off was due largely to the free-agent departure of Jayson Werth and, to a lesser degree, to the aging of the Phillies' core.) That took care of everything except relief pitching. While it was possible to run the same exercise for relievers, I instead opted to get a little bit creative. Surprisingly enough, my inspiration for this decision came not from the work of baseball analysts but from a football analyst, Aaron Schatz, of footballoutsiders.com, the author of the essential (if you're a football fan) *Football Outsiders Almanac*, an annual publication that clearly took its inspiration from Baseball Prospectus.

*　　*　　*

Years ago, Schatz discovered that teams that displayed a big disparity on third-down performance vs. first- and second-down performance tended the following year to perform at an overall level that more closely resembled their first- and second-down performance from the year before. For instance, in 2004 the San Diego Chargers had, according to Football Outsiders' unique data analysis, the NFL's third- and fourth-best offense, respectively, on first and second downs. On third down, they ranked 25th, resulting in an overall ranking of 15th. While everyone else, including probably the Chargers' fans, saw an average offense at the end of 2004, Schatz predicted great things in 2005 for San Diego. In 2005, the Chargers ended up having the third-best-overall offense in the NFL, a seemingly unforeseeable leap from average to elite. However, Schatz had predicted this turnaround, because he sagely observed that third-down performance, compared with first- and second-down, is a small-sample, high-leverage situation that disproportionately affects overall performance and potentially masks actual skill level.

Turning back to baseball, the smallest-sample-size, highest-leverage element of a team's performance is relief pitching. In fact, I found that when a team's bullpen performance as a whole is examined from one year to the next, in one very important way it mimics randomness. To predict the WAR of a team's entire bullpen for one season, it is more accurate to forecast a performance equal to the league average from the prior year than to use the team's actual prior year WAR. In other words, like all random sequences, it exhibits mean-reverting tendencies.

That seems like a very controversial statement, but savvy baseball GMs and analysts have known this for years. Bullpen pitchers, even high-profile closers, are highly interchangeable. Further, and this is another *Moneyball* tenet, teams are foolish to overpay for these skill sets when they are often easily found, cheaply, elsewhere. It must be acknowledged that the Yankees' Mariano Rivera is the exception to the rule. The consistency of his brilliance since 1997 is absolutely mind-boggling. Over his career, his season numbers have a ridiculously low standard deviation, no matter what statistic you look at. He's as assuredly the greatest reliever of all time as Wayne Gretzky is the greatest hockey player and *Seinfeld* the greatest situation comedy. Even so, here is the league ranking of the Yankee bullpen's WAR over the past five years entering the 2011 season:

Year	Bullpen WAR
2006	11th
2007	24th
2008	1st
2009	7th
2010	10th

Even anchored by the greatest, most consistent reliever of all time, the Yankees' bullpen performance as a whole fluctu-ates pretty significantly from year to year, if not quite as much as the average major league team's. Even with Rivera, in all but 2009, you would have come closer to estimating their WAR as a unit for the year by simply guessing the prior year's league average than you would have by guessing the Yankees prior-year performance.

I thought this was a pretty amazing finding and certainly not a consensus opinion among casual fans. So, rather than look at personnel changes within each bullpen, I simply assumed each team's bullpen WAR in 2011 would be 2.9 for National League teams and 2.5 for American League teams, the 2010 league averages. For the Phillies, a team whose bullpen registered 1.4 WAR in 2010, this projects to 1.5 additional WAR, or fifteen fewer runs allowed in 2011.

Put all three projection components together with the adjusted 2010 results and (ta-da!) the Phillies 2011 season has been modeled. Here is what my model predicted for the Phillies in runs scored and runs allowed for 2011:

	Runs Scored	Runs Allowed
Philadelphia Phillies in 2010	772	640
Adjusted for Cluster Luck	-27	21
Projected Change in Batting Performance	-51	

	Runs Scored	Runs Allowed
Projected Change in Starting Pitching		-70
Projected Change in Bullpen Performance		-15
2011 Projected RS and RA	694	576

After doing this for every team, I had a finalized model for the 2011 season that would serve as the basis for all of my wagers. My model yielded the following projected standings for 2011* (with change from 2010 in parentheses):

AL East		AL Central		AL West	
Boston	98-64 (+8)	Detroit	84-78 (+3)	Texas	87-75 (-3)
NY Yankees	94-68 (-1)	Chicago White Sox	82-80 (-6)	Seattle	81-81 (+20)
Baltimore	86-76 (+20)	Minnesota	77-87 (-17)	Oakland	79-83 (-2)
Tampa Bay	82-80 (-14)	Kansas City	73-91 (+6)	LA Angels	69-93 (-11)
Toronto	78-84 (-7)	Cleveland	73-91 (+4)		

NL East		NL Central		NL West	
Philadelphia	93-69 (-4)	St. Louis	89-73 (+3)	Colorado	91-71 (+8)
Atlanta	88-74 (-3)	Milwaukee	86-76 (+9)	San Francisco	85-77 (-7)

*Those reading with a calculator handy may have noticed that the Phillies projection of 694 runs scored and 576 runs allowed would come to a winning percentage of .584, or ninety-five wins in a 162-game season. The projected standings show only ninety-three wins, because once every team's projection was complete, total runs scored across the entire league needed to equal total runs allowed. All team projections were normalized to a 2011 run environment of 20,237 runs scored and allowed.

NL East		NL Central		NL West	
Florida	76-86 (-4)	Cincinnati	85-77 (-6)	LA Dodgers	83-79 (+3)
Washington	75-87 (+6)	Chicago Cubs	84-78 (+9)	Arizona	80-82 (+15)
NY Mets	74-88 (-5)	Pittsburgh	69-93 (+12)	San Diego	65-97 (-25)
		Houston	64-98 (-12)		

Now that the projections were completed, I compared them with the Las Vegas over-under lines for total wins in 2011. There were nine teams that had a difference of five games or more, as follows:

Over Bets: Projection > Over-Under Line		Under Bets: Projection < Over-Under Line	
Arizona	Over 72½ Wins	Florida	Under 82½ Wins
Baltimore	Over 76½ Wins	Houston	Under 72½ Wins
Kansas City	Over 67½ Wins	LA Angels	Under 83½ Wins
Seattle	Over 69½ Wins	Minnesota	Under 85½ Wins
		San Diego	Under 75½ Wins

These were the nine positions that I designated for a futures basket worth 10 percent of my starting capital. I would take the over—or, in trading-speak, "go long" four teams each for 1.25 percent of my starting capital and short five teams for another 1 percent each.

The portfolio had its first positions, but it would take six months to see if they would pay off. The real action was going to take place on a daily basis. It was time to figure out how to turn the full-season projections into single-game picks and compare them against the oddsmakers' daily line.

5

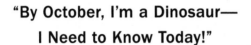

"By October, I'm a Dinosaur— I Need to Know Today!"

In the movie *Wall Street*, Marv, a fellow broker and friend of Charlie Sheen's Bud Fox, attempts to place an order with a floor trader. When he encounters a delay, he screams, "No, in ten minutes it's history! At four o'clock I'm a dinosaur!" Although the movie is more than twenty years old, that line is still a staple on trading desks across Wall Street, because it vividly describes the fleeting value of information. I felt the same way about my model's projections for the 2011 season. It was fine to have futures positions in place for a handful of teams, but between Opening Day and the start of the playoffs, more than 2,400 baseball games would be played. I felt the same way Marv did because I believed my model had an edge compared with consensus thinking, and I didn't want to have to wait around until October to see if that was true. I wanted to use the model every day of the season by applying its projections to single games.

Even without a model, casual baseball fans know the New York Yankees are better than the Toronto Blue Jays, who are better than the Kansas City Royals. But how much better are the Yankees than one team compared with the other? If the Yankees played each team twelve times in a season, how many games could they expect to win vs. each opponent? Having a full season outlook is all well and good, but if you want to put your money down now, you need to figure out how to make single-game projections.

Over the course of a full 162-game season, the best teams in each league will most likely win at least ninety-seven games, while the worst will lose that many. An average team, of course, would win exactly half the time, or eighty-one games. It takes ninety-seven wins (technically 97.2) for a team to win 60 percent of its games or, in sports-page and broadcasting parlance, "play .600 baseball." Conversely, a team that loses at least ninety-seven games (and therefore wins no more than sixty-five) is said to "play .400 baseball." This raises a very basic question for anyone trying to predict the outcome of a baseball game: If a .600 team played a .500 team, how often would the .600 team win? What if it played a .400 team? Or another .600 team?

To calculate the answer, long formulas with scientific names aren't needed, although they exist. The answer is intuitive to anyone who has ever watched a close basketball game. Picture your favorite team facing a one-point deficit with two seconds left in the game, about to send a 70 percent free-throw shooter to the line to shoot two free throws. What are the chances, after both free throws have been shot, that your favorite team is winning, tied, or still losing?

A fan that has taken a basic probability class knows there is a 49 percent chance the player will make both free throws. The math is simple. Since there is a 70 percent chance the shooter will make *either* shot, the chances of him making both are .70 x .70, or .49. There is only a 9 percent chance he will miss both attempts (.30 x .30) and, therefore, a 42 percent chance (.3 x .7 + .7 x .3, since there are two different sequences in which just one free throw is made) he will make just one of the two attempts and the game will be tied.

Returning to baseball, what's the win expectation in a single game for a team that wins 60 percent of its games against a team that wins 40 percent of its games? The logic is identical to the free throw calculation. If you were to randomly select a date from the baseball season when both teams played a game, there could be four different pairings of results: Both teams win, both teams lose, and either the 60 percent team wins while the 40 percent team loses, or vice versa. Here are the probabilities of those four pairings:

.600 Team	.400 Team	Probability	Calculation
Win	Win	24 percent	.6 x .4
Lose	Lose	24 percent	(1-.6) x (1-.4)
Win	Lose	36 percent	.6 x (1-.4)
Lose	Win	16 percent	(1-.6) x .4

Of course, if we're looking for games when the two teams play each other, they can't both win or both lose. So throwing those two outcomes aside, we're left with two outcomes: a 36 percent chance the .600 team wins and a 16 percent chance the .400 team wins. Only one adjustment is needed. Since those are the only two possible outcomes and they only add up to 52 percent, they must be adjusted to equal 100 percent. Therefore the .600 team would win 69.2 percent of the time (.36 / [.36 + .16]), and the .400 team would win 30.8 percent of the time (.16 / [.36 + .16]). So:

When a .600 team plays a .400 team, it is expected to win 69.2 percent of the time.

When a .600 team plays a .500 team, it is expected to win 60 percent of the time.

When a .600 team plays a .600 team, it is expected to win 50 percent of the time.

There are some interesting observations to be made from these calculations. To be a ninety-seven-win team, which will almost always result in a playoff appearance and most likely a division crown, a ball club must beat up on the worst teams in the league at a 70 percent clip. In other words, the best teams should beat the worst teams nearly three out of four games. Also, when it plays the best team in the league, an eighty-one-win team will play at the overall level *of the worst team in the league.* That is a bit surprising. An average, eighty-one-win team expects to win only 40 percent of the time vs. a ninety-seven-win team.

The relevance of this calculation is that I could now take my season projections and convert them to single-game-win expectancies. First, however, I looked at actual game results over the past few years. After all, this is just a theoretical calculation of probability. Let's check it against reality.

Over the five prior seasons (2006–10), there were twelve teams that finished with either eighty, eighty-one, or eighty-two wins. Those teams comprise the subset of .500 teams. There were eight teams that won at least ninety-seven games; they are the .600 team subset. Finally, there were thirteen teams that won no more than sixty-five games—the .400 team subset.

Results of Games in Which .400, .500, and .600 Teams
Played Each Other, 2006–10*

.600 Teams vs. .400 Teams

From 2006 to 2010, there were 136 games between the best and
worst teams in baseball. The .600 teams' weighted-average
(based on the proportion of the 136 games participated in) winning percentage was .611, and the .400 teams was .386. Therefore the .600 teams' winning percentage would theoretically be
71.3 percent. The .600 teams actually went 95-41, for a winning
percentage of 69.9 percent.

.600 Teams vs. .500 Teams

From 2006 to 2010, there were sixty-nine games between elite
and average teams. The .600 teams' weighted-average winning
percentage was .602, and for the .500 teams it was .497. Therefore the expected win percentage for the .600 teams is 60.4 percent. The .600 teams actually went 44-25, for a win percentage
of 63.8 percent. While the 3.4 percent spread between predicted and actual results is the largest of the three subsets, it's
still only a two-game difference in results over sixty-nine
games, the same as the subset above.

---

*Excludes the handful of interleague games that may exist in any grouping, due to the dif-
ference in overall league talent. For instance, during this period, a .500 team in the American League was better than a .500 team in the National League.

.500 Teams vs. .400 Teams

From 2006 to 2010, there were 155 games between average teams and the worst teams in baseball. The weighted-average winning percentage of the .500 teams was .497, and for the .400 teams it was .380. Therefore the .500 teams' expected winning percentage in these matchups is 61.8 percent. They actually went 98-57, for a win percentage of 63.2 percent—again, just a two-win difference vs. expectations across 155 contests.

In two of the three cases, the actual win percentage came within 1.5 percent of the estimate, while the estimate for the .600 vs. .500 teams was off by 3.5 percent. The number of games that fell into that second category—roughly one-half of the observed games in the other two categories—wasn't nearly as robust. Over an entire 162-game season, a 1.5 percent slippage rate totals about two to three games. This is a very acceptable slippage rate and tells me that if my overall projections are correct, I should be able to convert them into very reliable individual game projections. Again and again, analysis like this reveals the virtue of modeling a 162-game baseball season vs. efforts to handicap a sixteen-game football season in the NFL.

Turning to the first of six Opening Day games, Milwaukee at Cincinnati, I calculated each team's win expectancy. From the previous chapter, we know the projected final records for each team are nearly identical, with a one-game edge to the Brewers. (Note that the projected win percentage is derived from the Pythagorean theorem based on projected runs scored and runs allowed. The projected record is rounded based on the projected win percentage.)

	Projected 2011 Win Percentage	Projected 2011 Record	Opening Day Win Expectancy
Milwaukee	.531	86-76	.5080
Cincinnati	.523	85-77	.4920

A .531 team has a win expectancy of 50.8 percent when it plays a .523 team, so if there were no more adjustments to make, that would be our projection for the game. However, there are three other factors that must be taken into account, and they can all have a material impact on the initial calculation.

1. Lineup Changes

The projection for each team assumes a specific starting lineup based on each team's expected starters for the year. Anytime there are substitutions because of injury, platooning,* or simply rest, an adjustment to the projection is necessary. For instance, Milwaukee's regular right fielder, Corey Hart, began the season on the disabled list, and as a result Mark Kotsay took his place in the

---

*In a platoon system, a player with a specific trait—say, the fact that he hits left-handed—plays against pitchers who are right-handed but sits against left-handed pitchers. Another right-handed hitter will play against the left-handed pitcher. This concept baffled my wife, so I explained it like this: During college, there was a 7-Eleven in Blacksburg, Virginia, that never used to card me, so among my friends, I'd buy the beer when we stopped in there. However, in another part of town, we noticed there was a store that never carded African Americans. So at that store, my African-American friend would go in and buy the beer, while I would wait in the car. "That's a platoon system," I explained while my ballet-obsessed wife leaned back and nodded knowingly. I'm like the Rosetta Stone software program when it comes to translating the language of baseball.

lineup for Opening Day. Additionally, although Jonathan Lucroy was expected to start the majority of games at catcher for Milwaukee, Wil Nieves got the Opening Day nod. Based on the PECOTA projections, Kotsay and Nieves are inferior players vs. Hart and Lucroy. Therefore, the Milwaukee team I had projected to score 737 runs, and subsequently win eighty-six games, was not the same team that took the field in Cincinnati on Opening Day. Based on the differences in their expected WAR contributions, a lineup with Kotsay and Nieves instead of Hart and Lucroy would score sixty-two fewer runs over the course of an entire season. That would cost Milwaukee roughly six wins. There were no changes in Cincinnati's Opening Day lineup compared with its projection, so no adjustment was needed. As a result of the Milwaukee lineup changes, I now had a different projection.

	Projected 2011 Win Percentage	Projected 2011 Record	Opening Day Win Expectancy
Milwaukee	.493	80-82	.4683
Cincinnati	.523	85-77	.5317

2. Starting Pitcher Adjustment

It may not be necessary to calculate an adjustment due to lineup changes every game, but there will always be an adjustment needed to account for each team's starting pitcher. That's because a team's projection of runs allowed for an entire season is the sum of the expected runs it will allow across games started by its aggregate rotation. But, of course, every pitcher in a starting rotation is not the same. For instance, looking at Milwaukee, it was expected that the Brewers' five starting pitchers would provide the team with a total contribution of 15.7 wins above replacement. However, their Opening Day starting pitcher was Yovani Gallardo, projected to produce a 2011 WAR (assuming thirty-two starts) of 4.48. Similar to the logic used in the Justin Verlander discussion a few pages back, if Gallardo started all 162 games for Milwaukee, as opposed to his thirty-two projected starts, he would provide 22.4 (4.48 x 5) WAR, or 6.7 more than the projected starters. (In this equation, for simplicity, a 160-game season is assumed for all starting pitching adjustments. Thus 5 [160/32] is used instead of 5.0625 [162/32].) Therefore, for the purposes of calculating their win expectancy for this game, Milwaukee's projected runs allowed for the season would be lowered by sixty-seven runs. The Reds' Opening Day starter, Edinson Volquez, is better than the average starter on the Reds projected staff by an even greater margin than Gallardo, relative to his counterparts. As a result, Cincinnati's seasonal runs-allowed projection would be lowered by seventy runs for the Opening Day projection. Adjusted for lineup changes and the starting pitchers, here is the new win-expectancy calculation.

	Projected 2011 Win Percentage	Projected 2011 Record	Opening Day Win Expectancy
Milwaukee	.535	87-75	.4665
Cincinnati	.568	92-70	.5335

3. Home Field Advantage

One of the great mysteries of major league baseball has been the remarkable consistency of the value of home field advantage. Across every era of baseball in the past century—which encompasses changes in travel from train to airplane, a switch from predominantly day games to night games, and numerous league expansions, reducing the number of trips to the same city—the value of playing games at home has stayed roughly the same, at 8 percent. That is, home teams have consistently won 54 percent of games for the last one hundred years. The data is remarkable for its consistency. There has been only one decade when the home-team winning percentage deviated by more than +/- 0.5 percent. That was the 1930s, when it was 55.3 percent. In every other decade it has never been more than 54.4 percent or less than 53.5 percent. For example, from 1910 to 1919, home teams won 54 percent of their games, and from 2000 to 2009 they won 54.2 percent. There isn't one other part of baseball—not the rules, the scoring environment, or the venues in which the game is played—that has remained constant over one hundred years.

At the same time, based on a study conducted by Matt Swartz while he was a writer at Baseball Prospectus, no single team has ever had a persistent home field advantage in excess of 8 percent (with the exception of the pre-humidor*

*During the first decade of the Colorado Rockies existence, home runs were hit at record, and to some, alarming, rates at Coors Field. To combat the excessive home runs, in 2002 Colorado began storing baseballs in a humidor prior to their use in games. Since then home runs, and by extension total runs scored in games at Coors have decreased noticeably.

Colorado Rockies, circa 1994–2004). From one year to the next, home field performance is mean-reverting, and Swartz proves this in a number of ways, most convincingly by demonstrating that using a .540 win-percentage estimate for a team's home winning percentage for any year is more accurate than using a formula that relies on its prior year's home winning percentage. As such, the model will use an 8 percent adjustment for all games that do not involve interleague play.*

Turning back to the Brewers and the Reds, my prior calculation, which accounted for lineup changes and the game's starting pitchers, was essentially a win-expectancy calculation if the game were played on a neutral field. However, the game was in Cincinnati, so applying the 8 percent advantage to Cincinnati resulted in a further adjusted win expectancy:

	Projected 2011 Win Percentage	Projected 2011 Record	Neutral Field Win	Home Field Win Expectancy Adjustment	Opening Day Win Expectancy
Milwaukee	.535	87-75	.4665		.4238
Cincinnati	.568	92-70	.5335	1.08	.5762

*Based on fourteen years of data, home field advantage appears to be worth slightly more, perhaps as much as 10 percent, during interleague play, suggesting that there is some familiarity aspect to home field advantage. However, the limited number of interleague games played each year hasn't been enough to alter the league's overall home field advantage of 8 percent.

So, given the Brewers' and Reds' announced starting line-ups and their respective starting pitchers, the Reds would win a game played in Cincinnati 57.6 percent of the time. This is a big difference compared with season-long projections that foresaw the Brewers as the slightly better team in 2011. It's why fine tuning the model to account for lineup changes on a daily basis is critical to success.

Conveniently for those inclined to gamble, oddsmakers also post a line that contains *their* win expectancy for each game. Disagree and it's time to place a bet, because, as it's said on the trading floors at investment banks, "it takes a buyer and a seller to make a market." For this game, the oddsmakers posted the following line:

Milwaukee: -105
Cincinnati: -105

Although that's the simplest line possible for a baseball game, it still doesn't look anything like a typical listing you'd see in the newspaper for a football game, chiefly because there's no point spread. A primer on baseball betting is necessary because, to the uninitiated, determining the price at which to buy or sell when placing a bet on a baseball game can be as daunting as determining the currency exchange rate in a foreign country.* That uncertainty or discomfort could lead one to pass on an attractive opportunity.

And this was a situation where placing a bet made an awful lot of sense.

*Every time I find myself in a country where little English is spoken, my dining experience always follows the same path. I order dinner, via pointing and hand gestures, like a mediocre charades player, while the non-English-speaking waiter barely tolerates my existence. Then the check comes and, after a tortured calculation involving the exchange rate, I pay the bill and leave what travel books tell me is a customary tip. I mutter "thank you" in the native language as the waiter picks up the bill. Invariably, he or she collects the payment, looks up, and says (suddenly in fluent English, mind you), "No, *thank you*, sir!" I traded millions of dollars in stocks without making a math error, and yet I never seem to get out of a bistro in Europe without overpaying for an order of steak frites.

6

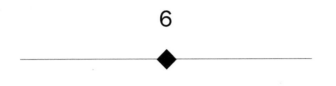

Betting on Baseball: a Primer

If Google existed just about twenty-five years ago and you typed "betting on baseball" into the search engine, without a doubt you would have gotten pages and pages of Pete Rose–related output. Players betting on games has been grounds for banishment ever since the Black Sox Scandal of 1919, when eight members of the Chicago White Sox conspired to throw the World Series in exchange for payoffs from gamblers who'd bet on their opponents, the Cincinnati Reds. Thanks to the mysterious disappearance of confessions made before a grand jury in 1920, among other factors, the eight players were acquitted of the charges in 1921. Despite the dispute about the extent of "Shoeless" Joe Jackson's involvement in the fix—immortalized in the films *Field of Dreams* and *Eight Men Out*—

there was little doubt as to what had happened, and baseball's existence appeared imperiled.

Baseball's owners took swift action, appointing a federal judge, Kenesaw Mountain Landis, as its first-ever commissioner and granting him broad powers under a "baseball's best interest" clause. Landis banned the eight White Sox for life, setting the precedent that any player who bet on a baseball game would suffer an identical fate. To this day, Pete Rose, baseball's all-time hit leader, remains banned from baseball for betting on it, and although not officially bound to MLB's ruling on Rose, the Hall of Fame adopted an identical rule that has kept Rose ineligible for induction.

Owing to its history, MLB takes this rule so seriously—in every team's clubhouse there is a sign warning players against betting on games—that there is very little likelihood that any current player has bet on a baseball game. But times have changed since Pete Rose's ban, and a Google search for "betting on baseball" currently returns a first page free of Black Sox and Pete Rose references. America's tolerance for gambling has evolved tremendously in the last twenty-five years, and the odds are overwhelming, due to self-selection, that if you picked up this book, you've placed a bet on at least one football game. Those odds drop—but are still significant, due to March Madness (a.k.a. the World's Largest Office Pool)—if "football game" is replaced with "basketball game." There are many, many passionate sports bettors and devoted baseball fans who place bets all year on football and basketball games yet never bet on baseball. Whether you bet on football and basketball games for the entertainment value of gambling or with the serious intent of making money, baseball betting is a much better alternative. If you disagree, give me this chapter to change your mind. By the end of it, I hope you see how tough a market baseball oddsmakers operate in.

To say gambling on sports in the United States is popular is an understatement. In 2011 there was $3.17 billion wagered on sports—just in Nevada. Industry observers conservatively estimate that legal wagering in Nevada comprises 5 percent of total betting across the U.S., with some saying Nevada represents less than 1 percent of a $380 billion global industry. In 2011 football accounted for 42 percent of the bets, and basketball accounted for 23 percent (per the Nevada Gaming Commission). Baseball, by comparison, accounted for just 18 percent of all sports bets. (Hockey, horses, soccer, boxing, etc., made up the other 17 percent.) Despite the fact that bettors wager more than three times as much money on football and basketball games as they do on baseball, they do so knowing this irrefutable and maddening fact: In almost all cases, the interests of the players they are betting on are not aligned with their own. That's because football and basketball wagers are governed by the point spread. Baseball wagers are not.

As most casual sports fans know, when two teams play football or basketball, oddsmakers designate the favorite in terms of points. The Green Bay Packers were a 3½-point favorite in the 2011 Super Bowl, meaning that if you bet on the Packers, you would only win your bet if Green Bay won the game by more than 3½ points. Conversely, a bet on the Steelers would win if Pittsburgh won the game or lost by fewer than 3½ points. To illustrate the misaligned interests of bettors and players, consider this fictional but not at all far-fetched scenario: With the score tied and less than two minutes left in the game, Green Bay has the ball at Pittsburgh's one-yard line, first down and goal. Pittsburgh has called its last time-out, while Green Bay has all three of theirs left. As Green Bay comes to the line of scrimmage, there is exactly 1 minute left in the game. What is going to happen?

To the chagrin of Pittsburgh bettors, if Green Bay runs a play, the Steelers will let the Packers score a touchdown to go up by seven points. Pittsburgh will (or should) do that because that is the only way it can get the ball back with sufficient time left on the clock to tie the score and force overtime. Green Bay, on the other hand, fearing the possibility of a fumble and knowing that a field goal attempt from extra-point distance is nearly a sure thing, will most likely snap the ball and take a knee at least once and possibly two times, running the clock down to less than ten seconds in the process. If the Packers execute this plan, they will win by three points. This, of course, infuriates Green Bay bettors, who want the Packers to score a touchdown. Both teams will be working to the detriment of the people who have bet on them.

When it comes time to kick the field goal, the roles of the bettors will again reverse. Now Pittsburgh bettors want the Packers to make the field goal, while the Steeler players are actively trying to block it, and Green Bay bettors want the Packers to miss the field goal, setting up the possibility of winning by six in overtime. This is especially gut-wrenching for actual Packer fans who have bet on Green Bay. They don't know what to root for. It's a completely convoluted situation, and it happens all the time in football—and basketball, too: Meaningless uncontested three-point shots at the buzzer, college teams with big leads emptying their benches to play seldom-used substitutes with a minute left, and teams dribbling out the clock without attempting a shot are the bane of basketball bettors.*

Would you ever tie your financial interests to someone who didn't share the same incentives that get you paid? It would be like agreeing to be Adam Sandler's agent and getting paid by the Oscar nomination instead of a percentage of box-office gross. That's exactly what can happen when you bet basketball or football. No such misalignment of incentives exists when

---

*You could fill a book with the crazy bet-altering events that have occurred at the end of sporting events, but one of my favorites occurred in the 1990s, when a buddy of mine in Las Vegas lost the last game of his five-team basketball parlay when John Starks, of the New York Knicks, leaped and snatched (not blocked but simply snatched with one hand) a ball out of the air as it approached the rim. The final buzzer sounded and goaltending was called on the Knicks. The Knicks easily won the game, but the last two points for their opponents turned my buddy's winning ticket into a loser. To this day, if you mention John Starks to him, he will reflexively pummel you—even if he's just about to serve Communion.

betting baseball. Baseball has no point spread; its bets are instead governed by the money line. When oddsmakers establish a favorite in a baseball game, it's expressed in terms of a percent chance of winning the game. This is called the money line, and, for example, the New York Yankees were a -150 favorite on Opening Day of the 2011 season. This implied that the Yankees had a 60 percent chance of winning the game (150 / [150 +100]—much more on this later). Whether you think there is a chance greater than 60 percent (making you a candidate to bet on the Yankees) or less than 60 percent (now you are a candidate to bet on the Tigers, their opponent) of the Yankees winning, whichever team you bet on will attempt to win the game. Each team's manager will employ strategies designed to optimize his team's chance to win the game and, by extension, your chances of winning the bet. From an emotional and entertainment standpoint, as well as from an investment standpoint, that makes betting on baseball a proposition superior to betting on football or basketball.

The house advantage for a casino in the game of roulette is 5.26 percent. On a standard roulette wheel there are thirty-eight equal-size slots, numbered 1 through 36 with two zero spaces colored green. Place a bet on any number and if it comes up, you will receive thirty-five times the amount of your bet, plus your original bet, in return. It's very easy to see that in roulette the casino pays 35–1 on an event that has only a 1-in-38 chance of happening. If $1 were placed on each of the thirty-eight numbers, the casino would collect $37 in losing bets, pay $35 to the one winner (and return the original $1 bet), and pocket $2 in profit. Over time, whether the bets are on single numbers, colors, or odd/even, the casino will always make $2 out of every $38 bet, for a profit margin, or house edge, of 5.26 percent. In craps, the house advantage on the basic pass/don't-pass bet is about 1.5 percent, but because most players also make higher-margin bets on hard numbers, the field, etc., the effective house edge exceeds 3 percent. The house edge in blackjack varies with the skill and knowledge of the player and can actually be negative for successful card counters, but, similar to the basic bets in craps, the effective house advantage is somewhere between 1 percent and 3 percent.

So what is the house edge in sports betting? Just like in standard casino games, the trick is to determine the difference in the true odds of an event occurring and the implied odds as reflected in the payout. For football and basketball, which both employ a point spread, it's as easy to calculate as it is for roulette. Each team, regardless of whether you bet on the favorite or underdog to cover the spread, will be listed at a price of -110. That simply means that the bettor must risk 10 percent more than he can win. In other words, the -110 price means you must bet $110 to win $100. If the sportsbook gets two different people to bet $110 each on two different teams in the same game, it is guaranteed a $10 profit on the $220 that was bet, resulting in a profit margin of 4.55 percent. That profit margin never fluctu-ates for sportsbooks on the standard point spread–based wagers that dominate football and basketball betting.

Baseball, on the other hand, has a house advantage that rarely exceeds 50 percent of football and basketball's and is usually quite a bit less. The explanation requires a little bit of history. Because betting on football and basketball is a seller's market, sportsbooks have no need to run sales, reduce prices, and lower their profit margins. Baseball, for the majority of its season, has no other sports competition, and sportsbooks are looking to attract any business in the dog days of the sports-betting summer. Long ago they cut their baseball prices from the standard -110 to -105. So if two evenly matched teams are playing, sportsbooks offer -105 odds on either team. Using the same logic as above, this means that over the long run, sports-books make $5 out of every $210 that is wagered, for a margin of 2.38 percent, nearly 50 percent less of a house advantage than in football or basketball. But the good news for baseball bettors doesn't stop there. While the house edge never fluctu-ates in football or basketball, in baseball the 2.38 percent house edge is as *disadvantageous* for the bettor as it gets.

Only two teams judged evenly matched by an oddsmaker will have a -105 price. As the oddsmaker moves the price of the favorite higher to -110, -115, -120, and so on, the price for the underdog moves as well, to +100, +105, +110, respectively. For each dollar bet, there is always a ten-cent difference between the amount required to win $1 with a bet on the favorite and the payout a $1 bet on the underdog will return. This spread is known in betting circles as the "dime line," and it is the number-one reason serious sports bettors should focus on baseball.

Thanks to the math inherent in the dime line, as the price of the favorite rises, the house advantage actually decreases. This can be seen most clearly by examining the difference in the implied odds of an individual wager. Implied odds are simply the percentage of time a bet would have to win to make one indifferent to choosing a side. For instance, if I offer an even money proposition, or 1-to-1 odds, on flipping a coin and getting heads, the implied odds are 50 percent. If you get heads 50 percent of the time, over the long run, you would break even on your bet. (Obviously, these are also the actual odds.) On a standard football or basketball bet with a $100 payout, losers pay $110 while winners collect $100. Because you must bet $11 to win $10, the implied odds of each team covering the spread are 52.38 percent ($11/$21). Mathematically, the implied odds formula is expressed this way: outlay / (outlay + payout). Since each team has implied odds of 52.38 percent, combined that comes to 104.76 percent. In gambling parlance, "juice" equals the sum of the implied odds in excess of the actual odds. Of course, there is just a 100 percent chance one team will win at the end of the game, so there is 4.76 percent of "juice" in the standard point spread wager, priced at -110. For comparison purposes, here is the standard football or basketball wager in table form. As a reminder 110 / (110 + 100) = .5238 for both sides of the wager.

	Price	Implied Odds
Favorite	-110	.5238
Underdog	-110	.5238

1.0476–1 = 4.76 percent of "juice"

Compare this with the amount of juice in baseball bets at different levels of implied odds. Here's the calculation for the dime-line wager between two evenly matched teams:

	Price	Implied Odds
Favorite	-105	.5122
Underdog	-105	.5122

1.0244–1 = 2.44 percent of "juice"

As the dime line increases, the amount of juice actually decreases:

	Price	Implied Odds
Favorite	-110	.5238
Underdog	+110	.5000

1.0238–1 = 2.38 percent of "juice"

	Price	Implied Odds
Favorite	-120	.5455
Underdog	+110	.4762

1.0217–1 = 2.17 percent of "juice"

	Price	Implied Odds
Favorite	-150	.6000
Underdog	+140	.4167

1.0167–1 = 1.67 percent of "juice"

Over the entire 2011 season the average favorite was priced at -142.

	Price	Implied Odds
Favorite	-142	.5868
Underdog	+132	.4310

1.0178–1 = 1.78 percent of "juice"

Remarkable, isn't it? The amount of juice on an average baseball bet is just 37.4 percent (1.78 percent vs. 4.76 percent) of the standard football and basketball bets. I know extremely savvy traders and sports bettors who are not aware of this vast difference, because they've never focused on betting baseball. It stands to reason that with a much smaller house advantage, there exists a far greater chance of making money betting on baseball than on football or basketball.

After writing a sentence like that, a voice in my head speaks, and it sounds a lot like my mother. "Joey, smaller house advantage or not, you still can't make money vs. a casino. Have you ever seen the lobbies? You don't decorate with Dale Chihuly sculptures unless you're winning. It's called a 'house advantage' for a reason, no matter how small." This is, of course, a salient point. Using roulette as an example, a casino could choose to increase the payout for correctly picking the correct number from 35–1 to 36.5–1. The implied odds of hitting a single number (1 in 37.5, or 2.67 percent) would still be greater than the actual odds (1 in 38, or 2.63 percent), and across all thirty-eight numbers the total difference would represent 1.33 percent of juice (38 x 2.67 percent = 101.33 percent). It's true that over the long run casinos would still have a gross profit on each roulette table. They might not have a *net* profit—paying the dealers, the cocktail waitresses, plus the overhead involved in running a casino might erase the table's gross profit—but even so, the players would always have a negative expected value. That's because, a priori, or before any single spin of the wheel, the true odds of each outcome are known with absolute certainty. This is true of any game you play against the casino,[*]

---

[*]Poker, of course, has a positive expected value for lots of players, but they don't play against the casino, which simply collects rent in the poker room.

and it's why the house cannot be beaten, except by expert card-counters in blackjack.

In baseball, as in all sports betting, the true odds of an event are only known with absolute certainty ex post facto, or after the event has occurred. Even then, observers should be careful not to confuse the results, ex post facto, with the true odds, a priori. The actual event played is only one possible outcome. It usually takes a great deal of distance, and many more observations, to determine true odds in a baseball game. For instance, on Opening Day 2011 the Colorado Rockies hosted the Arizona Diamondbacks and were listed as a -200 favorite, while the Diamondbacks were a +185 underdog. (The dime line does spread out to fifteen cents around the -200 area.) The implied odds of winning were therefore 66.67 percent for Colorado and 35.09 percent for Arizona. (Again, please note that even with a fifteen-cent line at this level, the juice is still just 1.76 percent, even less than the average bet across an entire season.) These odds reflected the pre-season expectations for both teams, as well as for their starting pitchers, Ubaldo Jiménez, for Colorado, and Ian Kennedy, for Arizona. Those expectations were wildly incorrect. Arizona ended up being a much better team than Colorado in 2011 (topping the Rockies by twenty-one games in the National League West), winning thirteen of the eighteen games they played. Kennedy finished fourth in the

National League Cy Young Award voting, while Jiménez had the worst year of his career. By the time Arizona visited Colorado in September, the Diamondbacks were actually favored in a game started by the unheralded Josh Collmenter. The result of that Opening Day game didn't prove it (although Arizona won 7–6), but by the end of the season it was clear that the true odds of the Arizona Diamondbacks beating the Colorado Rockies—in Colorado, with Ian Kennedy starting against Ubaldo Jiménez—were vastly different from the implied odds of 35.09 percent. I'd put them at about 50 percent, but no matter where an alternative calculation places the true odds, not one would have the true odds anywhere close to 35.09 percent. Ex post facto, we know there was positive expected value—and tremendous value, at that—in betting on Arizona on Opening Day. A model can detect that a priori. (In fact, I saw an Opening Day bet on Arizona possessing a nearly 4 percent edge—more on this in Chapter 7.) That prescience can never happen at a casino table game, and it's why you can't dismiss out of hand someone's ability, when betting sports, to overcome the house advantage.

This is where the "juice" comes into play, and the fact that it is minimal for baseball games has a huge implication for the casino and the bettor. The oddsmaker must attempt to use the small amount of juice, about 1.78 percent on average (1.76 percent in the Arizona-Colorado game, even with the expansion to a fifteen-cent line), to straddle the true odds of the game. As

I rehabbed my leg during the summer of 2011, I stumbled upon a visual analogy that demonstrated just how difficult it is to maneuver in a window that small.

Compatible with its Wii game console, Nintendo has a stand-alone game entitled Wii Fit. One of the activities on Wii Fit is a balance test. In it, the user stands on one leg in the center of a specially designed balance board. The board measures shifts from right to left, and the goal is to stand as perfectly centered on one leg as possible. While the user is balancing on the board, the deviation from centered balance can be viewed on the television screen. There are borders on either side of center, and the user must keep his balance within the borders. In time, the borders shrink and it becomes much harder for the gamer to maintain balance within the borders. It occurred to me as I worked on my balance that this is exactly the problem the oddsmaker faces. At the beginning, the wide borders represent the margin of error in setting football and basketball lines. By the time the borders have shrunk down to one-third of the starting width, there is almost no margin of error. This is what the baseball oddsmaker faces. Anyone serious about making money by betting on sports has to consider baseball.

The third factor that makes betting baseball more appealing than football or basketball is the ability to model the results. In analyzing the NFL, Aaron Schatz and his team at Football Outsiders have made huge strides in the last decade applying advances in statistical analysis to determine how and why certain teams win, as well as the contributions of individual players to winning. John Hollinger, of ESPN, among others, has pioneered that approach in analyzing NBA games. But the analysis of both those sports is far behind the field of research in baseball. In fact, their research is largely derivative of theory developed by baseball researchers years before. However, there are huge differences between baseball and the other two sports, which limits the modeling ability of the latter. In baseball it is much easier to isolate the performance of one individual, independent of other variables. For instance, from 1995–2002, you could model with a high degree of certainty that Randy Johnson would strike out 34 percent of the batters he faced. For eight years, it didn't matter what team he was on, what league he played in, what ballpark he pitched in, who caught the pitches he threw, or even who the opposition was; independent of all those factors, you could count on Randy Johnson to strike out 34 percent of the batters he faced.* That

---

*This from my wife: "You know what else you could model with absolute certainty? Randy Johnson's dickish behavior." Wow. I should explain. A perk of manning the trading desk at a hedge fund that trades actively is that brokers constantly offer tickets to area sporting events. One broker in particular had tickets to Oakland A's games in the first row behind the home-plate backstop. These seats had literally been built on the field, as an addendum to the original seating configuration at the Oakland Coliseum. I accepted a pair of tickets when the Yankees came to town in May 2005. Only because it was the Yankees, I successfully persuaded my wife, Caitlin, to go to the game and bring our infant daughter as well. Lily, being eleven months old, traveled in a BabyBjörn, strapped to her mother's chest and facing forward the entire game. To get to these seats on the field, we had to walk, single-file, through the same narrow maze of tunnels the umpires and the visiting players use to get to the field. As such, any trip to or from our seats put us in contact with players, especially before the game began. When we first walked to our seats, I smiled as, in front of me, a few different Yankees casually strolled down the tunnel after warm-ups and told my wife how beautiful our baby was, smiling at Lily and even shaking her wiggling feet as they

type of precision is not available in football, due to the inability to isolate individual performance. The same holds true in basketball, with the exception of free-throw shooting percentage. To illustrate this dependence, Aaron Schatz likes to say that, while we can make statements of certainty about baseball, in the NFL it's necessary to add caveats such as, "Playing behind the New England offensive line, throwing to Wes Welker, with occasional play-action fakes to the Patriots running backs, Tom Brady will complete 65 percent of the passes he attempts."

This means it's much easier to precisely determine the outcome of a baseball game than it is that of any other sport. Despite this ability to be more precise, the cost of applying this precision against the oddsmaker is considerably lower! And, as shown earlier, the very behavior being modeled (chances of winning the game) will be exactly the same behavior the players and coaches exhibit on the field. Betting on football or basketball is fun, just like playing roulette or a Wheel of Fortune slot machine. But the only value these table games offer is entertainment. Baseball betting, which provides just as much excitement as football or basketball betting, offers a bettor a much better chance of achieving a positive expected value.

---

walked by. A short time later, after a diaper-change run, Caitlin came back to our seats fuming and said, "Who on the Yankees is really tall and thin with stringy hair?" I told her it had to be Randy Johnson. "He just growled at Lily and me as we walked down the tunnel. Who would growl at a baby?" Suffice it to say, Randy Johnson remains an enemy in our household to the point that whenever the GEICO commercial featuring him comes on TV, I always have to lie when Caitlin asks, "We don't still have any GEICO policies, do we?"

Aligned interests between bettor and team. A materially lower house advantage. Behavior that can be modeled more precisely. Could there possibly be any other advantage to betting baseball over football? Well, if you had the opportunity to invest in a venture with a positive expected value, like ownership of a roulette wheel, would you prefer to own it for one hour or nine and a half hours? Funny things can happen in one hour; there is no guarantee of a profit even with the house edge. But over nine and a half hours, the natural fluctuations inherent in the game will smooth out, and the chances of losing money will be very small, approaching zero over time.

That's a relevant question to consider because there are 256 NFL games played each regular season, while there are 2,430 major league baseball games—nine and a half times more than the NFL.

PART TWO

THE LAUNCH

7

Bettor Up! Opening Day for the Model

Major League Baseball stretches Opening Day over multiple days—to allow teams to enjoy a relatively uncluttered spotlight for their first game of the season—before launching into a standard thirty-team, fifteen-game daily slate a few days later. In 2011, Opening Day was a two-day affair, March 31 and April 1. Over those two days, all thirty major league teams played their first game of the season and, with the exception of the Los Angeles Angels and Kansas City Royals in the American League and the San Francisco Giants and Los Angeles Dodgers in the National League, each team played only one game. Oddsmakers set these lines for all of the games:

March 31, 2011, Games					
Visitor	Starting Pitcher	Odds	Home Team	Starting Pitcher	Odds
Milwaukee	Yovani Gallardo	-105	Cincinnati	Edinson Volquez	-105
Atlanta	Derek Lowe	-135	Washington	Livan Hernández	+125
San Diego	Tim Stauffer	+160	St. Louis	Chris Carpenter	-175
San Francisco	Tim Lincecum	+105	LA Dodgers	Clayton Kershaw	-115
Detroit	Justin Verlander	+135	NY Yankees	CC Sabathia	-145
LA Angels	Jered Weaver	-145	Kansas City	Luke Hochevar	+135
April 1, 2011 Games					
Visitor	Starting Pitcher	Odds	Home Team	Starting Pitcher	Odds
Houston	Brett Myers	+240	Philadelphia	Roy Halladay	-260
Pittsburgh	Kevin Correia	+160	Chicago Cubs	Ryan Dempster	-175
Arizona	Ian Kennedy	+185	Colorado	Ubaldo Jiménez	-200
NY Mets	Mike Pelfrey	+160	Florida	Josh Johnson	-175
San Francisco	Jonathan Sánchez	+110	LA Dodgers	Chad Billingsley	-120
Chicago White Sox	Mark Buehrle	-110	Cleveland	Fausto Carmona*	+100
Boston	Jon Lester	-110	Texas	C.J. Wilson	+100
Minnesota	Carl Pavano	+105	Toronto	Ricky Romero	-115
Baltimore	Jeremy Guthrie	+165	Tampa Bay	David Price	-180
LA Angels	Dan Haren	-135	Kansas City	Jeff Francis	+125
Seattle	Felix Hernández	+100	Oakland	Trevor Cahill	-110

*Prior to 2012, Roberto Hernández played under the visa alias, Fausto Carmona.

Finally, I could decide which individual games to bet on. After having done so much work in the solitary confines of my apartment, the morning of March 31 felt like being back on a trading desk the morning before earnings were to be announced for a bunch of companies. On days like that, trading desks crackle with energy; based on weeks of work, decisions are about to be made that, depending on the quality of the work, will reward or punish the trader. I pored over each game, as if I were in front of a Bloomberg terminal studying the table of earnings expectations "the Street" had published.

Turning to the Milwaukee-Cincinnati game, I had taken into account the starting lineups, the starting pitchers, and the location of the game to convert my 2011 outlook into a single-game projection. As shown on page 78, the projection yielded a win probability of .5762 for the Reds and .4238 for the Brewers. Oddsmakers deemed this an even matchup, with both teams listed on the money line at -105. That converts into an implied chance of winning of 51.22 percent for both teams. My calculation deemed the Reds had a 6.4 percent (.5762–.5122) better chance of winning than the implied odds.

Applying the same steps as I had for the Brewers and Reds, I came up with the following list of teams with projected odds of winning in excess of the oddsmakers' implied odds.

March 31, 2011, Games	
Cincinnati Reds	6.4 percent
St. Louis Cardinals	14.13 percent
San Francisco Giants	5.04 percent
NY Yankees	6.98 percent
Kansas City Royals	9.87 percent
April 1, 2011 Games	
Philadelphia Phillies	0.13 percent
Chicago Cubs	1.65 percent
Arizona Diamondbacks	3.81 percent
Florida Marlins	2.76 percent
Cleveland Indians	3.46 percent
Boston Red Sox	5.79 percent
Toronto Blue Jays	2.97 percent
Baltimore Orioles	8.02 percent
Kansas City Royals	9.83 percent
Seattle Mariners	7.41 percent

That came to fifteen plays out of seventeen games—the other two games had implied odds that, thanks to the small amount of juice inherent in the prices, exceeded the projected odds for both teams. Therefore, with no positive edge, I passed on those games. The remaining fifteen-game basket was made up of seven favorites, seven underdogs, and one game deemed a toss-up (i.e., both teams were -105). In the case of some underdogs, like the Baltimore Orioles, I didn't actually think they were going to win. I thought the Orioles had just a 45.76 percent chance of winning. However, the implied odds in their +165 money line were 37.74 percent. Even though I thought they would lose, according to the model, the Orioles had true odds of winning that exceeded the implied odds by 8.02 percent.

It's very difficult for most people, even many professional traders, to invest in an outcome they don't think is going to happen. It's impossible to be an options trader with this mindset. For this reason, when interviewing prospective candidates on a trading desk, I liked to ask them how much they would wager on rolling a six with one roll of the die, based on two payouts I offered them: a 5–1 payout and a 9–1 payout. There is no right answer, but the candidate must recognize relative value; the amount bet on a 9–1 payout should be higher than the 5–1 payout. That's because the 9–1 payout offers a 6.67 percent edge (16.67 percent true odds vs. 10 percent implied odds) for the interviewee, while the 5–1 payout carries no edge for either party (16.67 percent true and implied odds).

Across the fifteen-game basket, the value of my projected edge ranged from 0.13 percent on the Phillies vs. the Astros to 14.13 percent in the case of the Cardinals vs. the Padres.

This brought up a very important question: How much should I bet on each game? Risk-averse individuals—at the risk of offending anyone, let's just refer to this type of person as my mother—would certainly suggest too little of a wager. They might be frightened by the concept of gambling, even if they were savvy in other areas of their life governed by finance, not realizing that an attractive risk-adjusted return—whether it exists in the stock market, a treasury bond, or a baseball game—is a prudent investment. (However, if they doubted the accuracy of the model, that's a perfectly rational reason to pass on an investment.) Another subset of the population, which includes many of my trading desk colleagues, might mistake an attractive risk-adjusted return as a sure thing, and just as surely as my mom would under-invest, many of my old colleagues would trample the word *prudent* on the way to place their bets.*

My approach—perhaps no surprise, given my background—is a bit different and is rooted in the concept of return on investment. As a result, getting the correct answer on how much to bet would take some more work, but there were two

---

*A few years ago, in an effort to entertain my friends and coworkers, I sent around an e-mail early on a Thursday morning, just hours before the start of the NCAA basketball tournament. I hadn't followed college basketball all year, but following in the footsteps of a couple of friends who wrote wildly entertaining college bowl preview e-mails, I used that same mailing list to create a similar NCAA tournament preview. In what I thought clearly established the e-mail as entertainment and not serious analysis, the first sentence read, "My annual quest to go 63-0 in the tournament begins in a few hours, and I have a feeling this year is the year I pull it off." Later that afternoon, as the last of the first set of four games was ending—dooming me to a 0-4 start to the day—I sent another e-mail with picks for the four games that would be played that afternoon. Instantly my phone rang. A very senior salesperson in another office was screaming in the background as his assistant said to me, "Mike wants to know why you have four more picks—he thought your e-mail this morning were your best picks of the day." I started to laugh, which was conveyed to Mike. He grabbed the phone and screamed at me, "Why didn't you tell me there were games you liked later today more than the first ones you picked this morning? Do you have any idea how much money I put on these games? I thought these were your best plays! You didn't tell me there were going to be more games!" I screamed right back at him, "How could I go 63-0 if I didn't pick every game!" After witnessing fifteen years of antics on Wall Street trading desks, that's still a top-three story.

things that I knew with certainty: The right answer would not be expressed as a whole number and begin with a dollar sign, and whatever answer I came up with, I should bet more on the game with the 14.13 percent edge than the game with the 0.13 percent edge.

Before entering the industry, most financial professionals invested in stocks and passionately followed the market. Whether it started with paper-route money, a bar/bat mitzvah windfall, or an allowance from their parents, the profit motive and a fascination with the stock market led them to investing and provided them with some experience tracking stocks. On a trading desk there is one trait that gives this pre-professional fascination away: They express price movement in dollars and cents. I've worked with trading assistants, research analysts, and even a portfolio manager who would say things like, "Amgen is up 20 cents. IBM is down a dollar." I'd tell them, especially colleagues on the buy side,* "That's meaningless." In return I'd get a blank stare and then some sort of defense like, "We're long 50,000 shares of Amgen. It means we're up $10,000. How is that meaningless?"

I'd concede that in a vacuum a $10,000 rise in the value of

---

*The "buy side" consists of entities such as hedge funds, mutual funds, insurance companies, etc., that purchase financial securities or research from investment banks. The investment banks, typically also broker-dealers, are referred to as the "sell side."

one of our holdings wasn't meaningless. However, running a hedge fund or a mutual fund isn't the same as managing your personal trading account. In a personal account, you're mainly concerned with making money. There's a reason a monthly statement from a stock broker, whether it comes from Fidelity, Charles Schwab, or Merrill Lynch, highlights a box on the top of the first page that shows how much the account has increased or decreased in value over the past month. When you have a personal trading account, your primary goal is to have more money at the end of the month than you had at the beginning.

For a professional such as a portfolio manager, a change in value, especially of just one stock, has no context and yields few clues about the performance of the fund and, therefore, its manager. When running a fund, relative performance is of paramount importance, as opposed to absolute performance, which is what an individual investor focuses on when he looks at his brokerage statement. As a result, stock movement should be expressed in percentage terms, or as it's called in the world of investing, basis points: 100 basis points equal 1 percent. This is why the Bloomberg screens of market professionals display stock movements in percentage terms as opposed to raw dollars and cents. If the biotech analyst tells me, "Amgen is up 18 basis points," it has more meaning. Perhaps the biotech analyst recommended, and successfully persuaded the portfolio manager to purchase, Amgen. However, this is a hedge fund, and in order to minimize the fund's sensitivity to gyrations in the overall market, the portfolio manager paired the purchase of Amgen with an equal-dollar-size short of Pfizer, a pharmaceutical company. (Recall from earlier that hedge funds commonly express their views on stocks in pairs trades as a method to reduce day-to-day volatility in the fund and reliance on the overall market to move in one direction.) As the trader, I will know all of our positions and know that Pfizer is up 75 basis points. Further, I see that the S&P is up 40 basis points. Now, Amgen's 18-basis point gain has meaning—and it means we're not having a good day. Yes, the Amgen position might be up $10,000, but not only is it underperforming against the short it's paired with; it's also underperforming the broader market. The analyst shouldn't have been as enthused as he was in proclaiming Amgen had risen 20 cents. Expressed in terms that highlight performance, profit (or loss) is simply the residue of performance.

In that sense, in developing a model with an edge over the oddsmakers, it would be incorrect to conclude that I, or anyone, should bet $100 a game or to take an approach that has as its goal a fixed profit of, say, $10,000. The first goal was to determine the size of the investment in the model or, really, the size of my fund. Once determined, I could begin calculating what percentage of the fund I was going to invest in a single game. That way, if I'm starting out a season with $1,000, and it's up to $1,500 in July, or my friends gave me $5,000 of their money to invest at any point of the season, determining the amount of money to bet on any one night is always a matter of percentages.

Lots of research on gambling and related literature can help determine the proper setting of those percentages.* In particular, the Kelly criterion, a money-management system that has been applied to the allocation of money for stock portfolio purposes, has long been used by gamblers. While familiar with the tenets and philosophies of this, and other systems in the world of gambling, I had a better place to turn. The risk management principles I'd employ for my baseball fund would come from the field of finance. Based on my front row seat through a dozen years of boom times and then tumult in the financial industry, I saw firsthand how risk should be managed properly and how Lehman Brothers, my employer of thirteen years, ignored the tenets of risk management related to self-preservation.

---

*The best book is probably Andrew Beyer's *Picking Winners,* considered a classic within horse-racing circles. The book, however, is far more than a how-to book for race handicappers. In the 1990s, I read an article by Jim Cramer proclaiming it the best book for anyone to read who wanted to trade stocks for a living. Along with *Reminiscences of a Stock Operator,* by Edwin Lefèvre, I heartily agree. In particular, Beyer's philosophy on bankroll management has relevance for any sports bettor.

8

The Sanctity of Future Earnings

At some point during their education, all business students are required to determine how much a company is worth. There are a number of different approaches, from the dividend discount model to a discounted-cash-flow calculation, but they all have a similar goal: to determine the present value of all the future earnings of a company.

These calculations not only involve a number of assumptions but are also very sensitive to small changes in those assumptions. The assumptions can be company-specific (future sales growth) or beyond the company's control (interest rate environment). No one can claim there is one "right" answer in valuing a company. It is still an extremely useful exercise, however, especially because the calculation yields an invaluable valuation insight to those who construct a model and fiddle with the assumptions: The bulk of the value of any enterprise lies in its future earnings.

Anyone who grasps this concept, who *really* understands the implications of this fact, is a candidate for CEO. Everyone else should be excluded from CEO consideration. Every manager—whether on the board of directors or in charge of a single production line within a vast enterprise—who understands that financial truth should know that no action taken to increase earnings in the current quarter can justify risking the future earnings stream. Working through the valuation models makes it clear that no amount of marginal earnings produced by a product or a division or even the entire company in the present exceeds the value of the future earnings of the enterprise, so nothing should ever be done that risks the existence of those future earnings.

Dick Fuld—the CEO of Lehman Brothers from the time it went public, in 1994, to the day it declared bankruptcy, in 2008—demonstrated firsthand that he didn't grasp the significance of this maxim. In fact, based on his post-bankruptcy statements to Congress and the sporadic interviews he has granted since 2008, he still doesn't. Dick continues to blame the Fed, Henry Paulson, other banks, and, most of all, rumor-spreading short-sellers for the demise of his firm. Until I hear Dick acknowledge that Lehman Brothers risked its entire existence—that he "bet the company," so to speak—on the American real estate market, and that it was recklessly irresponsible to do so and, further, that he takes full blame for it, I'll remain convinced he still doesn't understand what went wrong.

Lehman Brothers went bankrupt because it lost money on real estate investments. A lot of people will read that sentence and probably conclude that only fools invested in real estate in 2006 and 2007. There is some truth to that, since the entire banking industry (and Congress and the Fed) helped create a real estate bubble that was based on ridiculous assumptions— chiefly, that the value of real estate could never decline—while a few wise naysayers issued warnings from the sidelines. I may not have heard of the heroes in Michael Lewis's *The Big Short* until after its publication, but I had read plenty of diatribes from various commentators who railed against Alan Greenspan, American investment banks, and the perils of investing in real estate. The problem was I'd been reading them since 1994. To say, in 2007, that those invested in real estate should have listened to the prophets ignores that listening to them in 1994 or 1999 or 2004 meant forgoing huge profits in the intervening years. So the mere fact that Lehman invested in real estate isn't an unpardonable sin.

I view Lehman's 2008 investment holdings in real estate the same way I view investors who lost money in Pets.com or Webvan* in 2000. The investments were doomed due to unrealistic

---

*Guilty as charged.

or ill-conceived assumptions. It's important to realize, though, that while those assumptions look ridiculous today, in 2000 they were no sillier than the assumptions the initial investors in Amazon and eBay had made just a few years before. I don't blame Dick and the inner circle of Lehman Brothers management for placing a bet on real estate and losing money (the money of the employees whom Dick forced to own a third of the company, I might add); I blame them for placing a bet so unbelievably large that it risked the future of the entire company. Until the day comes that I hear Dick acknowledge *that* fact, I'll remain pissed off at him. And that's too bad, because I loved Dick Fuld.

In the fall of 1994, I was in my first weeks as a Stanford University MBA student. I had left the world of public accounting with the hope that an MBA from a top school could open the door for me to work as a trader on Wall Street. During those first weeks of classes, all of Wall Street's biggest investment banks sent teams of recruiters to Stanford. They'd typically make a presentation, convey what made their bank different from every other bank,* and then, over cocktails, introduce

---

*Invariably, it was "the people." Every bank you talked to insisted the people at their bank were different. For another perspective, though, ask any single woman in Manhattan over the age of 35 what she thinks. If she has been in New York since she graduated from college, there is a decent chance she's dated a man from a number of different banks. I strongly suspect her view (perhaps peppered with f-bombs) will be something along the lines of "They're all exactly the same."

themselves to the students they would be interviewing in another month or so for summer internships. All of the banks, that is, except Lehman Brothers.

Lehman Brothers didn't send a recruiting team, which always, always, *always* consisted of a firm's personable, enthusiastic, smooth, male managing director in charge of recruiting, flanked by half a dozen ridiculously attractive women. All of them exuded New York City sophistication and style, and every one of them, from the MD on down to the twenty-two-year-old, 110-pound recruiting associate, could drink for hours. No, Lehman Brothers sent its CEO, Dick Fuld.

Dick wasn't smooth, he certainly wasn't warm, and not many people have called him personable. That doesn't mean his speech wasn't effective. Delivered in what I would only call a brusque manner, it stood apart from every other bank's message. Dick came across as driven and unbelievably competitive. Some of the other banks jointly hosted panels that were essentially Q&A sessions. That would have never worked with Dick; his disdain for his competitors would have made for, at best, an uncomfortable situation.

After his speech, as was customary, there was a reception, and dozens of students took their turn gathering around Dick in small groups. In the ten or so minutes I was in front of him, there was none of the small talk that you usually got from recruiters. He greeted everyone with a firm handshake and a "Hello, I'm Dick Fuld." While I was one of four people in front

of him, he asked me, "Why are you interviewing with investment banks?" I sputtered something about my passion for the
stock market, how it consumed me not only while I did tax
work and financial planning for clients but also after hours.
The mention of stocks, as opposed to the desire to be an investment banker or a bond trader, provided Dick with an opportunity to expand on a point he'd made during his presentation.
Lehman Brothers, he told us, had an equity-division problem.
The bond department was best in class on the Street, investment banking was middle-of-the-pack but talented, but the equity department really needed help. "The equity division at
Lehman Brothers is going to stop being an employment shop
for friends and family from Brooklyn and Staten Island," he
said. "I want my equity division filled with people as smart as
the guys in fixed income, and it's going to start with MBAs like
you." We tittered at the Brooklyn–Staten Island reference, but
Dick never cracked a smile. It wouldn't be the last time I'd hear
Dick say something that only he didn't consider funny.* His

---

*Dick had lunch with the 1995 class of summer interns and asked us for questions. At the
time, the financial press teemed with stories about how Lehman could not survive on its
own and printed constant speculation about whom we would merge with. When asked
about a merger by one intern, Dick started to give his standard answer about fiduciary
duty to the board, etc., when he suddenly stopped. After a long pause, he fixed the room
with a gaze and said, "I'm going to let you ask that again, and just like Michael Corleone in
The Godfather, I'll answer the question truthfully. But you only get to ask it one time." This
time, when asked if Lehman would merge, he launched into a profane tirade against the
former bankers that at one time divided the firm and forced it into the arms of American
Express. At the end of his impassioned speech, he said, "No, I will never sell this firm, and
that's the only time you get to ask me that question," and with that he excused himself
from lunch. As he left, one of my classmates started laughing uncontrollably. Finally, he
composed himself and said, "Didn't Michael lie during that scene in the movie?"

speech concluded, he turned back to me and said, "You're going to like working at Lehman Brothers."

Just a few weeks into my two-year MBA program, and a full two years before the release of *Jerry Maguire*, Dick Fuld had me at "hello."

A classmate next to me said, "I think he just offered you a job." I'll never know if he did or not, but it didn't stop me from relaying that exchange to every single person I met along the Lehman interview path. I did get a summer internship, was offered a full-time job a year later, and traded stocks for Lehman for thirteen years. I watched the firm's equity division transform itself from a third-tier afterthought to a trading powerhouse. Just as Dick Fuld said it would. Even after the equities division tripled in size and moved from a boiler-room-type setup in 1995 to a state-of-the-art trading floor in 2002, I never forgot my first meeting with Dick Fuld.

I wanted to work for Dick Fuld because Lehman wasn't a white-shoe firm, inaccessible to those without connections. He wanted to create an equities division with smart, ambitious, exceedingly competitive people, and that was exactly the culture he created. It's not the people that are different from one bank to another; it's the culture. That's the message I took away from my first encounter with the CEO of Lehman, and so powerful was it that even years later, as the department harvested hundreds of millions of dollars in profits where once there were just hundreds of millions of dollars of revenue, I still felt as if I were part of Dick Fuld's equity division task force.

Embarrassingly, and at significant cost to my family's net worth, I never grasped the riskiness of the enterprise, mostly because the profit machine I was part of in the equity division didn't operate recklessly. In retrospect, however, even as early as that first summer I worked at Lehman Brothers, I could have known just how much risk the bank was exposed to at all times.

Summer internships for prospective associates, almost always MBA students, are designed to introduce the intern to different areas of the firm. There are many functions across research, fixed income, and equities, and a summer internship allows the future employee to get a taste of some of them. My ten-week internship, in 1995, started with five weeks on Lehman Brothers' central funding desk. Some of my other classmates were assigned to desks with self-explanatory products like mortgages, high yield (i.e., junk bonds), or treasuries. Others, like central funding, left the interns baffled. I reported to the central funding desk having no idea of its function within the firm. Realizing this, the recruiting department instructed all interns to create a document describing the desk we had been assigned to. Summarizing the desk's product, day-to-day activity, and the work of the salespeople and traders there, the document would educate the next intern to sit on the desk.

In the summer of 1995, I wrote this description of Lehman

Brothers' central funding desk. It was a full thirteen years before the firm declared bankruptcy:

Looking for Mr. Greenback: Central Funding's Daily Search for $20 Billion

"Hey, Moose, Rocco! Help the judge find his
checkbook, will ya?"

—Rodney Dangerfield, *Caddyshack*

For those who run the central funding desk, work must make them feel a little bit like Sisyphus, who you may recall was destined to roll a boulder up a mountain for all of eternity. Consider this: Each day, the three people who occupy the desk's crucial overnight seats are charged with the task of finding about $20 billion to fund the firm's fixed-income positions. After a harrowing day of buying money and screaming at summer interns, salespeople, traders, "the Cage," and, for good measure, summer interns, it is not uncommon for them to still be a billion dollars short with just minutes left before the Fed Funds wire "goes down." This results in a frantic rush to "help the judge" find his last billion dollars so the firm can remain liquid.

When the money is found, the day is over and the traders go home. But unlike other traders, who can ride a great trade for days or weeks, there is no time to relax or celebrate on the central funding desk. Because when they get to work the next morning, in the words of one of the overnight traders, "the fucking rock's at the bottom of the hill again."

Central Funding's Purpose

Imagine you are an investor with $3 million of equity in your brokerage account and no margin requirements. After evaluating the current bond market, you instruct your broker to purchase $23 million in bonds. However, you have to pay for those bonds by tomorrow. Consequently, you're short $20 million. You want to finance these bonds with the cheapest money available, so you look to the overnight cash market to borrow the $20 million. Finding someone (we'll assume it's a bank, but it could be any entity with excess cash) with the cash is easy, but with a leverage ratio of almost 7 to 1, the bank is leery about giving you money, even overnight, without any collateral. So to effect the transaction, you agree to give the bank $21 million (remember, you have $23 million) worth of bonds as collateral. The bank then gives you a $20 million overnight loan. You then take the $20 million and settle with your broker. And therein lies the plight of Sisyphus. The next morning, you owe the bank $20 million, and the cycle starts all over again. Thus the need for central funding.

Imagine the same scenario with one additional fact. At the same time you are hunting for cash, other, less wealthy friends of yours are searching for overnight money to finance *their* positions. However, owing to your high net worth, you have greater access to a lender's overnight money, so your friends offer to borrow money from you, at a rate higher than the lender's overnight rate. You see a chance to make money on the spread, so you make the loan to your friends, taking their collateral. This, of course, results in a higher funding requirement for you. In short, you'd end up trading a lot more than $20 million worth of money and collateral at the end of the day, but it would all have to net to a $20 million loan. With this scenario, it is quickly evident that central funding is no longer just a need for Lehman Brothers but an opportunity for the firm as well.

Central Funding at Lehman Brothers

Change the millions to billions, increase the 7-to-1 debt-to-equity ratio at least fourfold, and to a certain extent you've got Lehman Brothers' central funding desk in a nutshell. Essentially, the firm buys bonds on leverage and refinances the loans every night, while providing liquidity for others who are doing the same thing. (A note on the firm's leverage ratio: A look a Lehman Brothers' most recent year-end balance sheet reveals a debt-to-equity ratio of about 31 to 1. However, this is only a snapshot, taken on a predetermined date, of the firm's position. And, like anyone who knows when their picture is going to be taken, the firm combs its hair and applies makeup. One look at the firm's bond positions financed daily by central funding reveals that on any given day the firm's debt-to-equity ratio is nowhere near 31 to 1.)

The rest of the piece went on to describe the roles of specific salespeople and traders, as well as some trading terms unique to the desk.

A full five weeks after I wrote this piece, with just four days left in our summer internships, a number of factors converged to make me a notorious figure on Lehman Brothers' fixed-income trading floor. On Tuesday night of our last week, the recruiting department decided that the collection of essays had turned out so well, they bound them all into a book and, instead of just distributing them to interns, as we were originally told, passed them out to the roughly three dozen trading desks firmwide. Disastrously for me, central funding fell first in alphabetical desk order, so without a table of contents, my piece, with the *Caddyshack* quote, was the first page anyone saw when they opened the book. On Wednesday morning, shortly before noon, I was summoned to the recruiting offices from my desk on the equity trading floor, where I'd spent the second half of my summer. The head of recruiting said to me, "I just got a call from central funding and they want you to come down. They said it's urgent, but honestly I think they just want to bust your balls and have some fun with you."

Armed with that inside knowledge, I stupidly walked into the conference room adjacent the central funding desk smiling. After all, Wall Street trading desks are full of pranksters, and I had gotten along exceedingly well with the members of the desk. I'd even been invited to play on their softball team. This wasn't a Wall Street league either; it was a fast-pitch league on Roosevelt Island, where we played teams with names like

Bronx Drywall and Long Island City Piano Movers. I had no idea of the calamity I was about to walk into.

My smile instantly disappeared when I walked in and, before I could even sit down, a guy I thought I had made friends with that summer screamed at me, "WHO THE FUCK DO YOU THINK YOU ARE?!" with spittle flying everywhere. There wasn't one second over the next two hours that I thought anyone was joking.

I spent the rest of that day getting successively chewed out by increasingly senior people.* It was personal, it was fierce, and there was absolutely no doubt in my mind I'd lost my chance at full-time employment. Finally told to get out of their sight, I slowly made my way back up to the recruiting department. Their stunned expressions revealed that they, too, had learned this was no joke. The highest levels of senior management on the fixed-income floor had called the head of recruiting and told him that if a copy of my essay ever made its way out of the firm, he was going to be fired. Furthermore, the recruiting department had to account for every copy of the book and destroy them all.

The head of recruiting summoned the entire summer intern class to a meeting and informed us, in vague terms, that

---

*I later talked to someone on the central funding desk, and he said he'd never seen mob mentality gather so fast. When they came in that morning, everyone was joking about the piece, specifically asking Larry, the trader I'd quoted in the piece, "How did Joe know you had syphilis?" It changed abruptly when a senior salesperson whipped the desk into a frenzy aimed at me.

due to some errors in the book, each copy that we had been given the night before had to be returned immediately. For emphasis, we were told, to audible gasps, that if each copy wasn't returned by Friday none of us would be receiving his or her last check.*

Forget the reaction and whether my observations showed insight worthy of a job offer or incredible stupidity in documenting those observations. The seeds of Lehman's demise (and Bear Stearns's before it and that of every investment bank saved by TARP after it) are spelled out for all to see. The mechanics of the daily funding showed just how precarious and untenable a business model all investment banks operated under. Thirty-to-one leverage on reporting days, and higher than that inter-quarter, represents a deceptive, albeit not illegal, practice. Thirty-to-one was, is, and always will be a reckless, impossible-to-avoid-eventual-insolvency business practice. I just didn't realize it at the time.

The balance sheet of an investment bank, just like any other company's, is made up of assets and liabilities. Most of America's companies have physical assets such as property, like a manufacturing plant (Ford) or a fleet of trucks (FedEx) or warehouses and equipment such as oil rigs and silos (Exxon-

---

*There were forty-five of us in the summer internship program, and we were all paid $1,000 a week. Although none of the others knew specifically why we had to return the books, one of my classmates figured it out. He spent the next two days tormenting me, referring to my piece as "the $45,000 essay" and threatening to have T-shirts made up with the pages printed on the front and back.

Mobil). Some also have intangible assets like software code and patents (Microsoft). On the liability side, almost all have some sort of debt—whether in the form of bank loans or bonds or lines of credit—to fund their operations. An investment bank is different. It has few hard assets, just a workforce and a whole lot of investments. The liabilities are considered sources of funding: a bank's sole goal is for the investments to produce more income than the cost of funding. Why is 30–1 so reckless? Because at more than 30-1 (or precisely 33–1), if at any period of time assets are underperforming liabilities by more than 3 percent, the bank is, by definition, insolvent.

When evaluating the performance of investment managers, one gauge of riskiness is to measure how far the fund declined, from peak to trough, during its worst period. This is important because investors are emotional, and therefore it does little good to have a mutual fund return 20 percent over a two-year period if it suffered a 50 percent drawdown in the interim. Very few investors would have the stomach to ride out the 50 percent drawdown to ultimately enjoy the 20 percent appreciation. Returning to an entity that is leveraged 30–1, there is no investor alive, and never has been, who can avoid a 3 percent drawdown on their investment fund over a long period of time. I don't care if their entire portfolio consists of two-year treasuries funded by shorting three-year treasuries, probably two of the most correlated instruments possible; at some point there will be a market event that causes a dislocation between these two seemingly permanently correlated securities, and the two-year note will be up 17 percent while the three-year note is up 20 percent, or the two-year note will be down 2 percent and the three-year note up 1 percent, and in either case the result is the same: insolvency. That's a polite way of saying all the equity is gone.

That isn't necessarily a disaster. Plenty of individuals can live their life insolvent. A college grad with little or no money in the bank who buys a car, financing the entire purchase price, is insolvent the moment they drive the car off the lot. Anyone with a house that is worth less than the mortgage is probably insolvent. That doesn't change the graduate's or homeowner's ability to continue to work, pay bills, and go on with life. Either through future savings or an eventual rise in the home's value, the insolvency will disappear. However, there is one very important consequence of being insolvent. During that period of insolvency, it will be impossible to get a loan. No one with any sort of lending standards will loan new money to an insolvent party.

The problem with an investment bank becoming insolvent is that investment banks spend the whole of their days entering into lending and borrowing agreements. The moment counterparties realize a trading partner is insolvent, they won't do business with it, and a bankruptcy filing is imminent. Going back to the description of the central funding desk, you can see its ability to finance the operations would vanish instantly. For years and years investment banks everywhere bet their future existence on the ability to finance their operations with overnight loans—and, in Lehman's case, additionally bet its existence on real estate.*

I should have taken note, in 1995, of the intensity of the reaction to my piece of some of Lehman's senior managers. The vitriol directed at me, and the fear of exposure my two-page write-up induced, seemed incongruent with the offense. Nobody, at least as far as I knew, was doing anything illegal, and I believed the manner in which the desk operated had to be industry-standard for investment banks. I should have stepped back and said, Why the overreaction? Why the screaming references to *The Wall Street Journal* and the comment "We don't need another Michael Lewis around here"? (This was 1995, and these were *Liar's Poker*–era employees.)

I didn't ask myself those questions until June 2008.† At that time, I traded technology stocks in San Francisco for a Lehman

---

*Just three years after Lehman Brothers' 2008 bankruptcy, Jon Corzine duplicated this stupidity by bankrupting his firm, MF Global, in the same way, replacing real estate with eurozone bonds.

†Incredibly, due entirely to the fact that no one in the equity division ever found out about the central funding fiasco, I did get offered a job. A year later I stood outside the elevators on the floor of the cafeteria. The doors opened, but the car was too full to let me in, since I had a tray full of breakfasts for the trading desk. In the elevator was the senior salesperson on the central funding desk who had led the attack on me. He saw me, clearly a full-time employee now, with my badge and tray of food, and as the elevator doors closed, the look on his face was like the injured prison guard's in *The Fugitive* when, as he arrives at the hospital, he recognizes Harrison Ford pretending to be a doctor.

Brothers–sponsored hedge fund officially within Neuberger Berman but still under the Lehman umbrella. Three months earlier—and a few days before Bear Stearns went under, having been rescued by a $2-a-share bid by JPMorgan Chase and additional backstopping from the Fed—Lehman Brothers had announced that they would be shutting down our hedge fund. Two days after Bear Stearns's demise, Lehman announced strong first-quarter earnings, and CFO Erin Callan led a conference call that, for a couple months, was hailed throughout the firm for its effectiveness. But something was amiss, and this time at least, I figured that part out.

Friday, February 29, 2008—three weeks before that conference call—had marked the last day of Lehman Brothers' first quarter. (At the time, most investment banks, like Lehman, operated on a November fiscal year-end.) It had been a bad day for the stock market, with the S&P falling 2.71 percent. Our fund had dropped just three basis points, or 0.03 percent. At the end of each day, I sent an e-mail to a number of people in upper management and to the risk department. In the subject line it simply listed the performance of the stock market, and that of our fund, that day. The risk department wanted this information because Lehman was one of the owners of the hedge fund's management company. More importantly, it was the fund's largest investor, their initial $100 million investment having grown to more than $160 million.

Within minutes of sending my e-mail, I got a call from a

senior member of the risk department, an uncommon but not unprecedented development. "Joe," he said, "is your e-mail right? Did you lose 0.03 percent or 3 percent?" His question wasn't ridiculous—after all, the market had fallen nearly 3 percent that day, and he knew we entered the day significantly net long. "No, 0.03 percent is correct," I replied. "We actually had an excellent day. Our shorts significantly underperformed our longs to the point that it erased the losses associated with our net exposure to the market."

"Thank God," he replied.

I actually laughed out loud. "Thank God?" I questioned. "You're telling me the difference of 297 basis points on $160 million just made you say, 'Thank God'?" Left unsaid was the fact that he was a senior risk officer at a bank with a stock market valuation exceeding $50 billion. I knew it was the last day of the quarter and assumed he wanted to get an accurate valuation for Lehman's investment, down to the dollar, for reporting purposes. But those two words, "Thank God," had rattled me. The next four words provided clarity and were an omen for everything that was going to happen over the next six and a half months.

"Joe, every dollar counts."

The significance of management's overreaction to my central funding piece thirteen years earlier may have eluded me, but this didn't. I went home and told my wife, "Something's wrong. There is no way a senior member of the risk department should care about $5 million"—she looked at me for explanation—"which is the difference between the answer he feared and the answer that made him say, 'Thank God.'"

Before the next month was over, amid a defiant conference call that *proved* Lehman wasn't Bear Stearns, in the wake of a quarter in which the firm *raised* its dividend, Lehman management announced it was pulling its investment from our hedge fund. An investment up 60 percent in four years, easily beating the market with a fraction of the exposure of, say, an S&P exchange-traded fund (ETF). We were clearly a fund that provided the firm with positive expected value. Further, because it accounted for about 75 percent of the money in the fund, Lehman knew this would lead to the withdrawal of the outside money, the death knell for our fund. Since Lehman owned half of the fund's management company, it would damage itself even further. This didn't seem like a rational decision.

By the time June rolled around, we were winding down the fund, slowly selling off enough stock to return Lehman's investment in the form of cash, when I happened to meet someone I'd known from my early days at the firm. After the brief respite following the conference call in March, Lehman was once again under siege. My acquaintance, who worked in an entirely different area of the firm, happened to be in San Francisco and accepted my invitation to come up to our trading floor. Like every meeting held at Lehman Brothers during those last few months, we discussed the state of the firm. Since

I sat 2,500 miles from headquarters, I asked, "What's going on back there?" I was completely unprepared for the bitterness of my acquaintance, who had far more money than I did tied up in Lehman Brothers stock. "Joe, the firm is insolvent and everyone on the 31st floor knows it."

The 31st floor of 745 Seventh Avenue is where the Lehman Brothers executive committee sat.

"C'mon," I said, "everybody?"

"Everybody," came the reply, with a look into my eyes and a slight nod for emphasis.

We both knew that I knew a romantic relationship had existed between a member of the 31st floor and my acquaintance. Whether it still existed, I had no idea, and I didn't ask any further questions, because it really didn't matter. Whatever it was, enough of a relationship still existed that I concluded my friend had been party to a frank discussion. Turning back to our hedge fund, my friend remarked with a shake of the head, "Lehman isn't liquidating what it *has* to; it's liquidating what it can. You guys could be turned to cash in a matter of days." We went on to discuss the future of the bank, and the next few months unfolded exactly as my acquaintance had predicted. There was another round of layoffs that month, which included big changes in senior management. In July, the firm announced employees were going to be paid with stock. Sometimes that can be a savvy incentive to align the interests of employees with the firm. It can be a signal from management that it knows the stock is undervalued and it is going to help pass future wealth along to employees. Armed with my knowledge from the "known insolvency" discussion, I recognized the firm's motivation as akin to a start-up company so strapped for cash that it pays its vendors with scrip. That day in June, it all became clear to me. Three months later, Lehman Brothers filed for bankruptcy, the stock went to zero, and *the shareholders' claim on future earnings vanished.*

Lehman Brothers shareholders and bondholders got what they deserved. The senior members of management, led by Dick Fuld, deserve the ridicule and the permanent stain on their reputations that will follow them to their *New York Times* obituaries. You will never hear me say anything otherwise. However, Dick and anyone else who states there should have been a government-orchestrated bailout of some sort is absolutely right. It was essential to the American banking system— but not for the reasons often cited.

Here's why:

What happened to the future earnings of Lehman Brothers? Speaking from my thirteen years within the equity division, reinforced with subsequent stops at two other banks, one of which involved interviewing dozens of people from competing firms: The equity division at Lehman Brothers from 1996 to 2008 was staffed with the most talented traders and sales force on the Street. *A Colossal Failure of Common Sense,* by Lawrence G. McDonald and Patrick Robinson, gives a reader the same impression about Lehman's fixed-income department.

So what happened?

Similar to the setup in Ben Mezrich's book *Bringing Down the House*, it's as if a number of different card-counting blackjack teams inhabited Lehman Brothers. Both the equity and fixed-income divisions operated at different $10 tables grinding out a profit, if not every day, almost certainly every week, and without question every single month. The problem was, up on the 31st floor—or Club 31, as it derisively became known—management had empowered a small group of guys in the real estate division to play at the $10,000 table, downing Courvoisier like drunken rappers and, in the process, relegating the steady profits of the fixed-income and equity divisions to rounding errors.

The fact is the traders in fixed income and equity at Lehman Brothers made a lot more than $10 at a time. They made hundreds of millions of dollars over the course of a year. Their ability to make money didn't disappear when Lehman Brothers did. One week after the bankruptcy filing, with every bank in America afraid to do anything, due to their own corroded balance sheets, Barclays Bank, a member of the British banking system, bought Lehman Brothers' American operations for the sum of $250 million. (They also paid over $1 billion for the headquarters at 745 Seventh Avenue and its state-of-the-art trading floors.) They paid just $250 million for the operating assets, including the workforce and positions, or investments, that existed on the trading desks inside the building.

To this day, there are whispers and rumors from people who worked on those floors that within the first week Barclays had made billions just from the liquidation of trading positions in excess of the paltry $250 million they had paid. If true, billions of dollars that rightfully belonged to Lehman's creditors went overseas to a foreign bank. Further, every single *future* dollar earned—and it's been billions already—found its way not into the American banking system, which so desperately needed capital in the form of profits to reduce its collective insolvency, but onto the balance sheet of a British bank that itself may have crumbled without this gift from the American government.* Government action could have ensured the enormous value of the future operating profits of Lehman Brothers accrued to the American banking system.

As CEO of Lehman Brothers, Dick Fuld headed the management group that recklessly disregarded the value of the firm's future earnings. Decision-makers in the American government (and perhaps the bankruptcy court bowing to intense political pressure to act quickly) compounded the mistake by

---

*Barclays spent the rest of 2008 and early 2009 fighting insolvency rumors of its own. Unquestionably, the bank's decision in December 2009 to sell Barclays Global Investors, or BGI, its trillion-dollar asset-management business, to BlackRock for $13.5 billion did more to shore up its balance sheet and stave off the rumors of pending bankruptcy than anything else, but the billions in profits the ex-Lehman workforce produced for the coffers was an enormous help as well.

vastly underestimating the value of those earnings and subsequently allowed the bounty to leave our shores.

"What does all this have to do with betting on baseball?" you ask. More than meets the eye. It goes to the very heart of the question, "How much should I bet on my slate of Opening Day games?" It means that no matter what the endeavor, if you have an edge, a competitive advantage or a carefully constructed model with a positive expected return, you must avoid wiping yourself out with a single bet. Never make a bet on one day that imperils your ability to exist the next day.

I believed the model had an edge on the oddsmakers and therefore had positive expected value. In managing the pool of money I had dedicated to attempting to exploit that edge, my goal was to measure appreciation in basis points. A bet on one day—even one like St. Louis on Opening Day, which I calculated had a 14 percent edge—would never imperil my ability to exploit a similar edge the next day, the next week, or the next month.

If the CEO and executive committee at Lehman Brothers (and the other banks that were just as irresponsibly managed) had followed that guideline, the global financial meltdown that began in 2008 would never have occurred.

9

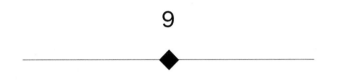

The Games Progress

I sent the model's selections to a short list of friends during the Opening Days of the season. During that time, I got the same inquiry from a number of them, and whether over e-mail or in a phone call the request was the same: "I want you to place bets on my behalf." After fielding this suggestion a number of times, the idea of a baseball fund took hold. One friend and I spent at least an hour one evening discussing how much fun it would be for him to come home from work, sit down in front of the television, open his e-mail, and learn what teams he had invested in that night. He laughingly added one caveat: "You can never bet my money against the Cardinals." "Oh," I said, "so you want me to be like one of those socially responsible funds that's restricted from investing in tobacco or alcohol stocks?" I chided. "And I thought you were a strict capitalist."

During that discussion, I started drawing comparisons to being a portfolio manager and realized that risk management would be paramount. I wasn't going to be risking my money and my friends' money because a game was on TV or because we liked the Yankees or any other reason relating to "gambling as entertainment." Over the course of April, the season's first month, I developed a schedule of capital management, which I applied to the model's picks for the entire year. The allocation schedule put a huge premium on capital preservation. That way, if the fund ever went belly-up using this schedule, it was because the model didn't work, not because the fund's manager had insufficient respect for risk or failed to apply the most basic tenets of prudence or risk management.

This is the lesson of the economic crisis. Failed firms and failed funds need to stop blaming "hundred-year storms" (which seem to happen every decade) for their demise and recognize that their own risk management shortcomings were to blame.

For all games in which the model projected a win expectancy greater than 15 percent, compared with the implied odds of the money line, I would wager 2 percent of the fund if the pick was an underdog. In the case of a favorite, I'd wager an amount needed to win 2 percent of the fund. I didn't expect this to be a common occurrence, and in fact in April only two games graded out with an edge greater than 15 percent. A 2 percent risk to the fund once every two weeks seemed prudent. As the perceived edge vs. the stated odds dropped, I would accordingly reduce the amount of the wager in a swift, non-linear fashion, so that the vast majority of the wagers would be for basis points of my existing capital, as opposed to percents. Based on Opening Day, with fifteen plays out of seventeen games, there would be a bevy of games to bet every day. Therefore, the amount risked had to be kept small, so that the fund could weather even a cold streak that was only remotely probable. I came up with this schedule:

Win Probability in Excess of Money Line–Implied Odds	Percent of Fund Risked
>15 percent	2 percent
>13 percent but <15 percent	1.5 percent
>11 percent but <13 percent	1 percent
>9 percent but <11 percent	0.5 percent (i.e., 50 basis points)
>6 percent but <9 percent	40 basis points
>3 percent but <6 percent	20 basis points
>0 percent but <3 percent	10 basis points

Turning back to the games over the first two days of the season, based on the above bet-sizing schedule, the fund fell 74 basis points, or 0.74 percent, with games listed in descending order of the perceived edge:

March 31, 2011, Picks	Price	Edge	Result	Change in Fund Balance
St. Louis Cardinals	-175	14.13 percent	loss	-2.63 percent
Kansas City Royals	+135	9.87 percent	loss	-0.5 percent
NY Yankees	-145	6.98 percent	won	+0.4 percent
Cincinnati Reds	-105	6.4 percent	won	+0.4 percent
San Francisco Giants	+105	5.04 percent	loss	-0.2 percent
April 1, 2011, Picks	Price	Edge	Result	Change in Fund Balance
Kansas City Royals	+125	9.83 percent	won	+0.63 percent
Baltimore Orioles	+165	8.02 percent	won	+0.66 percent
Seattle Mariners	+100	7.41 percent	won	+0.4 percent
Boston Red Sox	-110	5.79 percent	lost	-0.22 percent
Arizona Diamondbacks	+185	3.81 percent	won	+0.37 percent
Cleveland Indians	+100	3.46 percent	lost	-0.2 percent
Toronto Blue Jays	-115	2.97 percent	won	+0.1 percent
Florida Marlins	-175	2.76 percent	won	+0.1 percent
Chicago Cubs	-175	1.65 percent	lost	-0.18 percent
Philadelphia Phillies	-260	0.13 percent	won	+0.1 percent

After the first two days of the year, I was down 0.77 percent, or 77 basis points, really not that bad a result considering I dropped 2.63 percent on the only outsize bet of the group, when St. Louis lost 5–3 to San Diego.* In that game, St. Louis

---

*Some notes on the Change in Fund Balance calculations: St. Louis, with a 14 percent edge, graded out to a 1.5 percent play. The Cardinals were priced as a -175 favorite, so I

blew a 3–2 lead with two outs in the ninth inning and no one on base when the Padres' Cameron Maybin hit a game-tying home run. The Cardinals then lost in eleven innings. Losing the fund's biggest bet in that fashion certainly stung, but there were some incredible highs as well. Just an hour earlier, Cincinnati, a forty-basis-point play, scored four runs in the ninth inning to beat Milwaukee by one, and the next day the Phillies, a ten-basis-point play, scored three runs in the bottom of the ninth to escape with a walk-off, one-run victory. I started telling my friends known to frequent Atlantic City and Connecticut casinos that betting on a slate of baseball games is more exciting than a craps table. By the end of games on April 1, I was hooked.

The model and I had a date for the rest of the baseball season.

It's vitally important for any fund manager that finishes up for any period—be it a month, a quarter, or a year—to understand *how* they generated a positive return. It requires brutal honesty, but if the data is analyzed correctly, an objective evaluation is possible. It's not good enough to say, "The fund is up. That's all I need to know." The manager and investors need to know why, and they need to know if the fund is subject to undue risk.

had to risk 2.63 percent (1.75 x 1.5 percent) to win 1.5 percent. Kansas City, with a 9 percent edge on March 31, qualified as a 50-basis-point play. When it lost, the fund fell 50 basis points. The next day, the same-size play presented itself on the Royals, and this time, when they won the payoff was 63 basis points, 1.25 (because they were priced at +125) multiplied by the 50 basis points risked.

That's the only way to determine if the returns can be replicated going forward.

Let's say a hedge fund started the year with $20 million under management and finished the year up 22 percent, while the S&P 500 rose 12 percent. During the year, the fund's portfolio manager, or PM, invested 5 percent of the fund's assets in a very small publicly traded company, BuyMe, which subsequently appreciated 400 percent during the year as a result of a takeover by a larger company. Now how impressive is the fund's 22 percent return?

My analysis would be that the fund actually had a lousy year, and the PM isn't likely to replicate his market-beating returns in future years, *especially* if the fund grows in size. Complicating that conclusion further, the fund manager will *want* the fund to grow in size, and he'll market his 22 percent return vs. 12 percent for the S&P accordingly. I'd base my conclusion on the fact that one stock accounted for 20 percent of the fund's overall return of 22 percent. In other words, during the year, excluding the gains from that one stock—or, in Wall Street parlance, ex-BuyMe*— the fund rose only 2 percent, actually a very poor performance in a year that the market rose 12 percent. Upon hearing this, the

---

*The entire industry of finance loves the "ex-" game. "Ex-items" has become a category on earnings reports. Ex-items are used by companies as a way to mask losses and boost reported earnings to the point that it has become absurd. Every quarter there are some laughable examples of companies using ex-items in their financials, accompanied by clever spin in the press releases to try to meet earnings expectations. This used to lead to fun exchanges on the trading desk. Traders would try their hand at the "ex-" game as well, and you'd hear comments like this: "Ex-doughnuts, I'm thin." "Frank's never cheated on his wife, ex–business trips." "Ex-blackjack I walked out of Foxwoods a winner this weekend."

PM, offended by this evaluation (and they'd all be offended, in my experience), claims that it's not fair to exclude BuyMe's gain in the evaluation of his performance, because he *can* find an undervalued, obscure company every year. I'd find that assertion dubious. In any case, if the fund grows in size per his marketing efforts, his claim will become a moot point, because it will probably be impossible to commit 5 percent of a larger fund to a single micro-cap stock.* For the year that just ended, the gains may count, and the money made may be green, but if I'm an investor in that fund, I take those profits and get out of the fund as quickly as possible at the end of the year.

Which brings us to an evaluation of the model's first-month performance.

The Model's Results in April	
Total Return	+8.79 percent
Total Games Picked	340 (out of 398 played)
Record in Games Picked	166-174

How is the return so good with an under-.500 record in games selected? There are really only two possibilities: Under-

---

*Let's suppose BuyMe had a market capitalization of $20 million at the time of the portfolio manager's investment. The $1 million worth of stock he bought represented 5 percent of BuyMe. Even ignoring the increased reporting requirements, it's very difficult to accumulate more than 10 percent of any one company's stock. So if his fund grew fivefold, to $100 million, he'd roughly be limited to a $2 million investment in BuyMe. Now, if it appreciated 400 percent, it would contribute only an 8 percent return to his fund, not 20 percent. If returns are not scalable, then they are not repeatable as the fund gets bigger, which is why an analysis like this is valuable.

dogs made up a majority of the winning bets and, thanks to the mechanics of money line betting, it's possible to make money with an under-.500 record. Also possible: Success in a select few highly rated games overcame net losses elsewhere.

Return by Category of Team Selected		
	Win-Loss Record	Return
Favorites	78-89	-6.25 percent
Underdogs	79-73	+15.15 percent
Pick-'Ems	9-12	-0.11 percent
Total	**166-174**	**+8.79 percent**

Return by Wager Size		
	Win-Loss Record	Return
2 percent bets	2-0	+4.40 percent
1.5 percent bets	7-3	+3.31 percent
1 percent bets	11-4	+8.00 percent
50-basis-point bets	11-9	+0.95 percent
40-basis-point bets	29-29	-0.58 percent
20-basis-point bets	37-65	-7.44 percent
10-basis-point bets	69-64	+0.15 percent

The overall return was great, and the fact that the underdogs were huge winners while favorites were net losers didn't bother me. Indeed, that was almost trivial; in choosing 152 dogs vs. 167 favorites, the model didn't exhibit any apparent preference for favorites or dogs.

What did cause me some concern was the fact that the results were so dependent on a great performance in the highly rated games. I suspected 20-7 wasn't going to happen every month in the 1 percent and above wager size category, if ever again, especially if the model lost money at lower levels. That would suggest an edge really didn't exist to the extent I hoped and the return on the fund would experience wild swings based on the infrequent large bets. That would clearly be a trend to watch as the season progressed. Then again, if I didn't expect 20-7 to happen again, I couldn't reasonably expect the dismal 37-65 results to happen again at the 20-basis-point-bet level.

+/- 2 Percent Returns on Teams Bet On			
Boston Red Sox	9	11	+3.60 percent
Kansas City Royals	11	9	+3.47 percent
Baltimore Orioles	10	10	+3.21 percent
Seattle Mariners	13	12	+2.59 percent
		.	
		.	
		.	
		.	
Pittsburgh Pirates	0	5	-2.37 percent
NY Yankees	8	7	-3.34 percent
St. Louis Cardinals	8	11	-4.21 percent

Although different starting pitchers play a large role in the model's determination of a team's win expectancy, it was clear, based on at least eighteen plays on each team, that the model thought much more highly of Boston, Kansas City, Baltimore, Seattle, St. Louis, and, not shown, Arizona and Atlanta, regardless of who was pitching, than the oddsmakers did. For the most part this wasn't surprising. Four of those teams (Kansas City, Baltimore, Seattle, and Arizona) made up my long-futures basket, meaning I held them in higher regard than the oddsmakers even before the season started. St. Louis barely missed the futures-basket cut, so no surprise there, either. However, Boston and Atlanta appeared to be chronically undervalued based on oddsmakers' pre-season projections. Boston was listed as a team with a 97½ over-under. It was not priced like that on a daily basis. My eighty-eight-win projection for Atlanta actually matched the pre-season over-under, but again oddsmakers seemed to back off that assumption in posting a daily line.

Of course, the model didn't select all games based on the assumption that the selected team was undervalued. It's just as possible the model judged that the opponent was overvalued. So to complete the look at April's results, here are the returns by team bet against.

+/- 2 Percent Returns on Teams Bet Against			
LA Angels	10	13	+5.41 percent
Detroit Tigers	12	3	+4.56 percent
San Diego Padres	13	10	+3.46 percent
Oakland A's	8	6	+2.44 percent
		.	
		.	
		.	
		.	
Minnesota Twins	11	8	-2.54 percent

No surprise in the high number of plays against the Angels, San Diego, and Minnesota based on the pre-season futures basket of "unders." There were other teams, like Texas and Detroit, that were bet on and against at least ten times apiece, which suggests the model had more of a disagreement with oddsmakers over the quality of specific starting pitchers rather than either team overall.

Running the model, managing a pool of money, and immersing myself in a daily slate of baseball games turned out to be more fun than I could have imagined. At the same time I had shed my wheelchair and, although still tethered to New York for physical therapy and due to an inability to travel, I had begun to navigate the sidewalks around my apartment on crutches. I found myself engaging in baseball conversations with the doormen and my physical therapist, a fantasy baseball junkie. I used to equate hearing about someone's fantasy baseball team with being subject to a discussion about their latest round of golf, but now I found myself relishing our daily discussions about team construction. I hadn't cared this much about leaguewide happenings in baseball since I was a teenager. Unlike those years in the 1970s and 1980s, my consumption of out-of-town games wasn't limited to the range of an AM transistor radio or a weekly wrap-up on *This Week in Baseball;* I had the ability to watch any game I wanted to each night.

My love of trading stocks drove me out of bed each morning for more than a decade, even during the years I awoke at 3 A.M. to get to my trading desk at a San Francisco–based hedge fund. The success of the model, the thrill of trading again, and a love of baseball got me through that month of April and had me looking forward to the daily slate of games in the same way I anticipated getting to work to trade stocks.

10

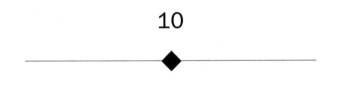

The Sweet Sound of Familiar Voices

There is a CD entitled *The Saint, the Incident & the Main Point Shuffle*. Available at no legitimate retail outlet, it's a two-disc bootleg recording of a Bruce Springsteen concert in February 1975, and I happen to own a copy. Although nominally the CD itself isn't really worth anything, to me it's priceless. The fifth track on the CD is listed as "Wings for Wheels," but it's actually the first known performance of rock and roll's perfect song, "Thunder Road."

Perfect is a funny word, because it appears to be an absolute concept with a definitive meaning. In truth, *perfect* is open for interpretation and comes in degrees. Take baseball's "perfect game." The definition is simple. Twenty-seven up and twenty-seven down. If no one reaches base over a full nine-inning game, the pitcher is credited with a perfect game. To date there have been twenty-three in major league history. Are they all really perfect? Of course not, or it wouldn't be so easy to rank them. In 2010, when there were two perfect games, Roy Halladay of the Phillies struck out eleven batters in his, but Oakland's Dallas Braden struck out only six. Halladay's was more perfect, right? But even Halladay allowed sixteen batters to hit the ball into play. To truly throw a perfect game, shouldn't a pitcher have to strike out twenty-seven batters? Even then, if it's done on more than three pitches to each batter, is it really perfect, or does tossing some balls in there simply change the degree of difficulty? *Perfect,* I acknowledge, has a degree of subjectivity to it.

"Thunder Road" is a perfect song.* It's the opening song on Springsteen's *Born to Run* album, and it's a rarity in rock and roll in that it has no chorus. It's simply a story told in an extended verse that covers a lot of ground over four minutes and forty-nine seconds. From a narrative perspective, there is the story of Mary, but it's the narrator's view of the world, and his struggle to find a place in it, that creates an arc. The first half of the song is saturated with sounds and images of resignation: the mournful harmonica, a radio playing Roy Orbison's "Only the

---

*My concept of perfection in other media: Art: Van Gogh's *Starry Night.* Commercials: Google's 2010 Super Bowl ad, "Parisian Love." The written word: Jim Murray's 1979 *Los Angeles Times* column lamenting the loss of his eye, probably the greatest sports column ever written. Movies: The montage that traces the married life of Carl and Ellie Fredricksen during the opening of *Up.* (I take back what I wrote earlier. In this case, perfection isn't subjective. This is the most perfect four minutes and twenty seconds ever seen in a movie. We will not argue about this.)

Lonely," and lyrics like "You ain't a beauty, but hey, you're all right." Realizing that his "dusty beach road" of a town has nothing else to offer, the narrator longs for more, and the second half of the song bursts with dreams of success and determination and the need to break free from the binding ties of the town he and Mary call home. With equal parts promise to himself and plea to his girlfriend, the song ends with the image of the narrator finding success while his town disappears in his rearview mirror—with or without Mary.

If aliens from a strange land came to America and demanded, "Tell me about this thing you call rock and roll," I'd reply, "It's about girls and cars and dreaming—but not necessarily in that order." And then I'd play them "Thunder Road."

In February 1975, Springsteen debuted "Wings for Wheels" during a concert at the Main Point, in Bryn Mawr, Pennsylvania. Shortly after that, he and the E Street Band disappeared into the studio to record the *Born to Run* album, and while the lyric "trade in these wings on some wheels" made it into the final cut of "Thunder Road," the one all fans are familiar with, the original version was never heard again, and apparently no other recordings exist. The existence of a recorded "first draft" is a rare treat.

We can never go into the kitchen with Nobu Matsuhisa and taste his early, experimental versions of black-cod miso, when it may have first been made with teriyaki and flounder. Movie buffs don't get to see the early drafts of *Rocky* to find out if the title character originally went by the name of Timmy Balboa. But because of the existence of "Wings for Wheels," we can see the evolution of "Thunder Road." Mary was originally Angelina. The words *Thunder Road* weren't even in it. The song had a standard verse-chorus-verse-chorus construction. It ended with the band breaking into an extended solo, extremely similar to the party music of beach or shag bands, and it even included a cringe-inducing verse in which Bruce rhymed "jive" and "alive." It was a catchy song but not very notable. It was the subsequent changes that made it perfect. Some are subtle but illustrate with clarity that Springsteen carefully chose, and probably agonized over, every word and, of course, every note in the song. A two- instead of a three-syllable heroine flows better. "*You* ain't that young anymore" became "*We* ain't that young anymore," a crucial switch that gives the song universal appeal. "Dirty road" became "dusty beach road," a far more evocative description. And so on.

It's a rare treat to see an artist perform at such a young stage in his career, when the greatness—even genius—is evident but not yet fully formed.

During the 2011 baseball season, I was reminded of that every time I watched Clayton Kershaw pitch.

The Los Angeles Dodgers drafted Clayton Kershaw with the seventh-overall pick in the 2006 draft. In 2008, at the age of twenty, he made his major league debut amidst a lot of fanfare. Kershaw pitched against the Phillies in both the 2008 and 2009

National League Championship Series, and I remember being vaguely offended at the hype preceding his appearances. In those games, the Phillies hit him hard, and he was wild, walking more batters than he struck out. By the end of the 2009 series I couldn't understand why Cole Hamels—clearly the better young, left-handed pitcher (in my biased mind)—didn't get the same type of accolades.

I didn't see Kershaw pitch again until April 21, 2011, when I tuned in to watch a Braves-Dodgers game. The model had called for a small play on Los Angeles, a -140 favorite, so I placed my bet and settled down with anticipation to watch Kershaw, whom the model loved. Kershaw was mesmerizing, taking a three-hit, one-run gem into the ninth inning. I love watching left-handed pitchers throw. Randy Johnson overpowered batters, Cole Hamels puts on a change-of-speed clinic in his best outings, and Cliff Lee has Greg Maddux–like command over the location of his pitches. Clayton Kershaw, however, was the closest thing I'd seen in nearly thirty years to my favorite left-hander of all-time, Steve Carlton. With a mix of devastating breaking pitches and a dominating fastball, Kershaw had batters up and down the Braves lineup flailing at pitches exactly like Carlton used to. His delivery isn't as smooth as the elegant Carlton's (the baggy, throwback uniforms the Dodgers wore that day didn't help), but he's the closest thing I've seen to an heir apparent. With that performance, he became my favorite pitcher of the season to watch.

Even though he lost a 2–1 lead in the ninth (after he retired the first two batters without incident, three singles and a walk followed, and suddenly the Dodgers trailed 3–2),* I knew I'd be tuning in for more Clayton Kershaw starts.

By May, it had been four months since the accident, and I still couldn't put any weight on my right leg. The X-rays looked exactly the same as they did post-surgery, confirming an ugly truth: My bones weren't fusing. With a combination of pain, worry, and opiate-based medications, my nightmares were equally dark: By this time the nightly replay of the accident in my dreams included my older daughter accompanying me across the street. She never got hurt, but she always witnessed the accident. I dreaded the nighttime.

I started staving off bedtime by watching West Coast baseball. It may have started with the idea of watching Clayton Kershaw pitch, but over the next few weeks it morphed into something else. I know it sounds hokey, but I turned on those games to be soothed by voices from my childhood—two old friends—and I took comfort in the nostalgia they triggered.

About the time my little brother turned five, he decided

---

*Despite this gut-wrenching turn of events, which seemingly erased my sure win on the Dodgers, they rallied with two outs in the bottom of the ninth to tie the game against the Braves' previously untouchable rookie closer Craig Kimbrel. (He hadn't given up an earned run yet that season.) The Dodgers won it in the twelfth inning on a Matt Kemp walk-off home run. If you want emotional thrills, there is nothing like betting on baseball.

that he would not follow the lead of his father and older brother and root for the Phillies, instead becoming a fan of the Los Angeles Dodgers. A 1974 Steve Garvey baseball card, his first, sealed the decision. Even at a young age, Doug had a rebellious streak. (Later, as he grew, our family described him as "conforming rigidly to his nonconformity.") Until I had left home for college, Doug never wavered from his love of the West Coast team that Phillies fans hated (due to two bitter playoff losses, in 1977 and 1978). He packed his room with Dodger memorabilia.

One of the unique pieces he owned was a 33⅓ rpm vinyl record commemorating Don Drysdale's then-record scoreless streak of fifty-eight and two-thirds innings pitched. The two-sided record ran nearly an hour and contained every game highlight during the streak, as originally called by Dodgers announcer Vin Scully. We used to pull out a portable record player and listen to that LP endlessly.* Even knowing Drysdale eventually set the record, listening to those replays we couldn't help but feel the original tension. In fact, for a brief moment, the streak actually ended before Drysdale broke the record. The San Francisco Giants had loaded the bases with nobody out, with the streak impressively long but not yet a record. Drysdale then hit a batter with a pitch. Streak over. Except the

---

*This joins "Do we need any blank tapes for the VCR?" and "I'm going to run down to Tower Records to get a CD" and "Those Red Sox fans sure seem like a nice bunch. I hope Boston wins a World Series someday" as sentences from my past that will never be uttered again.

umpire ruled the Giants' batter hadn't made a sufficient effort to get out of the way of the pitch and, consequently, simply ruled the pitch a ball.* Drysdale amazingly pitched out of that jam without giving up a run.

The beauty of that recording, however, is in listening to the play-by-play call of Vin Scully. Although I hated the Dodgers in the 1970s and Phillies announcer Harry Kalas provided the soundtrack to my youth, listening to that LP with my brother, I knew even at that young age: This is how you announce a ball game.

As I started watching late-night Dodgers broadcasts in 2011, I listened once again to the marvelous Vin Scully. Amazingly, at eighty-three years old, Vin Scully sounded better than ever, still better than all of the other announcers across baseball.† Even more incredibly, he works alone in the booth. And you know what? He doesn't need a partner, because he provides his own color commentary. I liken it to the vocal gymnastics of Michael Jackson, who could seemingly provide his own per-cussion backing just with his voice.

Scully's knowledge of the game is so complete, his grasp of history so strong, and his memory so sharp, he can interject his

---

*If that happened today—a Los Angeles (or New York) athlete on the way to a record, get-ting benefit from an umpire invoking an obscure rule—the Internet and Twitter would blow up from the onslaught of conspiracy theories.

†In a lot of cases, sadly, that's not saying much. There's no need to run down the teams with unbearable announcers, but I will say this: After listening to a couple of Chicago White Sox broadcasts this year, I now know why everyone I ever meet from Chicago is a Cubs fan.

own color to the point that you think there are two Vin Scullys. Of the following three examples, two are from a single broadcast of a game vs. the Phillies from August 2011. See if you can identify the one that is made up.

1. "The windup and the pitch. There's a soft pop-up to center field and Jimmy Rollins is retired on a lazy fly ball to Matt Kemp. Matt's allergic to shellfish, so the Dodgers have to be careful with their post-game spreads to protect their young slugger."

2. "Charlie Manuel looks on from the Phillies dugout as his starter mows down one hitter after another. Charlie's seen a lot of baseball in his life. You know, he was born in the backseat of a car in West Virginia."

3. "Victorino, tired of waiting, steps out of the batter's box. When the Phillies honored Shane with a bobblehead doll, it came complete with a hula skirt."

It's hard to pick the invented passage, isn't it?*

Since the Dodgers didn't play night games at home every evening, I also found myself frequently tuning in to late-night Padres games. I knew Vin Scully was still announcing Dodgers games but had no idea that Dick Enberg was the voice of the San Diego Padres. What a pleasant surprise. As a kid, I may

---

*Watching Dodger games over the 2011 season, I never did learn if Matt Kemp had any allergies.

have recognized the brilliance of Vin Scully, but on fall and winter afternoons and evenings, when I envisioned myself in a different place, Dick Enberg's voice carried me there.

Although born in my father's hometown of Allentown, Pennsylvania, one town over from my mother's hometown of Bethlehem, Pennsylvania, I only have memories of West Chester, Pennsylvania, where we moved when I was three. My father was an only child, and although my mother was the ninth of nine children, all of our relatives were within a short drive. Other than two different three-day drives to Walt Disney World, our family vacations were within easy driving distance of our home. I have few childhood memories of hotels or babysitters.

My childhood didn't solely consist of Little League Baseball, paper routes, all-day Wiffle-ball games, listening to Phillies games each summer evening on the radio, and kicking field goals, barefoot, with Tony Franklin at the Philadelphia Eagles training camp, which was located just beyond my backyard, but nearly so. That was the world I lived in; it had good parents and friends, and it provided me with a solid grounding. It was also small. By today's standards, it was positively provincial. By age twenty-one, the furthest inland I'd ever been was Niagara Falls. I was in my thirties before I saw, in person, any of my favorite teams play a game in a city other than Philadelphia. At ages five and seven, my daughters have Silver Elite status on Delta Air Lines, but I had flown on a plane precisely once before going to college.

My friends and I spent most days outside, even when there was snow on the ground. We'd play football or basketball until it got dark, and then I'd come inside to watch sports. If it were a Sunday, inevitably there would be a football game on TV from sunny Los Angeles, San Diego, San Francisco, or, on New Year's, (gasp) Pasadena. I'd shed my layers of clothes and consider my frozen fingers and toes as I gazed at these beautiful cities in California. I know there were other announcers, but I always associated those faraway West Coast oases with the voice of Dick Enberg.

I knew I needed to get away from home to grow up. When it came time to pick a college, I took a map and drew a four-hundred-mile radius around my home, in West Chester, Pennsylvania. Why four hundred? Because that was just about the limit of a one-day car ride, and the thought of flying to college carried the same air of incomprehension as, say, meeting Brooke Shields. I remember thinking, "I'd like to *see* California at some point in my life."

I could have gone to any college within the Pennsylvania state college system (ex–Penn State) tuition-free, because my dad was a professor at West Chester State College. My dad decided Shippensburg State College would be perfect, and we took a trip to visit the campus. Upon arrival, my first thought was "You have to be kidding me." If I went there, I'd never get out of Pennsylvania. I vowed there was no way I'd go to college anywhere close to home. Fortunately, tuition at Virginia Tech, deeply subsidized by the state of Virginia at the time, along with the availability of a co-op program (I worked at IBM during college), allowed me to get far away from home. My dad and I didn't see eye to eye on that decision at the time. Only years later did he confide in me that he realized getting away from home opened up my world and that he had been wrong. I am, however, still forced to drink beverages from a Shippensburg State mug extolling the 1981 state champion football team whenever I return home to visit my parents. It stands as a monument to both our disagreement and my dad's thriftiness. Nothing that functions gets thrown away in that house.

As I spent nights listening to Dick Enberg call Padres games in the spring of 2011, these memories and others came back to me. I remembered so clearly the determination I felt as a teenager, and in 2011 the memories were more powerful than mere nostalgia. They rekindled my will to get through this injury. A girl from the beaches of Southern California was my wife. My daughters, the granddaughters of Erminio and Martha Joan Peta, were San Francisco natives.

Those weekend afternoons of my youth spent listening to Dick Enberg call a game from sunny California didn't exactly put in motion the decisions that would lead to these events. Sitting with my brother in front of a record player and imagining the games almost 2,500 miles away that Vin Scully's voice conjured up didn't, either. Nor is it accurate to say that relating to the characters in a song inspired me and provided the courage

I needed to break from the small town that was my home, take chances, expand my world, and find out, on my own terms, about life. But they helped plant the seeds. Hearing those same voices again, more than thirty years later, while confronted with new obstacles, reminded me that by the time I left West Chester, I was so ready to find my own way. I didn't know the path I would take, and I didn't know the ultimate endeavor, but I left there filled with determination and a single goal: I was pulling out of there to win.

11

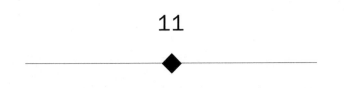

A Financial Field of Dreams

According to *Forbes,* which annually reviews the business of sports in America, Major League Baseball generated $6.4 billion in revenue in 2011. This is revenue from all sources, including ticket sales, stadium sponsorships, national television contracts, and local broadcasting rights. Per *Forbes,* operating profit amounts to a little less than 7 percent of total revenue, so MLB teams in the aggregate netted something less than half a billion dollars in 2011. The average value of each team is about $600 million, from nearly $1.9 billion for the New York Yankees down to $321 million for the Oakland Athletics. With thirty teams, that means the $6 billion-a-year industry is valued at about $18 billion.

Goldman Sachs generated between $3 billion and $4 billion

in revenue from just its various U.S.-based equity trading desks in 2011. The bulk of that figure comes from the trading of equities, equity-related derivatives, and convertibles. Morgan Stanley, second to Goldman Sachs in market share, generated a little less than $3 billion from its equity trading desks. Estimates put the total 2011 equity division trading revenue across all of Wall Street between $25 billion and $30 billion. That's more than four times the yearly revenue of MLB, and thanks to better gross margins, the stock-trading net income is an even greater multiple of MLB's bottom line. Many financial entities are worth more on their own than the entire industry of major league baseball.

So why is it that the Kansas City Royals have a much better idea of what their left-handed middle reliever is worth than Goldman Sachs does of its semiconductor trader? Because the Royals know how to collect, analyze, and interpret data.

Of course, it's not just the Royals. Thanks to the revolution started by Bill James, the sabermetric community uncovered a wealth of information about both the game and the business of baseball. As *Moneyball* chronicled, and as I've mentioned in earlier chapters, the discoveries eventually made their way to major league teams' front offices. The Oakland A's may have been early adopters, but today virtually every major league team has some sort of data analysis department under the purview of the general manager. Then–Boston Red Sox GM Theo Epstein's take on the Red Sox competitive advantage, revealed in a 2011 interview, is telling. It wasn't their passionate fan base, their regional sports network cash cow, their talent on or off the field, or their deep-pocketed owners. No, he said the Red Sox competitive advantage was the database they'd built over the last decade. Data, lots of it, and the ability to interpret it is as coveted within some organizations as a left-handed pitcher who can throw ninety miles per hour.

All this data hasn't changed just what happens on the field; it's changed the business of baseball as well. Front offices across the league know the marginal value of a win. In other words, teams can accurately estimate how many more tickets will be sold, how many more people will watch or listen to game broadcasts, and how much more merchandise will be sold for each additional win a team generates. That figure, on average about $5 million across all of baseball in 2011, varies of course by team, and even for each team by itself it's not linear. Take a look at the final standings for 2011 and it's obvious one more win would have had much more value for the Boston Red Sox or the Atlanta Braves than the Houston Astros or Minnesota Twins. However, when examined from the perspective of five- or ten-win blocks, the value of marginal wins is apparent for all teams.

Thanks to the creation of the wins-above-replacement, or WAR, metric, any team can reasonably estimate how many more (or fewer) wins any specific player will provide the team. With projection algorithms such as PECOTA, teams can, with declining levels of certainty over lengthening time periods, project WAR over four, five, or six years, allowing them to make educated guesses about a player's total value over the life of a proposed contract, in terms of both wins and money. The marginal cost of a win can now be easily calculated, since every team knows the cost of signing a free agent. Every team also knows what to offer in negotiations for those free agents. In the end it becomes a simple application of Economics 101: If the marginal value to a team exceeds its marginal cost, it should acquire the player.

Compared with the relatively unsophisticated methods of evaluating talent in the financial industry, you'd think major league baseball would have far more at stake in terms of enterprise value and potential profits. Ask a member of the Atlanta Braves' front office who their best starting pitcher was during the 2011 season and he'll probably tell you it was Brandon Beachy. "Brandon who?" a startled observer might exclaim. "Derek Lowe, a proven post-season ace, was the Opening Day starter. Tim Hudson was the ace of the staff. He's the workhorse you can depend on for two-hundred-plus innings, he won sixteen games, and like Lowe you paid him about $10 million. What about Jair Jurrjens, another multi-million-dollar pitcher, who had one of the best ERAs (2.96) in all of baseball? At one point during the season he was 12-3! Some scouts think Tommy Hanson, whose ERA was better than Beachy's, is the better prospect. How is Brandon Beachy even in the conversation?"

The GM (and if it's not the Braves' GM, I guarantee you a sophisticated GM from another team will be using this logic when he attempts to trade for Beachy) might reply, "Brandon Beachy was our best pitcher because he consistently displayed the best *repeatable* skill set of anyone on our staff."

Now, walk onto the trading floor of an investment bank and ask the head of any desk, "Who's your best trader?" Ask the head of a hedge fund or a mutual fund to identify the best portfolio manager and the best trader. Each trader has a profit-and-loss statement, or P&L, whereas a fund's return on capital functions as the scoreboard for portfolio managers. I guarantee you, based on my fifteen years of firsthand observation, after asking that question you will be shown the trader with that year's highest P&L and the portfolio manager with that year's best performance. Undoubtedly, these individuals will also be the best-paid and also very likely among the most senior members on the desk.

The difference? Financial industry managers point to the latest results. Baseball teams, using the advances in statistical analytics developed via sabermetrics, identify skill sets. They know that it's the possession of specific skills that is the most reliable predictor of future results. They also know, therefore, which results are repeatable. Using P&L or a fund's return as the sole determinate to identify a desk's best trader or a fund's best portfolio manager, respectively, is as misleading as using wins to identify a team's best pitcher. That's because both P&L

and portfolio returns in the financial industry, like wins in baseball, are highly dependent on factors beyond the control of the individual credited with the performance. In short, you need context.

From 2007 to 2010, Seattle's Félix Hernández and Kansas City's Zach Greinke didn't win as many games as Josh Beckett, Justin Verlander, or CC Sabathia, not because they didn't pitch as well but because their teams didn't score as many runs. You can be the greatest pitcher in the world, but if your team gets shut out, the best you're ever going to do is get a no-decision. The absence of context when making personnel decisions at the top of the financial services industry is astounding in light of the advances made in the industry of baseball. To accurately assess a financial professional's performance, you need to adjust for all the factors that influence bottom-line performance, the most prominent metric. In the case of traders and portfolio managers, those factors include access to capital, drawdown (or inter-period loss experience), product or sector specialty, and portfolio concentration.

Sabermetrics differs from the gathering of traditional baseball statistics as physics differs from accounting. Both disciplines use numbers, but the former makes discoveries while the latter merely tallies results. In baseball, sabermetrics allowed analysts to discover skill sets without being misled by metrics that often bear only a coincidental relation to them. No longer do sophisticated analysts look to a pitcher's wins or even his

ERA to determine skill; they look to his strikeout rate, his walk rate, and his ground-ball rate. That's because those statistics are better determinants of future success than ERA and wins. Even those outside the management of baseball teams have grown to understand this: Zach Greinke and Félix Hernández won AL Cy Young Awards in 2009 and 2010, respectively, despite win totals far from the league leaders.

The financial industry still uses accounting data. If it adopted a sabermetric-like approach, it'd be better able to evaluate the performance of its extremely well-paid employees. Nowhere would that be easier than in the evaluation of portfolio managers. Portfolio managers, or PMs, are the individuals in charge of deciding how the money in a fund gets invested. All funds have a stated benchmark against which their returns are judged. A fund dedicated to investing in technology stocks judges itself against a technology stock index like the Morgan Stanley High-Technology 35 Index, while a general stock fund with the freedom to invest in all sectors typically uses the S&P 500 Index, the most common benchmark. The goal of every PM, of course, is to beat the benchmark. To achieve this goal, the PM controls just two settings of the fund: market exposure and stock selection.

Market exposure is expressed as a percentage of assets under management, or AUM. Suppose a PM has $10 million of AUM. If he owns $5 million worth of stock at the beginning of the day while keeping the other $5 million uninvested, or "in cash," he is said to be 50 percent net long. If the next day, he shorts (sells stock he doesn't own yet) $7 million of other stocks, he would be 20 percent net short. If, on day three, he bought back $2 million of the stock he had shorted, he'd be "market neutral," the term for 0 percent net long. As this simple example shows, market neutral doesn't mean riskless (far from it, since the fund has $10 million worth of stock positions, $5 million long and $5 million short); it simply means after netting long and short positions the fund is indifferent to the market's direction.

If we were to tell the PM that the only stock he could trade was one that mirrored the performance of his benchmark, the S&P 500,* his ability to outperform his benchmark over any period of time would rest entirely on his ability to predict market moves. The PM would lower exposure when he had less conviction about a market advance, potentially turning short if he thought it would decline, and moving all the way to 100 percent short if he thought it was certain to do so. In the most simplistic example, if the fund had been 100 percent long for eleven months of the year and something less than 100 percent long for another month, the PM would have beaten the benchmark if the S&P declined during that month of decreased exposure. If the market rose that month, the fund would have lagged the index.

---

*Such a security exists under the symbol SPY, and it's technically an ETF, as opposed to a stock.

Stock selection as a determinant of PM success is more intuitive. Assume this time that the PM can hold no cash and therefore must invest the entire $10 million in stocks. In this case, his ability to outperform the S&P 500 will be entirely determined by his stock selection. Using a different approach to investing, market-neutral hedge funds require their PMs to keep a fund between +/- 5 percent net long or short. In this setting, too, the ability of the PM to select stocks—in this case, relative to one another—will determine his ability to beat the S&P. The market's overall direction will be irrelevant, with the exception of the small +/- 5 percent exposure setting.

In practice, it's a combination of these two factors, market exposure and stock selection, that determines a PM's success. As related as they may seem, however, success at these two tasks—selecting outperforming and/or underperforming stocks and predicting overall market moves—involves two entirely different skill sets. These skill sets are as different as speed on the base paths and power at the plate are in baseball, but I've never heard anyone explicitly acknowledge it or seen anyone make an effort to identify, let alone quantify, the presence of these skills in a PM. Yet it's easy to do and vital to understand.

In my four and a half years of running a hedge fund trading desk, I kept a complete database of our trades—an eleven-hundred-day trove of data that recorded every decision the PMs and traders made. I could go to any single day and determine our net exposure to the market and the performance of the stocks relative to our benchmark. What it revealed was fascinating. We had a PM who was a tremendous stock picker. Over any period of time—days, weeks, months, quarters, or years—he had an unwavering ability to buy, or go long, stocks that outperformed those that he shorted. In the parlance of the investment community, he created "alpha."

However, at the same time he was a very active trader, constantly adjusting his exposure to the market. It would not be uncommon at all to be net long 70 percent Monday, net long 10 percent Tuesday, and net short 10 percent Wednesday before returning to 50 percent net long by Thursday. When I'd examine the effect of our shifting market exposure, the results were eye-opening: Our PM was a horrendous predictor of overall stock market moves. It was absolutely uncanny. Over the four-plus years, no matter what period you examined, his periods of lower market exposure always coincided with the better performance by the overall stock market than his periods of high market exposure. Over the life of our fund, he possessed an amazing ability to persistently misjudge the daily moves of the market.

Our PM created alpha with stock selection and destroyed it with shifts in market exposure. Overall, his stock selection skills were so strong that he was a net creator of alpha—a valuable asset to the organization. If a potential investor looked at a prospectus for our fund, he'd note our fund beat the market over its life by a pretty convincing margin, and therefore the

PM created alpha. This is a true but incomplete summary of his skill set. Think of it this way: He was a plodding slugger who tried to steal every time he got on base. Getting thrown out frequently didn't entirely wipe out his value as a home-run hitter, but it sure watered it down.

To achieve the highest return possible, the PM, in charge of nearly a quarter-billion dollars at one point, should never have been allowed to alter his market exposure, just as a baseball team would never let the slugger continue to amass steal attempts. Even worse, within our fund we had a trader who possessed the skill set our PM lacked. Every single day during the life of the fund, the trader wrote a note solely focused on the short-term direction of the market, ending with a bullish, bearish, or neutral stance. Again, over eleven hundred days, the results of his analysis were unmistakable. The market did better by a substantial margin when he was bullish than it did when he wasn't.

Ron Shandler, a pioneer in the use of sabermetrics for fantasy baseball purposes, proposes a simple rule: Once you display a skill, you own it. The PM, through four and a half years of consistent demonstration, owned the stock-picking skill, and the trader owned the market-reading skill. I once calculated that the return of the fund in excess of its benchmark, already high to begin with, would have more than doubled if the PM would have simply maintained a fixed schedule of market exposure—for example, something like 60 percent net long when the trader was bullish, 25 percent when neutral, and -10 percent when bearish.

When presented with this overwhelmingly conclusive data, the PM either ignored or belittled it. Celebrated for the whole of his career, he refused to acknowledge that he lacked a skill set. This is not an uncommon attitude among PMs. As Nassim Nicholas Taleb, author of *Fooled by Randomness* and *The Black Swan,** points out repeatedly, it is common for highly compensated PMs to think high pay and infallibility are correlated. Rebuffed by the PM, I took this data to the head of the asset management division, who reported directly to the CEO of Lehman Brothers, the largest investor in the fund.

Lehman Brothers, at the time, was at the forefront of investment banking, a company with a market capitalization exceeding the entire value of Major League Baseball. It had grand plans to develop (they used the word *incubate*) hedge funds it could eventually spin off, raise money for, and market as internally developed hedge funds. The head of the asset management division—a group that included the hundreds of billions of dollars run by dozens of managers within Neuberger Berman—had responsibility for developing and marketing the organization's PMs.

He had no interest in my analysis.

---

*This book is a staple on the shelves of traders. Hence, when *Black Swan,* starring Natalie Portman, came to theaters, a common joke on the trading floor was "That movie was *nothing* like the book. You wanna talk about tail risk, though? When Mila Kunis came on stage in that leotard...."

I may as well have been Bill James going around to the front offices of teams in the early 1990s, warning against the dependence on batting average.

The head of asset management told me our fund needed better salesmen. Using a baseball analogy, he planned to combat disappointing attendance with added pressure on the marketing department to put more fannies in the seats, rather than bothering with trying to improve the talent on the field, which would have produced more wins and led to sustainable attendance gains.

I'm just scratching the surface with this analysis. For instance, the beautiful thing about a database is the ability to creatively sift through it for less obvious discoveries. In the case of the PM who is terrible at shifting exposure based on how the market does the next day, or "day T," using the database, management could look at how the PM's exposure would have performed on day T-1. If the performance is much better, it provides strong evidence that the PM is a chaser. In other words, he let the market's performance on Tuesday effect his view of the market on Wednesday.

Now, not only has management identified a deficient skill set; it's also discovered the cause. Just like a prospect's inability to hit pitches coming in over the inside part of the plate, this weakness, once identified, can be addressed and possibly corrected. What organization, what industry, wouldn't want to possess this sort of insight about its most important and most expensive assets?

There are hundreds of sizable mutual funds and hedge funds, all employing dozens of PMs, that should be performing this type of analysis. They should know exactly what skill sets the individuals in charge of millions of dollars of client assets possess.

Another way to think about this kind of analysis is that the ability to pick stocks and the ability to read the market are as different skill sets as hitting and fielding are in baseball. Letting a PM with an above-average ability to pick stocks but a below-average ability to predict market moves do both would be as ill-advised as an American League team in 2010 letting Vladimir Guerrero, a horrendous fielder at the end of his career, don a glove and walk to the outfield when he could be the designated hitter instead. He creates incremental value with his bat, but no American League team should let him destroy some or all of that value by letting him try to field batted balls.

In the case of my fund, Lehman Brothers put Guerrero in the field despite having a defensive specialist sitting on the bench. Not even much-maligned Texas Rangers manager Ron Washington would do that. Wait a minute... what?*

---

*Game 1, 2010 World Series: Ron Washington started Vladimir Guerrero in right field against the Giants at AT&T Park, in San Francisco, site of one of the most expansive right fields in Major League Baseball. Guerrero promptly made two errors in a game the Rangers lost.

12

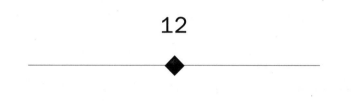

Taken Out to the Ball Game

"Daddy! I see grass!" cried Calista.

And with that, a vision of Philadelphia's Veterans Stadium, circa 1972, spread out before me.

By the middle of May 2011, I'd returned home to San Francisco, since my leg had shrunk sufficiently for the transcontinental flight. No longer lugging a discolored and unbendable leg that looked like it belonged on Shrek, I rejoined my family for the last few weeks of the school year. The first round of interleague play began on Friday, May 20, 2011, and it presented some challenges for the model, as American League teams playing in National League parks would be losing the services of their designated hitter, and in American League parks, National League pitchers would have to face a much tougher number-nine hitter. In response, I made what I thought were appropriate adjustments, but since the model wasn't designed for deviations in rules for the eighteen or so interleague games each team plays, I wasn't entirely comfortable venturing money on those selections. So I shut down betting for the weekend.

Coincidentally, that same morning our neighbor offered me a pair of tickets to the next day's game between the San Francisco Giants and their cross-bay rival, the Oakland A's. The timing was perfect. Although I was still on crutches, I had just shed the ten-pound boot I'd worn since my surgery, which enabled me to move around our home more confidently. Plus it sounded like a perfect opportunity to actually watch a baseball game in person for the first time in 2011. So I took my youngest daughter, Calista, then almost five years old, to her first baseball game.

My household is decidedly pink. From the time my oldest, Lily, then nearly seven, could walk, I've been up to my elbows in tutus. Calista followed in her sister's footsteps, although she did show slightly more interest in round things that bounced or could be kicked and thrown. Still, a trip to a baseball game hadn't seemed a likely destination until she'd learned "Take Me Out to the Ball Game" a month earlier and it had became a favorite. When I had explained to her that everyone sings it at games, she announced that she wanted to go so she could sing that song "at intermission of the football game." I let the double faux pas pass, thankful I had gotten her to agree to a sporting event of any kind.

Ever try to define a color? Without referencing another color, it's very hard, especially if you're dealing with shades. However, when it comes to emerald, I have no trouble. Emerald is the color of the sun-drenched grass you spot from the bowels of a baseball stadium as you ascend to your seats, and it's sublimely beautiful. Honestly, I don't know whether it's because stadiums are generally dank, damp, concrete bowls you need to navigate like a maze or if it's because you're always in darkness on the way to your seats or even if it's because, as a kid, you equate grass with playing. I do know that that first sight of the field is always striking. It's my very first memory of going to a baseball game with my father. I'd seen plenty of Phillies games on television by the time I was seven, and yet I couldn't believe how bright green—yes, *emerald*—the field looked when I spied it through the many ramps we walked up to get to our seats. We were in the infamous 700-level of the tiered, concrete bowl that was Veterans Stadium. On this spring Saturday, imagine my delighted shock when Calista, who had never watched a game on TV and who continually referred to our outing as a football game,* noticed a sliver of the field as we rode up the escalators to our seats and shouted, "Daddy! I see grass!"

Over the years, the stock market, pricing, and probability came largely to replace baseball as my passion, but baseball was

---

*At one point during the game, she noticed the oversize glove beyond the left-field bleachers that is an AT&T Park landmark and exclaimed, "Look at the big football glove out there!"

my first love, as a participant and as a spectator. When I was a kid I would have done any task or endured any hardship to go to a baseball game.* Hearing my daughter—who will never collect a baseball card, play an inning of ABPA or Strat-O-Matic, or don a Little League uniform—make the same connection to the game that I did when I was her age truly took my breath away.

My reaction was ridiculous; I was tearing up at a baseball game, and not only had it not started yet; I didn't have any money riding on the game! It was fitting that the first time I recognized an intergenerational connection between my daughter and me occurred at a baseball game. Baseball has been a significant part of life for generations of Americans. Like no other sport, traditions and appreciation for the game are passed from parent to child (sons *and* daughters!), creating indelible memories while at the same time marking time and providing milestones. I know both have happened in my family.

Earlier that weekend, Calista's older sister, Lily, who is likely to reach puberty without knowing if a baseball is in-

---

*At least, that's what I believed. Take 1981, when the Phillies opened the season against the Cincinnati Reds. At that time, the Reds always played the first game of the season, and it was filled with pomp and circumstance. On this particular Opening Day, Major League Baseball honored a number of the Iranian hostages, the fifty-two Americans held captive in Iran for 444 days, until January 1981. While honoring them, MLB announced that every hostage would be given lifetime passes to all major league stadiums. Well, this was too much for me to take, and I blurted out, "They're so lucky!" My mother immediately launched into a lecture about how good a life I had and the meaning of sacrifice. She then turned to my father for support. He just looked at me, smirked, and said, "He couldn't make it through the evening locked in his room without dinner." If I had ever been kidnapped, my father, the ex-Marine, would probably have ignored the ransom demands just to toughen me up a little.

flated, stuffed, or wound, wanted help with her multiplication tables. She asked me what eight times seven equals. In explaining the answer, I added that it's one of the most special numbers in all of sports. I don't know if she'll ever be able to define a hitting streak, but she just may remember that fifty-six represents a man who came from San Francisco, got married to the most famous movie star in the world, and was loved by her grandfather, Pa Peta, even though he hated the Yankees, because Joe DiMaggio was the greatest Italian American ever to play the game.

For my mother, baseball, the game around which her all-male household of a husband and two sons revolved, has turned into an unfortunate yardstick that measures my father's declining mental capacity as he succumbs to Alzheimer's-related dementia. As his physical health has worsened and his energy has waned over the past decade, he has slowly but irreversibly become housebound. Still, she could always count on his anticipation of that day's Phillies game. Sadly, in the past few years, that has changed as well.

My father told many stories about 1950, the golden year, amid a forty-year drought, that the Phillies were contenders. That year ended in a trip to the World Series, but the loss—a sweep at the hands of the hated New York Yankees—rankled my father. Twenty-some years later, while still in grade school, I could recite the 1950 Whiz Kids' starting lineup from all the stories I had heard about them from my dad. By 2009, when the

Phillies-Yankees rematch he had waited fifty-nine years for finally arrived, my dad couldn't even tell my mom who was playing in the World Series, despite the fact she had the television on nightly. Forgetting your kids' names might be the cruelest nail in the coffin that is Alzheimer's, but when my mom realized Phillies' games weren't registering with my dad, she knew she'd lost a significant portion of the man she'd spent her entire adult life with.

My grandmother gave birth to my dad just three months after she arrived in America from the Reggio Calabria region of Italy. Born in 1929, my dad, like many children of the waves of new immigrants, grew up in challenging times. Stigmatized at a young age due to his non-English-speaking parents, and saddled with an embarrassing name instantly announcing his own immigrant status, Erminio Joseph Peta made two choices: He adopted baseball as his favorite sport, and he set out to master the English language. Years later, those choices intersected on my personal atlas at the corner of Childhood Drive and Adolescent Humiliation Avenue. When I first started playing Little League Baseball my dad was my coach. By then, he was also an English professor, so my teammates and I not only learned infield and dugout chatter, we learned *grammatically correct* infield and dugout chatter. During one practice I was taking infield grounders when a hard roller took a bad bounce and hit me square in the nuts. My teammates gathered around in a mix of worry and, given our age, laughter. While they giggled and my dad approached, I moaned, "I wish I was dead." Dad called to one of the assistant coaches to bring him an ice pack. Then he leaned down to offer what I thought were sure to be some encouraging words. Clutching my balls, I looked up at him expectantly. "I wish I *were* dead," he corrected while looking me in the eye. "Subjunctive form of the verb *to be*."

That moment may have humiliated me at the time and given my teammates years of laughter, but many years later, as a single professional in Washington, D.C., I cherished the memory. My father introduced me to baseball, encouraged me to collect baseball cards, was my first Little League coach, and bought season tickets to the Phillies for several years when we probably had other pressing expenses. I owed him.

In 1992, I had tickets to the first Opening Day at Baltimore's Camden Yards, so, naturally, I invited my father, then retired in Florida, to the game.

I'd never seen a crowd arrive so early. We stepped through the gates two hours before the first pitch, and it wasn't long before every seat was full. Camden Yards had drawn rave reviews for its beauty and its upscale concessions, and fans wanted plenty of time to tour the facilities. During pre-game ceremonies, the Orioles trotted out all their great players from the past to take the field and cut a ceremonial ribbon before the first pitch was thrown. Near the end of the ceremony, they had one more player to go, one of the most beloved players in Orioles history. Completing his introductions, the master of ceremonies announced, "And now, the greatest third baseman in the history of baseball...." Remember my background: I was a boisterous twenty-six-year-old and a lifelong Phillies fan, so I naturally shouted out, "Hey! Mike Schmidt's here."

The remark didn't go over well with devotees of Brooks Robinson—also a Hall of Fame third baseman—who filled our section. In particular, an overserved gentleman (recall that everyone had been there for at least an hour) one row down and a couple seats over took exception to my remark and loudly insisted I had just disrespected everything Baltimore stood for. My father stood up and played peacemaker, diplomatically returning everyone to their seats. What came next was as out of character as my mother buying shots in a bar. My dad has never possessed a particularly sharp sense of comic timing, but Bill Murray himself couldn't have delivered his next line better. Having just defused a heated situation by citing the setting and the beautiful day, and with everyone having just settled back into their seats, my dad leaned forward and said, "Anyway, sir, they did say the *greatest* third baseman of all time."

That's what's great about a trip to the ballpark with your father or child. You never can tell if you're going to create a memory as simple as the wonder of a green field popping up into eyesight or as unlikely as a father-son bleacher brawl.

There's an expression on Wall Street, often attributed to Warren Buffett, which goes, "They don't ring a bell at the top." There's tremendous wisdom in that adage, because while in retrospect it's easy to pinpoint the day that the market (or even a specific stock) reached an all-time high that looks unlikely to ever be attained again in the foreseeable future, at the moment it happened it was impossible to recognize. That's because, unlike market bottoms, which usually have a crescendo feeling to them accompanied by investor panic, a market top generally passes without fanfare, indistinguishable from the series of tops that preceded it.

You know when else they don't ring a bell? For parents, they don't ring a bell the last time you read *Goodnight Moon.* They don't do it the last time you watch *Sleeping Beauty* and they don't do it the last time you help your daughter put on the same article of clothing she's wanted to wear every day as a toddler. Instead, a couple years after the fact, you find the book on a shelf, the DVD in a box, and the tights with the pink ballerinas on them in the back of a drawer. You can't for the life of you remember the last time you read the book, danced to "Once Upon a Dream" with your daughter on your feet, or helped put those tights on. But you do know that now she reads to herself at bedtime, she dances, alone, to Taylor Swift, and the tights—well, the tights wouldn't even make it over her knees.

I thought of all this on the night of May 21, 2011, the first time I shared baseball with my daughter. It seems poignancy, like market bottoms, can sometimes be evident as the moment unfolds. Baseball—the game that caused me to save paper-route money to buy Topps cards, the game for which I'd sprint home from the bus stop in middle school to play APBA with my brother, the game for which I'd fallen asleep countless nights with a transistor radio earpiece in one ear, and the game that my father adopted to announce that he loved America— was the same game that made my youngest daughter squeal, "Daddy! I see grass!" the first time I took her to a ballpark.

13

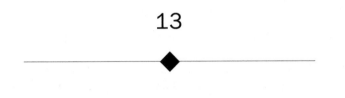

First Quarter Results

With games played every single day (except around the All-Star game, in July), the baseball season never lets up. By May 18, every team had played at least forty games, or a quarter of their 162-game season. As is the case every year, a handful of teams had gotten off to starts vastly divergent from the analysts' pre-season expectations. The 2010 AL Central–champion Minnesota Twins were in last place, with a record of 13-27, the worst in baseball. That put the Twins on a pace to lose a whopping 109 games and win just fifty-three. At the start of the season, they were expected to win about eighty-five or eighty-six games, based on the total-win over-under of 85½ set by oddsmakers. Even my projection, reflecting extreme bearishness on their 2011 prospects compared with conventional wisdom, had them winning seventy-seven games, a far cry from their pace at the one-quarter mark.

At the other extreme, the Cleveland Indians (72½ over-under; seventy-three wins by my projection) started the year 26-14, the best record in baseball. Their start projected to a 105-win season. Between those two extremes, other teams were deviating from my or the oddsmakers' expectations. Which raised the question: How much should the model factor in what actually occurs during the season?

Like so many other statistically based baseball puzzles, someone else had already tackled it. Fascinated (or, probably more accurately, tortured) by the Royals' hot start in 2003, Rany Jazayerli, a Baseball Prospectus co-founder and passionate Kansas City Royals fan, took on this very issue in the spring of 2003. At the start of the 2003 season, the Royals, coming off of eight straight losing seasons, including a franchise-worst one-hundred-loss season the year before, started the year 14-3. Jazayerli wondered if a team's start is an accurate indicator of how it will play the rest of the season. Over his three-part series, published at baseballprospectus.com, he concluded that there is significance to a team's start. He found that, after thirty-five to forty games, a team's record in the current year predicts more than 50 percent of its final record ($r^2 > .50$ once a team plays somewhere close to forty games).

It didn't take a nine-thousand-word, three-part series to come to that simple a conclusion; there was a great deal of detail to absorb. I applied Jazayerli's findings conservatively, and by May 19 I began to reduce the weight of my pre-season projections from 100 percent, replacing it with actual results. I continued to do this as each quarter-season was completed. Consistent with all my modeling, I didn't use a team's actual record at any of these mileposts; I used its theoretical Pythagorean theorem record, based on runs scored and runs allowed, and I stripped out the effects of cluster luck in converting actual runs scored and runs allowed to theoretical figures.

By the end of May, a handful of my friends aware of what I was doing became insistent. "You have to start betting on these games for me. Don't even tell me what you're doing. Just let me know how we did afterwards."

If you've ever been undecided about buying a stock and elected instead to track its progress for a period of time, inevitably the following occurs: The stock goes straight up, you kick yourself for not buying immediately, and then you buy at higher prices. It's as if the law of supply and demand taught in all Economics 101 courses has been suspended. Demand *increases* as the price goes up. Well, demand to get in on the action as dictated by the model reached the point where I agreed to place bets on behalf of a few other people. Of course, I should have waited for the model to hit a rough patch, because just like the investor who chases a stock higher, it seems the moment the stock is bought, the ascent ends.

The end of the fund's ascent wouldn't occur until June, because May's results resembled a stock that keeps climbing higher in price.

The Model's Results in May	
Total Return	+12.03 percent
Year-to-Date Return	+21.87 percent (compounded monthly)
Total Games Picked	368 (out of 420 played)
Record in Games Picked	199-169

Rather than adjusting my bankroll on a daily or even weekly basis, I recalculated only the notional amount of a bet (2 percent, 1 percent, and so on) based on the size of the fund at the beginning of the month. In other words, I'd compound my return monthly. Comparing May's results to April's, a few themes emerged. As in April, the model found an edge in more than 85 percent of games played. The overall record and the resulting return for the month were much better, however.

Return by Category of Team Selected		
	Win-Loss Record	Return
Favorites	124-83	+6.63 percent
Underdogs	64-75	+2.17 percent
Pick-'Ems	11-11	+3.23 percent
Total	**199-169**	**+12.03 percent**

Return by Wager Size		
	Win-Loss Record	**Return**
2 percent bets	7-1	+10.20 percent
1.5 percent bets	1-0	+1.88 percent
1 percent bets	9-6	+2.61 percent
50-basis-point bets	13-14	-2.53 percent
40-basis-point bets	41-34	+2.16 percent
20-basis-point bets	53-66	-5.13 percent
10-basis-point bets	75-48	+2.84 percent

In May, the model was a little more inclined to select favorites than in April. Favorites accounted for 207 of the 368 games chosen, or 56 percent, compared with just 42 percent in April. Satisfyingly, looking at the two months combined, the model showed net winnings on favorites, dogs, and pick-'em games. Although the returns were top-heavy for the second month in a row, this time the model showed a net gain, in total, in the ten-to-forty-basis-point tier where the bulk of the selections occurred. For some reason, the twenty-basis-point level continued to bedevil the model, even with net winnings above and below it. However, there was no evidence that this was due to anything but a statistical anomaly.

+/- 2 Percent Returns on Teams Bet On			
St. Louis Cardinals	13	5	+3.52 percent
Arizona Diamondbacks	16	8	+3.33 percent
Chicago White Sox	8	5	+3.22 percent
Milwaukee Brewers	15	6	+2.93 percent
.			
.			
.			
.			
Colorado Rockies	7	9	-2.09 percent
Texas Rangers	8	5	-2.52 percent

+/- 2 Percent Returns on Teams Bet Against			
LA Angels	15	13	+5.99 percent
San Diego Padres	14	10	+3.76 percent
Minnesota Twins	14	7	+2.69 percent
.			
.			
.			
.			
Kansas City Royals	2	4	-4.19 percent

It didn't appear the oddsmakers were making significant adjustments to their lines, despite two months of play and, in some cases, drastic lineup changes. For instance, the model started the season quite bearish on the Minnesota Twins' prospects relative to expectations. Therefore, in those early weeks of the season, when the model picked against Minnesota, to varying degrees, on a nearly daily basis, it was expected. However, by May the Twins had been decimated by injuries. Obviously, based on my daily inspection of the lines, the oddsmakers didn't find this as significant as the model did. Sure, the Twins' daily odds dropped: In April the sum of the implied odds of all their games totaled 12.99 games, and in May it totaled 11.94. With the Twins playing twenty-six and twenty-seven games, respectively, in those months, oddsmakers had dropped them from an eighty-one-win team to a seventy-two-win team. While that looks like a nine-win drop on the surface, there were some mitigating factors. For one, the Twins played fifteen games on the road in May vs. eleven in April. Adjust for that and oddsmakers really dropped the Twins' expectations by only seven games.

Granted, there may have been differences in opponents, but the oddsmakers still didn't move dramatically enough. The Twins regularly trotted out a lineup in May with Drew Butera and Trevor Plouffe in place of Joe Mauer and Justin Morneau. (While Trevor Plouffe—primarily a weak-hitting, poor-fielding shortstop—didn't play first base, the Twins shifted other fielders around the diamond with Morneau out, effectively making Plouffe his replacement.) That's a ten-win drop by itself. That should have resulted in a huge drop in win expectancy from April to May, but it didn't.

Either the oddsmakers never understood how weak the Twins' offense was as a result of mounting injuries, or they didn't grasp the implications of the weakness. By the time the season had ended, the Twins nine starters on Opening Day lineup, combined, would start just over half of the season's remaining games—by far the lowest rate in the league. In other words, for about half of their games, Minnesota started nine players entirely different from those they had on Opening Day, all of them bench players or minor league call-ups. To be sure, the model took some lumps over the next two months as Minnesota seemed to defy its prediction of total collapse, but by the end of the 2011 season, the Twins had the worst record in the American League.

14

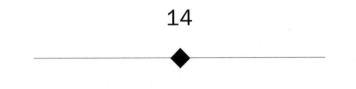

The Mental Discomfort of Being Behind

Over the past twenty years, thanks partially to the repeal of the Depression-era Glass–Steagall regulations in the late 1990s, Wall Street investment banks became the dominant force in global finance. During their rise in prominence, Alan Greenspan headed the United States Federal Reserve System. As chairman of the Federal Reserve board, Greenspan had a lot of explicitly authorized powers, but he also deftly furthered his influence over the American financial system: Despite occupying a government position designed to be insulated from political pressure, Greenspan was one of the most effective lobbyists inside the Beltway. Greenspan's frequent appearances before Congress felt more like lectures from a professor than typical congressional testimony. A master of obfuscation,

Greenspan probably didn't want to be so clearly seen as lobbying. Over the years, though, one message emerged clearly: The chairman thought American banks needed less, not more, regulation.

Greenspan's suggestion that banks didn't need to be closely regulated stemmed from his long-held belief that no one had a bigger interest in policing the banks than the banks themselves. Due to counterparty risk and self-interest, Greenspan surmised that bank managements would be so vigilant, so versed in the complexities of modern financial instruments, and so adept at risk management that Congress had no need to create agencies or pass laws to augment their oversight.

Deep breath.

That theory came under severe strain starting in 2008, and, to be fair, even Greenspan eventually admitted he had a flawed premise. Surely, after the demise of Bear Stearns, the bankruptcy of Lehman Brothers, TARP, and the bailouts of AIG and Fannie Mae and Freddie Mac, Wall Street management teams would approach risk differently.

As if the needless 2011 bankruptcy of MF Global—caused by Jon Corzine's recklessly increasing the firm's leverage ratio to more than 30–1—isn't enough of an exhibit, I'll relay my last experience on Wall Street. Nomura Securities, the largest financial institution in Japan, had by 2009 greatly expanded its international banking capabilities with the purchase of Lehman Brothers' non-U.S. operations out of bankruptcy a year earlier. Nomura recognized that the U.S. market represented its only hole in building a truly global investment bank. Management decided, therefore, to transform its minor U.S. presence into a full-service broker-dealer. To that end, in the first quarter of 2010 Nomura hired Pascal Bandelier, a friend and former colleague, to head its U.S. equity trading desk. In my nearly fifteen years on Wall Street, I'd met some very intelligent, astute, and successful people, but Pascal easily had the most innate grasp of risk. By hiring the thirty-year-old, Nomura announced to competitors and customers alike that its ambitions to transform its U.S. presence were serious.

The chance to work for Pascal and to help create a culture of risk like we'd known at Lehman had enormous appeal. In my interviews with management, its message echoed what Pascal had told me; Nomura had no interest in becoming a second-tier player. It had top-five, bulge-bracket ambitions, and its hiring in sales, research, and trading mirrored that goal. All that talent, often the best performers at other banks, is expensive. During interviews, I expressed my worry that an industrywide decline in trading volumes and a decade-long compression of commissions made it impossible to cover the labor costs with commissions alone. The stark, mathematical reality of the business was that additional revenue needed to be generated through risk-taking or, as it's known in the business, principal trading. In explaining that I embraced this reality, I drew upon my experience at a hedge fund. We didn't make money every day; there were a lot of days we lost material amounts of money. In fact, we only made money about three days a week, on average. However, the fund had an unmistakable positive expected return over time, because the PM, the analysts, and the traders picked stocks and gauged the market well. It was a great example of Warren Buffett's business philosophy of preferring to have "a lumpy 15 percent over time than a smooth 12 percent." (Buffett originally penned this line in Berkshire Hathaway's 1996 letter to shareholders. Interest rates, and therefore expected rates of returns on investments, have dropped sharply since then. Still, the sentence makes sense today—and I'll use it going forward—as a philosophy, even if the numbers should actually be adjusted lower.)

Now imagine grafting a few hundred thousand dollars of commissions each day onto that business model. It wouldn't remove the jaggedness of the profit line that slopes up from the bottom left to the top right, but it would move the entire line higher. Twelve percent smooth had no chance of paying the bills that any new entrant in the U.S. broker-dealer market would incur, let alone the expenses that Nomura, with its top-five ambitions, had rung up on its talent shopping spree. Twelve percent smooth wouldn't pay the bills, but fifteen percent lumpy might.

Consistent with the message I received during interviews,

by hiring Pascal management signaled to its employees, customers, and competitors that it understood this reality—and it wrote it into his contract. In addition to being paid a percentage of the profits *he* generated from principal trading, Pascal would also be paid a percentage of the profits that *I* or anyone else generated. Although I relished the challenge, it put considerable pressure on me: I was one of just three people on the principal-trading team Pascal had created. As such, I traded very lightly and took very small positions in my initial days at Nomura. During August, I created a book of positions totaling about $14 million. The book held about $7 million of long positions and $7 million of short positions, so it was roughly market neutral, and a month out of the gate I had made just under $1 million. I had gotten lucky. I'm not being modest; I had no doubt whatsoever in my ability to generate principal profits over the long term. It's just that $1 million in a month on a $14 million, diversified, market neutral portfolio represents an unsustainable return. Mathematically, it meant that my longs outperformed my shorts (or my shorts underperformed my longs) by 14 percent in one month. (The return on my $7 million of longs had to beat my $7 million of shorts by $1 million.) Any return that high contains elements of luck. Still, it was a good start and happened to attract the eye of very senior management.

At the beginning of September, the trio of traders tasked with launching the business and generating principal returns boarded a plane to meet with the Asia-based global head of equities. Upon arriving in Seoul, South Korea, we had dinner with him and members of the local office. I don't pretend to understand the mores and customs of the Asian business world, so for the most part I kept my mouth shut. However, over a post-dinner bottle of whiskey (this was one custom I grasped instantly—in Korea, workers drink after-hours like *that* is their job), he slid next to me and said, "I hear you're making me some money."* I smiled and talked about the business we were building, but before I could get very far he waved an arm to cut me off. "I want you guys to be big," he told me. "If you don't have enough runway in America, call me and I'll put the positions on in Asia. I want you to be BIG."

This should have sent up more flags than an Olympic village. He had no interest in discussing risk, questioning *how* I had made money, what plan I had, etc. Just be big. To drive his point further, he later told Pascal, "If the three of you make $50 million in principal trading by the end of March, I will give all three of you a week at my house in Ibiza—with your families."† The global head of equities had sent us an unmistakable message: Take big risks. Unfortunately, even though I recognized

---

*This is one of the most common ego-trip management techniques on Wall Street. There is a certain type of person who always wants to let you know you work for him and that he controls your future. Without near-parodies like this, Jon Stewart might be out of business.

†Translation: "I have a house in Ibiza and you don't." See previous footnote for explanation.

the recklessness of this approach—from the top dog, no less—I told my wife of his promise. By the time I got home we had travel books covering our coffee table and an Antonio Banderas–narrated DVD entitled *So You've Decided to Visit Ibiza* looping on the TV.

The real takeaway, of course, was the lack of concern the global head of equities of a large international bank had for risk management. I'd later learn from a member of the Asian management committee that the global head was under budget in virtually every region worldwide. Apparently, $50 million in additional profits from the U.S. region would have done a lot to plug those holes. A little more than six months after our meeting, he was removed from his position and left the firm.

However, just before his removal, he ordered a complete change in the U.S. risk profile. In conjunction with the U.S. head of equities, he fired Pascal fewer than four months after our official launch and installed a new desk head. The new head immediately conveyed the change in the firm's risk policy by sending the traders an e-mail, sporadically rendered entirely in capital letters,* stating that we were banned from soliciting trades from customers in stocks that were reporting

---

*I have come across two men in my career who haphazardly used all capital letters in portions of their e-mails, and both of them stood five feet tall. Statistically inclined readers might argue whether this is causation, correlation, or coincidence, but that misses the point. It's simply hilarious.

earnings before the next trading day. On the day a company reports earnings, unsurprisingly, its shares traded spikes to a multiple of its average daily volume. However, the day before, volume is nearly always above normal as well, since investors position themselves in anticipation of the earnings release. As a market maker, it's imperative to have a presence with customers and in the marketplace the day before earnings come out; many of the investors placing bets the day before earnings are the same ones reacting to the reported earnings the next day. If a market maker or broker knows who did the trading the day before earnings, they have the inside track for grabbing market share the next day.

Predictably, under this new risk standard our market share instantly plummeted, sending management into a new panic. In response, the new desk head, in a desperate attempt to attract orders, started making spectacularly risky after-hours and pre-opening markets in stocks that had just reported earnings. As a desk, we were lurching from one standard of risk to another like economist Milton Friedman's "fool in the shower," who, lacking the poise to make thoughtful incremental changes, adjusts the hot and cold knobs too quickly, alternately freezing and scalding himself in the process.

This type of desperate performance-chasing, throwing money at a hot trader and then changing organizational strategies midstream, is very reminiscent of the mismanagement of baseball teams in the seventies and eighties, typified by George

Steinbrenner's Yankees. Over the years, baseball management has wised up considerably, and there is much more emphasis on identifying the skill sets of players rather than fixating on their results. Management at investment banks should be doing the same thing.

Baseball researchers get ridiculed by traditionalists for the alphabet soup of newfangled statistics they create. WAR, VORP, and their ilk are harder to grasp than basic counting statistics like RBIs and wins, but that's because they measure skills and evaluate talent more accurately. Accounting is easy. Physics is hard. But the latter allows for far more advances in understanding our environment. My question isn't why baseball has created so many different acronyms in evaluating performance; my question is why haven't other industries done the same?

I wanted to help change that on a Wall Street trading desk, and Pascal and I had started to do so. We thought that management needed a better way to compare traders beyond a simplistic profit-and-loss statement. At the same time, traders needed to know that to truly *earn* a bonus they had to generate excess profit above what someone else or a machine in their seat would produce—the replacement-level concept in baseball.

For instance, sell-side traders don't get to pick which stocks they trade, let alone what side (long or short) of a trade a customer will stick them with. This is part of the business. I may not want to be long Oracle—in fact, due to a recent announcement from competitor Salesforce.com, I may think Oracle is about to go down a dollar over the next day or two and is therefore a screaming short—but if a large mutual fund calls and says it's selling me 300,000 shares, all I can do is try to pay a price a few pennies below the quoted market, plus charge a commission, in return. As is true in a lot of businesses, customers have that power. As such, liquidating unwanted positions is a large part of the sell-side trader's job. There is no right way to liquidate a position, but there are wrong ways. It turns out one of those wrong ways mirrors an error of judgment that dogs the majority of major league managers.

Imagine this scenario: top of the eighth inning, men on first and second, and no one out, with the visiting team trailing by two runs. Based on my observations, a significant number of major league managers will call for a bunt, especially in the playoffs. There will be some evaluation for what the batter might do if he swings away, but in the eighth inning it would surprise no one to see a National League manager pinch-hit for the pitcher and still call for the bunt. If the sacrifice succeeds, there will be runners on second and third with one out, and while a single will now score both runners, the manager also has his eye on a subsequent sacrifice fly to score one run. That's "manufacturing a run" in traditional baseball parlance, and based on the way certain announcers breathlessly extol the virtues of this strategy and the value of "small ball," you'd think they were watching a prodigy at work. In fact, the opposite is true. In short, the manager has employed a strategy most likely to tie the game, and traders fall prey to the same mental flaw, which leads to sub-optimal decisions.

Take another look at this strategy through a win-probability prism. A visiting team down by two runs during the top of the eighth inning with runners on first and second and nobody out has a 31 percent chance of winning the game.* Should it execute its manager's goal and tie the game by the time the inning is over, its chance of winning rises to ... 39 percent. That's right: The home team wins 61 percent of games that are tied going into the bottom of the eighth inning. Should the visiting team's attempt at manufacturing a run in this situation work as follows—bunt sacrifice out, sacrifice fly, third out—the visiting team will have cut the deficit to one run, and the manager, and most announcers, would likely be happy. ("By manufacturing a run, the Nationals have cut the deficit to a manageable one run as we enter the bottom of the eighth. . . .") Unfortunately, a visiting team trailing by one run after seven and a half innings has just a 13 percent chance of winning. The manager's "work" in manufacturing a run actually reduced his club's chances of winning the game significantly—a 58 percent drop, in fact, from 31 percent to 13 percent.

It's a terrible decision to employ a strategy designed to tie

---

*All win-expectancy calculations are courtesy of a theoretical calculator available at hardballtimes.com. The empirical results can be viewed for any specific year, beginning in 1951, at baseballprospectus.com.

the game or cut a deficit to one run. In the example above, the reason the visiting team, despite facing a two-run deficit, has a nearly one-in-three chance to win the game three batters into the top of the eighth inning is that it is in position *to take the lead*, subsequently needing only six outs to win the game. A team should never squander its upside in this situation, yet managers constantly do, due to the mental discomfort produced by trailing. Because of that discomfort, and their desire to avoid it, managers have a tendency to pursue strategies aimed at reducing their chances of being behind instead of maximizing their chances of winning.

Consider a trader faced with the need to liquidate a large block of stock. It's not possible to hit a button and sell a considerable amount of stock at the current price, so the trader has to be patient while the whims of the market move the price of the stock like a feather in the wind. In watching prices gyrate, every young trader, and far too many experienced ones, tend to do the same thing: sell as many shares as possible if the stock begins to rise, thereby exerting enough selling pressure on the stock to drive the price back down to his or her cost basis. However, if the price of the stock falls after the block is purchased, the trader tends to do nothing. They're gripped by the fear of adding to the selling in the marketplace, pushing the stock even lower. Sometimes this discretion is rewarded and the stock begins to rise. However, the moment the stock gets back to the purchase price, the trader will assuredly begin to sell shares "like their hair is on fire," in the words of one of my favorite Lehman colleagues, a keen observer of trading behavior.

After "I thought I told you *extra* cheese on my chicken parm—what the hell good are you as an assistant, anyway?" the second most common expression I heard during my years on the trading floor may have been "Lord, get me back to even and I'll never get long again."

The problem with that approach is exactly the same as the manager playing to tie the game. Since there is no "correct" way to approach block liquidation, neither patience nor panic by itself is the problem. However, if you're patient when the stock is down and a frantic seller the moment it's up, you will never make money in the long run. Make no mistake: Each block of stock that needs to be liquidated, in the short term, has an expected loss from the current market. There is a loose analogy to the uncertainty principle in quantum mechanics: The mere act of participating in the market changes the market to your detriment. Offering stock for sale tends to reduce the price you can get for it. However, that expected loss is greater if, just like the manager playing to tie, you systematically take away your upside. If, alternatively, we instructed a monkey to sell every block of stock at a designated linear pace over time, the upside is preserved. However, some traders know their stocks, know the market, and recognize that selection bias is unequal across customer orders. As such, trader judgment has value, and traders should be given discretion to use their judgment in pacing their liquidations.

That's one approach. Not all traders possess this skill in judgment, however, and, frankly, their marginal value to management isn't that much more than a monkey's. Over time, given enough repetitions, attentive managers will learn which traders create value with their judgment and which destroy it. Hence, I created for Pascal's use "additional loss above replacement monkey," or ALARM. Traders on the desk didn't want to be triggering an ALARM on a regular basis.

Another task for management is compensating its traders. Like good baseball managers, truly skilled employees are rare and have a lot of value. An organization benefits from properly compensating these producers. The problem for managers at banks is that even though traders always point to their P&L when lobbying for year-end bonuses, P&Ls are difficult to compare. A trader with an $18 million year-end profit might trade telecom stocks at a bank with the top-ranked telecom analyst on the Street, as well as a team of bankers in the sector ranked number one in closed deals. On the other hand, a trader of biotech stocks may work at this same firm without any biotech research, analysts, or health-care bankers. He has a year-end P&L of $12 million. A team of research analysts costs money, and so do investment bankers. An expensive sales force exists to distribute that research, etc. All of that effort accrues, in the form of orders, to the telecom trader, with little or no effort on his part. Additionally, telecom stocks generate more volume than biotech stocks. All of these costs, including the employment cost of the trader and his assistants, can be quantified and presented as the cost of trading a specific set of stocks. This way, you can compare disparate P&Ls and determine a "trader upside above cost" (or, in a nod to the rap music coursing through the headphones of the largely male traders as they come in each morning, TUPAC).

Maybe the biotech trader actually deserves a higher bonus than the telecom trader with a bigger bottom line. Maybe the bank's management would find it useful to know who is actually *creating the most value,* instead of overseeing the highest P&L, but without creations like TUPAC and ALARM, they'll never know.

If investment banks really want the best talent on their trading desks, management needs a systematic approach to identifying top traders that resembles the talent-evaluation methods of baseball's forward-thinking general managers. At the same time, baseball general managers would do well to teach a little more game theory to their on-field managers and heed the lessons of the best stock traders.

But, most important, professionals in other industries shouldn't be mocking baseball for its collection of acronym-heavy statistical analyses. They should be embracing the practices in their own industry.

15

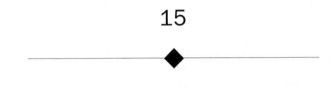

June and the Vexing Minnesota Twins

Nearly half of the games played in June were interleague games. From June 17 through the end of the month, American League teams and National League teams played each other as they have since 1997. (Owing to the presence of two extra teams in the National League, there is always one traditional series between a couple of National League teams occurring at the same time.) In 2011, there was also a weekend of interleague games played in May and July. I knew interleague games would cause a problem for the model, because its backbone—projecting runs scored and runs allowed—was based on the 150 games or so each year that teams played under their own league's rules, not the handful of games they played under the other league's rules. (The American League, of course, uses a designated hitter in place of pitchers batting, as it has since 1973. For interleague play, games in American League parks use designated hitters, while games at National League venues do not.)

Additionally, comparing player values, in terms of WAR, for players from the American League and National League is not a perfect comparison, because the level of play in each league is different. For the past few years—and it only got magnified in 2012, with the defection of Albert Pujols and Prince Fielder to the American League—the average player in the American League has been better than the average player in the National League. I had known this and made adjustments I thought were appropriate, but I still dialed down the capital-allocation schedule for interleague games.

Even with the more conservative approach to capital allocation, the model lost money for the first month in June. The loss of 4.16 percent wasn't just due to interleague play, however, as traditional league games accounted for 2.8 percent losses.

The Model's Results in June	
Total Return	-4.16 percent
Year-to-Date Return	+16.80 percent
Total Games Picked	339 (out of 400 played)
Record in Games Picked	178-161

Even with the half-month of interleague games, the model identified a perceived edge at the same rate as during the first two months of the season. There was nothing unusual about finding a preference on 85 percent of the games played, and the overall win percentage of 52.5 was actually better than the 51.6 percent the model posted through the end of May. A winning record with an overall capital loss suggested that there must have been some losses not only on favorites but on favorites that the model calculated had a big edge.

Return by Category of Team Selected		
	Win-Loss Record	Return
Favorites	110-85	-4.17 percent
Underdogs	52-68	-0.12 percent
Pick-'Ems	16-8	+0.13 percent
Total	**178-161**	**-4.16 percent**

Return by Wager Size		
	Win-Loss Record	Return
2 percent bets	2-2	+0.6 percent
1.5 percent bets	1-3	-4.24 percent
1 percent bets	8-6	-0.45 percent
50-basis-point bets	11-10	-2.32 percent
40-basis-point bets	26-26	+0.69 percent
20-basis-point bets	49-50	-0.20 percent
10-basis-point bets	81-64	+1.76 percent

The model did indeed take some lumps on its biggest plays. The overall loss would have been a lot worse without the solid showing on the small-size bets that made up the bulk of the total plays.

+/- 2 Percent Returns on Teams Bet On			
No 2 Percent Winners			
.			
.			
.			
.			
Colorado Rockies	6	6	-2.46 percent
Chicago White Sox	1	6	-2.80 percent

+/- 2 Percent Returns on Teams Bet Against			
LA Angels	9	5	+5.04 percent
Florida Marlins	17	4	+3.14 percent
.			
.			
.			
.			
San Francisco Giants	9	13	-2.86 percent
Minnesota Twins	8	14	-7.92 percent

Here we see the true cause of June's losses. The collective monthly loss of 7.92 percent betting against the Twins ended up being the worst monthly performance for any single team bet on or against for the year. The model simply thought the Twins had a far-below-average ability to score runs, combined with, at best, league-average pitching. Thanks to the replacements it was forced to use due to injuries to their projected starters, each day the Twins took the field in June, the model saw a sixty-win team, or, in other words, a one-hundred-loss team. The Twins went 17-9 during June (14-8 when the model bet against them), winning games at a .654 pace that translated to a *one-hundred-win* season. A divergence that huge guarantees losses.

The timing of the losses was terrible. I had been sharing the model's daily selections with a small group of like-minded friends and, by June, had even started placing bets on behalf of a couple of them. It wasn't long before the criticism began.

One buddy, new to baseball betting but a veteran football bettor, cornered me via e-mail and asked, "Why do you keep betting against the Twins?" I explained that the Twins were regularly trotting out a lineup with four or five bench players. "Oh," he dismissed me, "you can't follow lineup changes. I subscribe to the notion that they're all major league players capable of having a good day at the plate."

He'd clearly never seen Twins catcher Drew Butera swing a bat.

Seriously, of course, my buddy's logic was as hopelessly flawed as a poker player shoving money into a pot while holding nothing but an inside straight draw under the belief that "any card is capable of coming up next." And yet I had to seethe silently, because the Twins' strong performance in June gave my buddy the confirmation bias he needed to gloat.

With gritted teeth, I viewed June's poor results as a small-sample-size fluctuation, since that month's games accounted for just 16 percent of the total season. Unfortunately for the fund and my bankroll, the difference between the model's projection for Minnesota and the Twins' actual performance wasn't just a one-month problem.

16

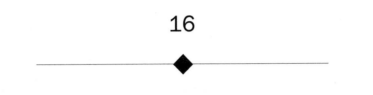

What Las Vegas Can Learn
from the Trading Floor

Michael Lewis's extraordinary writing career began with a depiction of gambling on a trading floor. In the opening pages of *Liar's Poker,* Lewis's seminal account of his time on Wall Street while a bond salesman at Salomon Brothers, he writes that the Salomon bond traders loved to gamble, and their game of choice was liar's poker.

Over the past couple of decades, liar's poker (the game) has gone the way of the Quotron machine and handwritten tickets as a trading-floor staple, but the prevalence of gambling remains. Texas hold 'em has replaced liar's poker as the poker game of choice among the current generation of traders, and after-hours dice and blackjack games have a small but devoted following, but by far the most popular form of gambling on the trading floor is sports betting.

When I came to Wall Street, I expected to participate in some big, creative, complex sports pools.*,† I had no idea I'd actually create one of the most enduring.

Gambling on a trading floor goes hand in hand with the job. If you work on the trading floor at an investment bank, regardless of the product your desk specializes in, which could vary from a mortgage security to a convertible bond to NASDAQ stocks, its primary purpose is to trade with customers. Customers, as everyone from baristas to car salesmen knows, hold a special position within the chain of business. A bank's trading desk is no different. If the customer wants to buy, the trader must sell, and if the customer is selling, the trader—and, by extension, the bank—is going to have to buy the stock, regardless of how the trader would like to be positioned in the underlying security. The only term left to negotiate is the price.

---

*The floor of the NYSE ran the biggest NCAA basketball pool I've ever seen. For $100 you picked the Final Four, and if you got it exactly right, you won, splitting the pot with all other correct entries. Not only did many of the thousands of people working on the floor participate in the pool; nearly all of the "upstairs" traders (people like me who traded stock from the trading floors of their firms) from dozens of NYSE member firms, got involved as well. There were rumors the total pot regularly exceeded $1 million. According to local lore, the pool organizers used to take all those $100 bills and, during the duration of the tournament, store them with some nuns on Staten Island.

†It's common knowledge on Wall Street that any story involving the antics of floor traders at the NYSE is complete and utter bullshit unless it contains two of the following three elements: Staten Island, the Catholic Church, and a box of six dozen cannoli. By this maxim, the preceding footnote meets all standards of responsible journalism.

Welcome to the world of market making,* where traders are required many times a day to risk money on a security, equipped with incomplete information and a range of possible outcomes. Price the merchandise correctly, understand the probability of the entire range of outcomes, know the company behind the stock, as well as the way the stock itself trades, and, given a large number of trades over an extended period of time, you will likely be profitable. This is gambling, plain and simple, and no one who believes in capitalism, or the benefits of liquidity in the stock market for both shareholders and America's companies, should pretend otherwise. For the best traders on Wall Street, though, it's gambling *with an edge,* which makes it a profitable proposition for their employers and, ultimately, the traders as well.

What's the edge? Risk management, intimate knowledge of the marketplace, and discipline. Take the example in the prior footnote. If a customer sells a market maker 500,000 shares of Microsoft at twenty-five cents, the trader will collect a commission, typically four cents, on the order. If the stock is trading at twenty-seven cents at the time of the transaction (two cents being a fair discount for instant liquidity on 500,000

*The phrase "market making" exists because a customer might call up and say, "Make me a market in Microsoft." The trader doesn't know if the customer is a buyer or seller. A typical reply would be, "I'll buy any part of 500,000 shares at twenty-five cents or sell you 500,000 at thirty cents." (Unless a stock is trading over $100, like Apple or Google, the dollar amount is usually omitted during pricing.) The trader has just made a market and will be long or short Microsoft seconds later. (It's considered poor form for a customer to ask for a market and then not trade or counter with different terms—for instance, "I'll buy 100,000 shares at twenty-seven cents.")

shares of stock), the market maker has a cost basis in the stock six cents below the market. If he or she has properly priced the merchandise, and uses discipline in liquidating it, over time the trader should be able to sell the stock, on average, two or three cents below the current price of the stock and, when the commission is factored in, net his employer three or four cents per share in the process.

Gambling with the purpose of making money is often confused with gambling as entertainment or, in the worst case, addiction. In their otherwise superb book on the demise of Lehman Brothers, *A Colossal Failure of Common Sense,* Lawrence G. McDonald and Patrick Robinson make that exact error. Midway through the book, in an effort to show the reader how great a risk-taker a senior bond trader at Lehman was, McDonald recounts a trip to a casino he took with the trader. Playing multihand, high-stakes blackjack, the trader lost well over $100,000 in a couple of hours. McDonald marveled that the trader didn't get rattled but, instead, continued to increase his bets until, down a couple hundred thousand dollars, he had a total of $60,000 riding on six hands, all crappy ones, with the dealer showing 11. The dealer, in dramatic fashion, ended up busting, and mayhem ensued. The trader tackled McDonald with joy and said, "Never give up when you're down, because luck will turn," and proceeded a few hours later to walk out of the casino up a couple hundred thousand dollars. McDonald describes the night in utter awe, admiration, and undying respect for the trader.

I despise that passage. McDonald convincingly spends the rest of the book explaining that there were many brilliant, insightful, and savvy bond traders and analysts at Lehman who understood exactly how precarious a position the management, led by Dick Fuld, had put the firm in. He undermines the book's premise with that passage. The bond trader never had an edge in the casino; he was a thrill-seeker, an action junkie, and nothing else.

No one should assume that someone who loves to gamble would make a good trader. Stories like the one about McDonald's trader in a casino simply fall into the category of "gambling as entertainment." Unless you are a professional card-counter playing blackjack, nothing about playing table games in a casino is anything other than gambling as entertainment. It is an endeavor with negative expected value, and the exact odds and variance of outcomes are known a priori. It may be immensely fun—I'm partial to half a dozen or so friends gathered around a craps table—but make no mistake about it: When a bunch of us are huddled around a craps table at the Bellagio, only MGM Resorts qualifies as an investor with an edge. The rest of us are merely paying for entertainment.

On the other hand, risking money while possessing an edge, and while exercising prudent risk management, makes someone a trader. My first boss on Wall Street provided me with a vehicle for developing those skills.

*   *   *

Matt Johnson began running Lehman Brothers' NASDAQ trading desk when he was just twenty-nine years old. In the eight or so years that he headed the desk, he turned it from a break-even (at best) operation, irrelevant within the market structure of other broker-dealers, into a cash-creating juggernaut rivaling the profitability of far more prestigious trading desks at Goldman Sachs, Merrill Lynch, and Morgan Stanley. Although he was only two weeks older than me, Matt was a managing director at Lehman when I first walked onto his desk as a summer intern, in 1995. Instantly captivated by the atmosphere on the desk and the pace of trading,* I'd found my calling. I started on the desk full-time in December 1996.†

As the summer of 1997 came to a close, nearly all non-work conversations turned to the upcoming NFL season and the Jets' and Giants' prospects. Online gambling hadn't exploded in popularity yet, so the concept of the Las Vegas "over-under" wins total was somewhat new. I had been to Las Vegas earlier in the summer and had a list of the over-under propositions for

*Not only was screaming at co-workers, competitors (market makers at other firms), and computer screens permitted, it was essential.

†My first day on the desk was the morning after then–Fed chairman Alan Greenspan's "irrational exuberance" speech. That day the NASDAQ set a record for shares traded. I answered phones all day in a language I barely knew, screamed myself hoarse, dodged shrapnel in the form of shattered phones from my desk colleagues, and never left my desk for food, water, or a bathroom break. As a phone-answering clerk, I didn't risk a single dollar all day, and yet that was the most scared, by far, I've ever been at work. I also knew I'd be trading stocks for as long as I could.

total wins for every NFL team. Some of the traders and salesmen wanted to place bets, but, I explained, you had to go to Vegas to do it. Las Vegas posts a regular-season win total for each team, and one can take either side of the bet for a 10 percent surcharge paid only if your bet loses. For instance, you might see the Broncos listed as follows:

Team	Wins	Over	Under
Denver	6½	-110	-110

One could bet either over or under 6½ regular season wins to win any amount. To win that money, though, say, $50, the bettor would have to risk 110 percent of the amount, or, in this case, $55. (It's not possible in this example, but in the case of ties, all bets are fully refunded.)

Matt Johnson overheard this conversation, turned his entire musclebound body in our direction (since the granite block that was his human form never seemed to twist), and boomed, "Peta, I want you to have on my desk tomorrow two-sided markets for every NFL team. I want to trade these things like stocks, and you're going to take the other side." A two-sided market means to simultaneously quote different prices at which a customer could either buy (the higher price, obviously) or sell without knowing the customer's intentions.

The next morning, I placed a sheet of paper on Matt's desk with markets for all thirty teams. The spread, or the difference between the bid and offer for each specific team, was one game. (For example, the Bears were 7–8, or "seven by eight," meaning they could be bought at eight or sold at seven. In other words, I, the market maker, would pay $7 for shares of the Bears, or if someone wanted to buy, I would sell shares for $8.) I told Matt each market was good for up to 500 shares, after which I would move the market. (For instance, if Matt bought 500 shares of the Bears at eight, I would move my market—just like a stock price changes during the day—upward to 7½–8½.)

In addition to using a bid–ask spread (as opposed to the 10 percent of juice Vegas charged), I had thought up a number of twists. First, total wins included playoffs. Second, and most important, this wasn't standard over-under betting; this would pay off like a stock. The market I quoted was the price to buy or short each team, and like a stock you were buying or selling shares. The final value of those shares would be the number of games the underlying team won, including, as mentioned, playoff wins. This added a huge level of interest, because it meant the magnitude by which any team exceeded or fell short of their pre-season market was important. Each team plays sixteen regular-season games, but once you add in the complexity of determining the probability for a certain team to play multiple playoff games, the allure increases. If, for example, you bought a hundred shares of the Green Bay Packers at $10 and they won eleven regular-season games, your position would be in the money by $100 at the start of the playoffs. If they ultimately won the Super Bowl, the Packers win total would finish at fourteen, and you'd win $400. If they won only eight games in the regular season and missed the playoffs, you'd lose $200. Finally, I told Matt I would make new markets every Tuesday during the season so teams could be traded all year. This may have been the most appealing aspect of all.

Matt took a look at my markets and announced to the desk, "Joe Peta has made markets for every single NFL team this year. I don't want to hear anyone's opinions if they're not going to back them up. I'll make the first trade right now. I buy 500 Jets at 4½!" This was the equivalent of scattering hot dog bits at the beach. My deskmates swarmed me like seagulls, and before I knew it I had positions in a dozen different teams.

Matt's trade was interesting. The year before, the Jets had won one game. I made the initial market in 1997 at 3½–4½, meaning I would buy the Jets at 3½ wins or sell them at 4½ wins. Matt had just bought 500 shares at 4½. When my desk cleared, he walked over to me. "Peta," the former nose tackle on Penn State's 1986 NCAA championship team told me quietly (or what passed for quietly when he spoke), "what you don't understand is how important coaching is in football. Bill Parcells will make them a .500 team." After Matt had bought his 500 shares, I moved the market to 4–5. Now I was a little scared: Eight wins meant I would be out $1,750 to Matt. In fact, I was more than a little bit scared. Deeply in student loan debt, living alone in New York City, and earning just $70,000 a year, I, a lowly assistant on the desk, had just taken the other side of bets from senior salesmen and traders. Matt seemed pretty sure he had just taken me for a little less than $2,000. What had I gotten myself into?

Later that afternoon, a guy from another desk on the trading floor walked over and said, "I hear you make markets in NFL teams." I handed him a paper with the latest markets on it. "I'll sell you 200 shares of the Jets at 4." I stamped a ticket, gave him a receipt, and smiled. I'd bought back 200 of the shares at 4 that I'd sold Matt at 4½. Much of my panic subsided as I thought to myself, I might be on to something here.

This may appear to have been gambling, and of course it was in the sense that I had money at stake that hinged on the results of football games. But this was also trading in its purest form, and Matt Johnson knew it. After the season was over, he confided in me that he wanted to raise my profile on the desk, give me experience making markets, and, most important, see how I handled risk in practice. "Do you know what the vomit zone is?" he asked. Given that many of Matt's questions were rhetorical, even if he was the only one who knew it, he continued before I could respond, "It's trying to make a putt to win a hole from six feet. Doesn't matter if you make them on the practice green; no one knows how they'll do until it matters." As I paid him his winnings (the Jets actually won nine games), he added, "I like to see how young guys do in the vomit zone. You did well." Within a year, I was promoted to a full-fledged market-making position responsible for fifty or sixty of my own stocks to trade every day on Lehman Brothers' behalf.

There was no doubt at all that some of the insights I'd gained running the football markets made me a better trader of stocks and risk manager. Consider the following revelations I had over that first season:

◆ On the surface, it looked like people were buying and selling shares of stock in a single team. In truth, they were making a series of money line bets on every game that team would play before the season started. For instance, if someone bought 100 shares of Philadelphia at 8, they were risking $800 if the Eagles won zero games, and could win $800 if the Eagles won sixteen. (For this example, I'm ignoring the possibility of playoff wins.) That meant that they actually had just made a $50 bet on the money line of every Eagles game before the season started. As the seller, I had the opposite bet. Trading any derivative (and shares of an NFL team in this format are a derivative, because the ultimate value of each trade is derived from the number of games the underlying NFL team won) requires understanding the components of the derivative and how to hedge those components. In this example, anytime the Eagles were an underdog, I could perfectly hedge my exposure that week by betting an amount on the money line required to win $50. Since it would take less than $50 to do that (since the Eagles were an underdog), the difference would represent a profit no matter the outcome of the game. In the alternative, I could also bet $50 on the Eagles plus whatever points the line provided that week. While this is an imperfect hedge,* if the Eagles lost the game but covered the spread, I'd win not only my bet but also the $50 from my short.

◆ In making the markets, while it was important to have views and realistic markets on each team, as long as active trading existed across the league the more important factor was making sure bids and offers for the entire league evenly straddled the total number of games to be played (267 in today's thirty-two-team NFL: 256 regular-season games—sixteen a team—and eleven playoff games). Traders learn quickly that, in the long run, getting killed in one stock doesn't matter as long as your other stocks are priced correctly and attract a lot of vol-

---

*Hedging is the act of reducing risk. A perfect hedge removes risk entirely. If you're long a company's stock in your 401(k) account that you don't want to sell for long-term investment planning, but you're worried about the company's prospects over the next few months, shorting an equal amount of stock in your brokerage account is an example of a perfect hedge. In the example above, the perfect hedge always guarantees me a profit, albeit a small one. The imperfect hedge removes the guaranteed profit but allows for situations where I can make a much larger amount of money, although that will occur infrequently.

ume. In the case of the NFL markets, more than anything else I wanted volume in as many teams as possible.

◆ Being short (or long) three different teams in a four-
team division is the same as being long (or short) the
fourth team. (The fourth team has six out of sixteen
games, or 38 percent of its season, against the three
teams I'm short.) That makes me synthetically long the
fourth team. Again, this is a great lesson applicable to
derivatives specialists, and traders learn quickly that ignoring the general correlation of the equity markets is
foolish. (Derivative theory is complicated, but in intro-
ductory derivatives courses, one of the first things taught
is that the owner of a put is synthetically short the underlying stock and the owner of a call is synthetically
long the stock.) Even though I didn't actually own a
share of the fourth team, since I was synthetically long
it, I'd want to make it less attractive for anyone else to
sell it to me. In this case, a market maker should lower
the price of the security he's synthetically long, making
it less likely he'll buy more and more likely he'll sell
shares of the fourth team in a division. This is a good
idea because . . .

◆ Being short four teams in a division or a dozen teams in
a conference or nearly all thirty-two teams in the NFL
makes it virtually impossible to lose money. Unlike
stocks, which can theoretically rise to any price, there

are a finite number of games any NFL division, conference, or league can win, and a spread market guarantees
the sum of the offers, or prices at which teams are sold,
will exceed that finite number. That's a guaranteed profit
for the market maker, and it's why an effective risk manager lowers the prices of teams he has no position in if he
is short all the other teams in the same division.

From the perspective of NFL fans on trading desks, this is
one of the greatest football pools ever invented. Like any market, as volume grew it became advantageous to lower spreads,
which attracted even more volume, which for a market maker
trumps all.

Little did I know how widespread these markets would become. More than ten years later, after Lehman Brothers went
bankrupt, I traveled with UBS to Chicago to visit an account.
In discussing mutual friends in the business in Chicago, a
trader at the account said to me, "Thanks for bringing up that
name. I have to call him this morning and sell some Bears." He
explained that his friend had a salesman at Barclays (the former
Lehman Brothers) through whom he could buy or sell NFL
teams. "We settle up with our friend, but the main book is kept
by some New York traders. It's the greatest pool I've ever been
in."

Las Vegas is missing out on a huge potential product. Struc-
tured like this, over-unders trade all year instead of just in the

pre-season. The inclusion of playoff wins adds an additional element of excitement. Since the customer payouts (and losses) increase with each win, it adds a level of interest that will attract a whole new type of gambler. Unlike over-unders, the bettor can switch sides, as often as every week, if his opinion changes. All this would drive increased transactions, and because of the spread between buying and selling, each transaction would contain a bit of an edge for the house.

Las Vegas should turn to Wall Street for other ways to increase interest, traffic, and, ultimately, bets in their sportsbooks. First and foremost, there should be a ticker tape lining the walls of the sportsbook. A conglomerate like MGM has a huge competitive advantage here. Every time a bet gets placed at an MGM property's sportsbook, the transaction should be posted on a ticker tape. Everyone loves to see their own stock trade cross the ticker; the same thing would happen in the sportsbook. Most important for the casino, however, a whole breed of tape studiers would emerge, convinced they could find patterns in the tape. Eventually, they'd risk more of their money. To that end, the sportsbooks should turn over all their data to the public. A potential bettor should instantly be able to walk into the sportsbook and observe, "Seventy-five percent of the money is on Denver this week, but only 52 percent of the total number of bets are. Hmmmm. That means the size of the average bet on Denver is larger than the average size on Oakland. And yet the line hasn't moved. The pros must know something." Whether or not that has any meaning is irrelevant; bettors will *think* it has meaning, and if they think so, some of them will inevitably act on it in the form of a bet. Providing data to customers and installing a ticker tape would increase betting and keep customers in the sportsbook longer.

The takeaway is that sports betting, portfolio management, and Wall Street trading are all interrelated. There are some innovations in Las Vegas, primarily pioneered by Cantor Sports, a division of the broker-dealer Cantor Fitzgerald. If the management at the sportsbooks thought more like a Wall Street market maker, they'd see that product innovations like the constantly trading NFL markets present a huge new market with sizable profit potential that hasn't been explored—yet.

17

Pete's Tavern Revisited

When it comes to watching baseball in a bar in any city with a major league baseball team, the choices are as varied as the cities themselves. In San Francisco, there's MoMo's, populated by hip, tech-savvy young professionals and featuring plenty of outdoor seating across the street from the most beautiful stadium in America. For a more traditional Fog City experience, there's Lefty O'Doul's, a bar so revered by legendary Phillies announcer Harry Kalas it was joked his luggage used to be sent directly there, allowing him time for a few extra songs at the piano between games. Murphy's Bleachers and the Cubby Bear border Chicago's Wrigley Field, but I contend that the Wrigley Field bleachers aren't only the best place to watch a baseball game in America; they're also the best *bar* I've ever been to.

The National, in Orange County, and the Sports Column, in Denver, are essential stops for anyone with tickets to an Angels or Rockies game. Sick of the obnoxious Red Sox fans sitting next to you in a restaurant, church, stadium, or subway? There's a decent chance you can get them to turn on themselves in the cannibalistic manner of crocodiles by asking them which is the better Boston sports bar, the Four's or the Cask 'n Flagon.

In New York City, for the last twenty years Mickey Mantle's was probably the first place toward which out-of-town baseball fans gravitated. It closed permanently in the summer of 2012, but the truth is that in Manhattan there is a great bar on virtually every block. Most New Yorkers' watering hole of choice is in their own neighborhood. My preference for the best bar in New York City to watch baseball games in may have no chance of appearing on a list of the city's best sports bars, but it had a huge influence in my life as a post-thirty-year-old baseball fan.

As July 2011 drew to a close, even though I looked like Verbal Kint (Kevin Spacey) in *The Usual Suspects* when I walked, my physical therapy had advanced to the point that I could move my treatment to San Francisco. As I spent the last week of July packing up to return to California, I spent one of my last nights in New York City in the Manhattan bar that I most associate with baseball, Pete's Tavern.

* * *

I moved to New York City in 1996, a lifelong Phillies fan who had virtually ignored the American League. When playing APBA baseball as a kid, I never opened the American League player cards, I rooted for the National League in every World Series, and while living with Orioles fans in my dorm at Virginia Tech, I derisively referred to the American League by its traditional nickname, the Junior Circuit. On top of that, my formative baseball years occurred during the reign of the owner-as-insufferable-bully that marked the first couple of decades of George Steinbrenner's ownership of the New York Yankees. So obnoxious was the free-spending Steinbrenner that you didn't even need to be a fan of a competing American League team to dislike the Yankees. So when I became a full-time New York City resident during the summer of 1996, there was very little chance I'd turn into a fan of the Yankees.

Pete's Tavern changed that in a little less than three months.

During the fall of 1996, I may have been an employee of Lehman Brothers, but the truth was, by the firm's design, I didn't actually have a job. The path to a seat on a trading desk at a Wall Street firm for a newly minted MBA traditionally goes through three stages. First, the candidate must get a summer internship. From there, a vote is taken by the firm's decision-makers, and successful candidates receive an offer to join the firm's full-time associate program the next summer. The following fall, after graduation, the associate goes through a three-to-four-month training program that culminates with dozens of interviews on trading desks across the firm. My associate class had roughly 50 aspiring traders and salespeople looking for full-time seats. While we were told there were jobs for all of us, the truth is only forty of those seats, tops, could be considered anything close to desirable for someone looking for a job with a career path. Getting a seat on a trading desk is a high-pressure game of musical chairs for anyone in an associate class at an investment bank.

That fall, I had a terrible time finding a desk that wanted me as a full-timer. It didn't help that I wanted to join only one of two: the desk that traded NYSE stocks or the one that traded NASDAQ stocks. Nothing seemed to be going right; even the strongest element of my résumé, an MBA from Stanford, was a decided liability.*

Meanwhile, the Yankees were finishing the 1996 regular season as division champs for the first time in fifteen years. Despite the fact that we were in competition for a limited number of jobs, my associate class spent most of the fall socializing with each other after work. As we ate and drank our way through the city's restaurants and bars that fall, I mentioned to a classmate that playoff games attracted a huge amount of people to

---

*I approached my interview on the desk that traded NYSE stocks prepared to impress everyone with my intelligence, drive, and love of the stock market. The first person I sat with ignored the résumé I set in front of him and, between bites of a massive egg-cheese-and-bacon sandwich, asked, "Where do you come to us from?" I told him I'd just gotten an MBA from Stanford. "Cool," he said, "it's a long commute to get here by seven, but I do it every day." I started to chuckle politely, thinking he was making a New York–California joke. As he continued, I realized he lived in Connecticut and thought I'd just gotten my degree from the University of Connecticut at Stamford.

the bars. A longtime resident of the city, he explained that despite all the different sports teams that claim New York City as their home, there was a buzz to the workplace, to the bars, to the entire city when the Yankees did well that none of the other teams could match.

By the time the World Series started, my career prospects looked bleak. I had been rejected from the NASDAQ desk, far and away my number-one choice, and because of my indiscreet summer essay while an intern, I had essentially been black-balled by the entire fixed-income division. I was in debt to the tune of six figures. The furniture in my apartment, on the southeast corner of 18th Street and Irving Place, consisted of little more than a mattress on the floor and a real-life cliché: a TV placed on an overturned milk crate.

A couple of weeks later, after pleading for a chance to make my case directly to the most senior members of the NASDAQ desk, I was granted a fifteen-minute meeting with a group of senior traders and salespeople to do so. Evidently convinced by the passion for stocks and market-making I conveyed during that meeting, they gave me my chance, and I would make the most of it. But on the evening of October 23, I sat on my mattress, worried about my future at Lehman Brothers, and turned on the TV to watch Game Four of the 1996 World Series.

Pete's Tavern is on the northeast corner of 18th and Irving. Billed as the "oldest original bar" in New York City, Pete's, which opened in 1864, is famous for remaining open during

Prohibition while disguised as a flower shop. It's also said to be the place where O. Henry penned the Christmas classic "The Gift of the Magi," and Pete's has memorialized the very booth where O. Henry supposedly wrote the story. Ludwig Bemelmans wrote the opening lines ("In an old house in Paris all covered in vines") of the endearing children's book *Madeline* on the back of a menu at Pete's.* President John F. Kennedy and his son JFK Jr. both took their future wives on dates there. And, on an October night in 1996, it's where I became a Yankees fan.

At the top of the eighth inning of that night's World Series game, the Yankees came to the plate against the heavily favored Atlanta Braves trailing 6–3 and down two games to one in the series. Although my prior twenty-five years as a baseball fan provided me with zero inclination to root for the Yankees, I really, really disliked the Atlanta Braves. The year before, they had moved from the NL West into the Phillies' division, won the World Series, and looked poised to dominate the division for years to come. Resigned to the fact that a win in the 1996 World Series would probably be the second of many for the Braves, I was looking for a reason to root against them.

With runners on first and third and one out during the top of the eighth inning, backup catcher Jim Leyritz came to the plate as a pinch hitter representing the game's tying run. Pitching for Atlanta was its hard-throwing reliever Mark Wohlers.

---

*Let this stand as proof that if an aspiring author with writer's block walks into Pete's Tavern hungry, the menu is better used to solve the former condition than the latter.

With the count 2–2, Wohlers hung a slider over the middle of the plate, and Leyritz absolutely clobbered it for a no-doubt-about-it home run the moment it left the bat.* As the ball took flight, I bolted upright in bed, realizing that the Yankees had just come back from six runs down, scoring the last three runs off of Atlanta's best reliever. What really caught my attention, though, was the incredible amount of noise that filled my eleventh-floor apartment through the open window next to my bed. I have never heard anything as loud as the roar that came out of Pete's Tavern that night.†

Down at Pete's, the cheering and chanting went on and on even after the Yankees were retired without doing further damage that inning. With the game tied, and Atlanta, as the home team, possessing an extra at-bat, the Braves had a clear advantage going forward. Still, the cheering kept coming. I took the elevator down to the lobby of my building, walked across the street, and entered the bar. I crammed my way in and, despite knowing no one but the bartenders there, immediately became part of the Yankees faithful. By the time the Yankees dodged trouble in the ninth inning and then won in extra innings, I had high-fived, hugged, and chugged beers with ev-

---

*Baseball historians say the last installment of the Yankees dynasty, dormant for more than thirty years in 1996, began that night, with the swing of Jim Leyritz's bat. They will get no argument from me.

†I lived in that apartment for eight years, four of which would feature Yankees World Series victories and trips to the Super Bowl and the NBA Finals by the New York Giants and Knicks, respectively, but nothing ever matched the intensity of the cheering that night.

eryone around me, transformed from a despondent would-be Wall Street trader to a jubilant Yankees fan. Three nights later, when the Yankees completed their remarkable comeback in the Series to win their first championship since 1978, I was back in Pete's Tavern, from the first pitch of the game.

Being a Yankees fan had its benefits when, in 2001, I met my wife. Thanks to her crush on Tino Martinez, the Yankees are the only team I've ever seen Caitlin actively root for. We were married in the summer of 2003, and by October of that year, a newly pregnant and exhausted Caitlin went to bed with the Yankees seemingly hopelessly behind during Game Seven of the AL Championship Series vs. the Red Sox. As I stayed up watching the game in another room, she retired with the instructions "Let me know if anything happens." Nearly two hours later, I burst quietly into the room to tell her the amazing news. As I approached the bed, Caitlin rolled over half-asleep, smiled, and said, "The Yankees won," as the cheers from outside continued to spill into our open bedroom window. Pete's Tavern had served as the local news station and already delivered the sports report to her.

Resigned to the fact that my injuries and the need for regular physical therapy made it unrealistic for me to look for a job in New York City, my family and I spent June and July 2011 in our Manhattan apartment before packing up and moving back to our home in San Francisco. It was a bittersweet period; I spent the last week of July saying good-bye to friends. When it came to one last night out with Matt, my best friend from college and the man who introduced me to Pete's twenty years before, we agreed that our last night should be spent watching the Yankees at Pete's. As they had done so many times while I was a resident of New York, the Yankees won, 4–1.

18

Clinging to Profits in July

For portfolio managers with a high degree of flexibility in how they invest the assets they oversee—especially those at hedge funds—one of the tenets of the asset management game is "Don't play from behind." Following that advice is easier said than done, of course, because there is no switch to hit in January that puts a fund ahead of its benchmark. However, a PM can implement a strategy that minimizes the chances of falling behind early in the year. Golfers are sometimes said to follow a strategic path on certain holes that "takes double bogey out of the equation." That approach to course management, as it's known in golf, is analogous to a PM primarily concerned with poor performance early in the year on either a relative or absolute basis.

For instance, suppose a PM at a hedge fund begins the year quite bearish on the overall market. The PM could short stock to the extent that their fund begins the year, let's say, 40 percent net short. If the S&P 500 falls 2 percent during the first week of January, then absent any +/- alpha* generated via stock selection, the fund will be ahead of the market by 2.8 percent (market down 2 percent, fund up 0.8 percent). However, if the market rises 2 percent that first week, the fund will find itself 2.8 percent behind the market.

PMs quickly learn that running a portfolio from a net short position is a high-risk strategy, because when the market moves the fund wins or loses twice, once on an absolute basis and once on a relative basis. (This is not true when running 40 percent net long. The PM, with market-matching stock selection, will be up on an absolute basis but down on a relative basis, or vice versa.) In the world of asset management, running short is a double-edged sword. Therefore, when not falling behind is of great importance, a PM might be better off taking a more conservative approach to expressing bearishness by starting the year with net zero exposure. If the market falls 2 percent, the PM will still have a 2 percent lead on the market, but if the market rallies 2 percent to start the year, the PM is only 2 percent behind. The reason for this approach is twofold. Investor money, especially at a hedge fund, is rarely sticky. Within pre-

---

*Alpha is simply the value, positive or negative, that a portfolio manager adds or subtracts from the performance of the fund.

scribed periods of notice, investors can always take out their money and walk away. Thus, starting a year in the hole can lead to redemptions. This is a perilous development for a hedge fund; in order to raise cash for the exiting investor, it will have to sell some of its holdings, which can put additional downward pressure on the holdings of the fund—a fund which is already having a bad year. Even without redemptions leading to that sort of downward spiral, losing can lead to sub-optimal, even desperate, decision-making, which inevitably worsens the problem.

I thought of this at the end of July because the model suffered a second-straight losing month. July's return of -7.99 percent was notably worse than the 4.16 percent loss in June. Fortunately, the fund had a big lead going into June, so I still had a solid profit for the year and, therefore, the confidence to stay the course. I had to admit, though, especially when it came to the Minnesota Twins, by the end of July I began to wonder if I was evaluating things correctly. Maybe my friend who advocated ignoring lineup changes in June, I bitterly thought to myself, had a point.

The Model's Results in July	
Total Return	-7.99 percent
Year-to-Date Return	+7.47 percent
Total Games Picked	340 (out of 395 played)
Record in Games Picked	163-177

The win percentage of 47.9 percent represented the worst of the year, but unlike April, when the overall record also fell below 50 percent, a good performance betting underdogs didn't rescue the fund.

Return by Category of Team Selected		
	Win-Loss Record	Return
Favorites	96-62	-5.14 percent
Underdogs	62-105	-3.38 percent
Pick-'Ems	5-10	+0.53 percent
Total	**163-177**	**-7.99 percent**

Return by Wager Size		
	Win-Loss Record	Return
2 percent bets	3-1	+2.10 percent
1.5 percent bets	2-5	-3.30 percent
1 percent bets	2-6	-5.19 percent
50-basis-point bets	5-10	-2.81 percent
40-basis-point bets	27-23	+2.95 percent
20-basis-point bets	58-56	-0.51 percent
10-basis-point bets	66-76	-1.23 percent

Like June, one bright spot did emerge looking at July's overall results. The bottom three categories, where the majority of the picks occurred, made money netted together. So the problem for the second month in a row was the handful of games the model identified as having the greatest edge vs. the odds-makers' line. And for the second month in a row, betting against the Minnesota Twins caused the model its largest problem.

+/- 2 Percent Returns on Teams Bet On			
Arizona Diamondbacks	12	2	+6.10 percent
Cleveland Indians	5	11	+2.32 percent
		.	
		.	
		.	
		.	
Seattle Mariners	3	13	-2.09 percent
Washington Nationals	7	12	-3.28 percent
Chicago White Sox	3	6	-4.31 percent

+/- 2 Percent Returns on Teams Bet Against			
LA Dodgers	9	5	+2.99 percent
San Diego Padres	13	5	+2.42 percent
		.	
		.	
		.	
		.	
Philadelphia Phillies	2	11	-2.58 percent
Florida Marlins	7	16	-4.98 percent
Minnesota Twins	11	16	-6.00 percent

The Minnesota Twins played twenty-nine games in July, and the model determined that an edge existed in betting on their opponent in twenty-seven of them. In June, there were twenty-six Twins games, and the model targeted their opponent for a bet twenty-two times. Often these were some of the fund's largest bets for the month. Unfortunately for the fund, the Twins went 33-22 over the two-month period, causing the fund a whopping 14.56 percent drawdown (before compounding) in those games.

While I wasn't about to pretend that all substitutes who donned a major league jersey had the same ability (as had been suggested to me by my mocking buddy in June), I did begin to doubt my assessment of the Twins' replacements, so I took a hard look at Minnesota's results and the performance of individual players vs. the model's outlook. Nothing I uncovered changed my view that Minnesota had compiled results in June and July far above the skill level of the players in their lineup. In going 33-22 over this two-month period, a .600 pace over 162 games that would lead to ninety-seven wins, the Twins had scored 239 runs while giving up . . . 239 runs. That means they played like a .500 team over fifty-five games and somehow managed to play .600 baseball. That represented a 6–7 win difference I instantly deemed non-repeatable—or, more succinctly, lucky. As I looked deeper into the performance of certain hitters and pitchers, I uncovered strong evidence of cluster luck as well and concluded the Twins were fortunate to have played their opponents to a draw in terms of runs scored and runs allowed.

This didn't placate my friends who, if they came aboard in May (or, worse, June), were down solidly for the year. The cheerleading that had been present in April and May, as well as the pleas from some to place bets on their behalf, had ended. The losses had created some doubt for me as well, but they vanished once I dug into the results on the field. I didn't know what the future held for the Twins, the model, or the fund for the last two months, but I was going to stay the course, because I had as much conviction as ever that the model had the right read on Minnesota and the oddsmakers were far too optimistic.

PART THREE

♦

SUCCESS

19

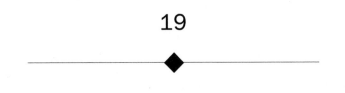

Focusing on the Wrong Data

Question: What do all of the following situations have in common?

1. On April 5, 2011, the New York Yankees hold a 4–0 lead over the Minnesota Twins entering the eighth inning. Their newly acquired setup man, the highly regarded Rafael Soriano, pitches ineffectively to the six batters he faces. When manager Joe Girardi comes to the mound to replace him, there are two outs, bases loaded, and the Yankees' lead has been trimmed to 4–1. Instead of handing the ball to Mariano Rivera, the greatest reliever of all time, to defuse this critical situation, Girardi turns to David Robertson. Not until the

top of the ninth, with the score tied 4–4, does Girardi make use of Rivera.

2. After a decade of playing in the World Series of Poker's Main Event, a player announces with pride that he has never been knocked out during the first day of the tournament.

3. *The New York Times* runs an article in June 2011 trumpeting the fact that while Derek Jeter spends time on the disabled list, his replacement, Eduardo Núñez, has committed fielding errors, implying a drop-off in production despite Núñez's stretch of potent hitting. The headline reads, NUNEZ FILLS IN FOR JETER WITH HITS, ERRORS, HOPE.

4. In 1999, more than half of the most-traded stocks on the NASDAQ market are priced in excess of $100. The difference between where a customer can sell stock (the "bid") or buy stock (the "ask") is known as a spread. In the absence of commissions, which is how the NASDAQ operates in the 1990s, spreads are the key to market-makers' profit margins, and in 1999 spreads are at an all-time high. Simultaneously, trading volumes soar to record levels. A sector head on the trading desk at Lehman Brothers tells his traders that no one should be losing money to customers and that they should strive to minimize their loss ratios. Traders will be judged, and therefore compensated, on their loss ratio.

5. A hedge fund manager gets into an argument with the COO, who is responsible for finding new investors, about the concept of "marketable returns," insisting that "absolute returns are all that matter."

6. Ron Washington, manager of the Texas Rangers, starts Yorvit Torrealba at catcher for Game Three of the 2011 World Series, breaking with the Rangers' post-season precedent to date. There are no apparent strategic reasons for moving his extremely hot hitting catcher of the post-season, Mike Napoli, to first base and benching Mitch Moreland in the process. Responding to reporters' questions, Washington says Torrealba deserved a start.

7. During the late 1990s and early 2000s, the business press, perfectly exemplified by *Barron's* infamous "Amazon.bomb" cover story, relentlessly mocks Amazon.com's stockholders and management for believing in a company that has not only never turned a profit but doesn't have plans to turn a profit anytime soon.

8. A new entrant in the U.S. broker-dealer market, despite operating in a business with razor-thin margins, highly entrenched competitors, and shrinking industry revenues, nonetheless immediately begins to take market share. A few months after launch, senior managers change trading desk leadership and completely retool the company's risk profile, citing minuscule net profit margins as the reason.

9. The Pittsburgh Pirates, a team mired in an eighteen-year streak of consecutive losing seasons, stun baseball observers by playing .530 baseball after their first one hundred games of the 2011 baseball season. About to enter the last third of the season and play their first meaningful August baseball games in nearly a generation, the Pirates play three extra-inning games over a six-day stretch. They lose all of them while their best reliever—nay, pitcher—Joel Hanrahan, does not throw a single pitch over thirty-nine innings of play. Two days later, however, Hanrahan pitches the ninth inning of a blowout loss, entering the game with the Pirates trailing 11–5, presumably because of that common managerial refrain, "He needed the work."

Answer: Despite the wide range of situations, they all illustrate real-life examples of focusing on the wrong data point, or managing to the wrong metric. It's a rampant problem across industries with little in common on the surface. Taking a look at each situation clearly illustrates the perils of managing to the wrong metric and what organizations should do to combat this error.

1. Misuse of the Yankees Bullpen
I am intimately familiar with the Yankees-Twins game on April 5, because the model assigned a 13 percent edge for the Yan-

kees, just the second game all year that possessed a >10 percent edge. Yankee ace CC Sabathia took the mound for New York, while the Twins started Brian Duensing, their lightly regarded fifth starter. The Twins also rested one of their top two players, former AL MVP Justin Morneau, replacing him with Jason Repko, a lifetime .227/.304/.365 (batting average/on-base percentage/slugging percentage) hitter. That's not even equivalent to the hitting line of an average catcher (.249/.319/.381 in 2010), and catchers are, on balance, the weakest hitters in an American League lineup. Yet Repko replaced, in Morneau, an elite hitter (.345/.437/.618 in 2010) at baseball's strongest offensive position (.264/.350/.452 in 2010 for the average first baseman). Although oddsmakers had the Yankees as -205 favorites (implied win percentage of 67.2 percent), the model assessed the Yankees' chances of winning to be 80 percent.* From the perspective of a Yankees fan (or bettor) the game unfolded perfectly. Three batters into the bottom of the first inning, the Yankees led 3–0. Sabathia cruised through the Twins' lineup, tossing seven innings of two-hit, one-walk baseball before be-

*Upon learning of my model, thoughtful colleagues ask, "Where do you have an edge?" They're not being cynical; they just know what having an investment edge is. I cite examples like this. The line for this game, which initially got posted the night before, never moved from Yankees -205, even after the lineups were announced, showing Repko starting for Morneau. Forget about Morneau; any team that replaces their merely average-to-below-average first baseman with Repko would cost itself at least five wins over the course of a season. (Repko hit a decrepit .226/.270/.286 in 2011.) Take five wins from a team and their odds of winning any single game drop by more than 3 percent—a good bit more vs. the premier teams in their league. Say whatever you want about the model's assumptions regarding Sabathia, Duensing, or even the Twins and Yankees in general; the fact that the price of betting on the Yankees didn't move from -205 whether Morneau was playing or not means one of those quotes is mispriced. That's an edge.

ing lifted for reliever Rafael Soriano, with the Yankees leading 4–0 at the top of the eighth.

The Yankees had signed Soriano to a massive three-year contract during the off-season. Behind Mariano Rivera, Soriano was immediately viewed as the second-best reliever on the team. He therefore became the bridge from the Yankees starting pitcher to Rivera. When Yankees management decided to spend $35 million on Soriano, it was fully aware that David Robertson was already on the team. Over three seasons and 134 games of 3.99 ERA pitching, Robertson had made an impression on Yankee management. By signing Soriano, management indicated that it did not have confidence in Robertson's ability to assume the bridge role. Nothing that could have occurred over the first week of the season should have changed that view.

When Soriano ran into trouble, with two outs and the bases loaded but the Yankees still holding a 4–1 lead, Joe Girardi decided Soriano's stuff that night wasn't good enough to finish the inning. You can quibble with that decision; Soriano has been a stud out of the bullpen for most of the last decade, but maybe Girardi, a former catcher, saw something in Soriano's velocity or pitch movement that warranted the switch. The Yankees needed just four more outs. It's difficult to imagine a potential ninth-inning situation as crucial as this one: This is almost certain to be the most important at-bat of the game. Retire the next hitter and even the pitching coach would have a decent chance of holding a three-run lead with just three outs to go. Hell, a pitcher with an 18.00 ERA (like, say, an eighteen-year-old prospect in Class A minor league ball) would save the game in the ninth inning more than 50 percent of the time, since a pitcher with an 18.00 ERA allows on average two runs to score each inning. Managers must deploy their best asset at this point, because it's the most important moment of the game. Stated another way, the next at-bat has extreme leverage.

Instead of Mariano Rivera, Girardi brought in the pitcher that the Yankees had already determined, after a winter of reflection, wasn't as good as Soriano, not to mention Rivera. One batter later the score was tied. When Rivera finally did get the call, at the top of the ninth of the now tied game, he promptly retired the side. Needless to say, the Yankees lost in extra innings, and nine miles south, in TriBeCa, I was beating my head against my crutches.

2. Poker Tournament, First-Day Play

Skilled poker players know—whether it's in a 7,000-person, nationally televised event, a one-table sit-and-go tournament, or the weekly poker night with the boys—there is one, and only one, goal: win the most money. Every other measure of success players can dream up—"I never lose showdowns," "I always make it to day two of the Main Event," and my favorite, from a friend whose wife used to play with him, "My wife will *never* knock me out of a tournament"—runs counter to the only goal that matters. In tournaments, astute players feast on those just trying to make it to the cash line from what's known as "the bubble." (In tournament play, only about 10 percent of the entrants participate in the prize pool. When there are just a few more than 10 percent left in a tournament, the group of players with the fewest chips are said to be "on the bubble.") The very first advice a beginner poker player, who invariably plays too many hands, gets from an experienced player focuses on managing to the *right* metric: "You're not trying to win the most hands. You're trying to win the most money."

3. Obsession with Errors

When I was in high school, I read *The Umpire Strikes Back*, by Ron Luciano. A former American League umpire who could have performed stand-up on *The Tonight Show*, Luciano had written a hilarious book about his time in the big leagues. It was so entertaining, and I read it so many times, that when my tenth-grade English teacher asked me who my favorite author was, I answered, to her complete bewilderment, "Ron Luciano."* In the book, Luciano described the fielding genius of shortstop Luis Aparicio on a sharply hit ball, straight up the middle of the playing field. Luciano explained that from his position be-

---

*Years later, in an episode of *Seinfeld*, NBC executives asked aspiring screenwriter George Costanza who he read, and he answered, "I like Mike Lupica." I thought the *Seinfeld* writers had somehow cribbed that from my life.

hind home plate he had seen that exact same hit, with that exact speed and trajectory, hundreds of times before over the course of his twenty-year umpiring career. It was always a single into center field. Except this time Aparicio got to the ball and threw the runner out at first. Wrote Luciano, "I wanted to call time out and go over to Aparicio and thank him for doing that."

At a time when few had heard of Bill James, let alone advanced statistics, Luciano described the way the sabermetric community today measures defensive prowess. Plays made—as tracked by assists and putouts, *not errors committed*—is the way to judge fielders. I believe errors are a completely meaningless statistic. In fact, by distorting ERA, errors do considerable harm in measuring pitchers' effectiveness, because ERA is the one statistic that traditionalists and sabermetric analysts agree has at least some value as an evaluation metric. For example: The Cubs, Phillies, and Yankees are all at home during the top of the first inning with two outs and nobody on base. The third batter in all three games grounds a ball sharply up the middle. Derek Jeter, maligned (fairly) for his lack of range at any stage of his career, dives* to his left but can't get it. Starlin Castro—the young Cubs shortstop known to Chicago's

---

*I'm in no way a Jeter basher, arguing (perhaps foolishly, perhaps not) during the nineties that I'd rather have him on my team than A-Rod or Nomar Garciaparra when they were the big three of young superstar shortstops. However, so many bloggers have ridiculed the frequency with which Yankees announcer Michael Kay says, "Past a diving Derek Jeter," that acclaimed sportswriter Joe Posnanski has suggested all restaurants in New York City should have a menu item named Pasta Diving Jeter.

North Side fans for his propensity to sometimes toss the ball randomly around Wrigley Field—comes up with the ball but throws wide of the bag, allowing the runner to reach first base. The Phillies' Jimmy Rollins fields the ball cleanly and throws the runner out. If the next hitter homers, think of how ridiculous the different results will be based on traditional scorekeeping. In the Phillies' case, the homer would lead off the second inning. Their pitcher would be charged with an earned run. In the Yankees game, the two-run homer would result in a 2–0 deficit with both runs charged to the pitcher. In the Cubs game, although the score would also be 2–0, the pitcher would not be charged with *any* earned runs. Incredibly, his ERA would be lower than the Phillies pitcher's, who merely trails 1–0. Yet Castro and Jeter did *exactly* the same thing. They failed to convert a batted ball into an out.

Baseball announcers, Gold Glove voters, and baseball reporters (like the one at *The New York Times* who implied that Eduardo Núñez had hurt the Yankees when he replaced Derek Jeter in the field) have got to change their fixation on errors. It's the wrong metric. Made plays, not errors, are what matters.

4. NASDAQ Spreads in 1999

I worked on Lehman Brothers' NASDAQ trading desk all through the incredible tech bubble of the late 1990s that culminated in the heady days of NASDAQ 5,000 in early March

2000. Trading volumes exploded, new hedge funds sprouted up weekly, and, without question, there were certain customers who were more demanding than others. One of the senior traders at Lehman used to look at the runs for the traders in his sector at the end of the day and see, for example, that although they had all executed four million shares of traded stock, one trader had a P&L double another's. He'd investigate and determine a specific customer was to blame for the lower P&L, which led to his pronouncement that we needed to stop doing business with these customers, because they were harming our gross margins. There was nothing wrong with his analysis of the P&Ls; there *were* certain customers whose orders were invariably less profitable. But the key to that finding was "less profitable," not "unprofitable." Thanks to triple-digit stock prices in virtually every large-cap stock on the NASDAQ, spreads were at an all-time high never to be seen again. The trading of NASDAQ stocks used to be a spread-based, not commission-based business, so high stock prices and wide spreads were gifts from the heavens for brokers. It was virtually impossible for any single customer to be unprofitable given enough business. Taking offense at lower-margin business—taking it personally when a customer insisted that you take a hit every once in a while—turned out to be exactly the wrong attitude. In a high-margin environment, regardless of the business or industry, management should do everything possible to get every single piece of business in the door, because, on the margin, each additional customer adds profitability. (Because of the incredible advances in computing power that revolutionized NASDAQ trading, at the time there was effectively zero marginal cost to doing more business.) The metric to focus on in this case was the bottom line, not gross margins.

5. Absolute Returns Aren't Necessarily Marketable Returns

It's a shame that managing other people's money can lead to sub-optimal decision-making for the owner of the money. Although Warren Buffett would rather make 15 percent lumpy than 12 percent smooth, that is not true for a lot of investors. In the case of many institutional investors (e.g., fund-of-fund investors), it's often exactly the opposite of what they want. To attract and retain investor money, hedge funds need to have a certain type of performance. Returns are path-dependent, meaning that if the fund gets to a desirable end result (beating the market by 5 percent) in an undesirable manner (with huge swings each month relative to the market), it will neither attract nor retain outside money. It's hard for some portfolio managers to comprehend—and it's a flaw in the structure of asset management—that the value of their enterprise (the hedge fund) would be worth more with lower but smoother returns. For the good of the hedge fund, they must focus on marketable, not absolute, returns.

Focusing on the Wrong Data

6. Torrealba Gets a Start

By dint of my job experience as a tax accountant and a stock trader, I've spent my entire career working for organizations that rely on a large number of people to work as a team in close quarters. I haven't encountered a work environment yet that wasn't enhanced by a manager who possessed excellent interpersonal skills. Conversely, working for a jackass sucks. It destroys morale, reduces productivity, and ultimately damages the organization. Recognizing the value of these soft management skills, I differ from some sabermetric-based baseball analysts, who view team chemistry, a manager's "people skills," and the mood of the clubhouse as meaningless. I take it as significant that the Rangers' manager, Ron Washington, is regarded as a "player's coach" and is loved by the players on his team. It's probably consistent with his approach to make a gesture of loyalty to a veteran player like Yorvit Torrealba. The problem is he shouldn't do it in the third game of a World Series tied one game apiece.

Torrealba started ninety-five games at catcher for the Rangers during the 2011 season. By the World Series, though, it was clear that another catcher on the team, Mike Napoli, was by an extremely wide margin the better hitter. However, Washington apparently felt he couldn't let Torrealba, a ten-year veteran, miss starting his first World Series game. So in Game Three, he moved Napoli to first, benching Mitch Moreland in the process, so that Torrealba could get the start he "deserved." Not only is Mitch Moreland a better hitter than Torrealba under any scenario; he's also a better fielder than Napoli, so Washington weakened his team in two different ways. I believe in the effectiveness of interpersonal skills, and baseball has some wonderful stories on that topic.* But in this case, a gesture of loyalty to Torrealba came at the expense of giving the other 24 players their best chance to win a World Series ring. A "player's coach" should be regarded as the one who gives his players the best chance to win the game.

7–8. When to Ignore Short-Term Profits

The story of "Amazon.bomb" and the ambitious broker-dealer are very similar. In the case of Amazon, it was journalists and many outside analysts who couldn't grasp the idea of ignoring near-term profitability. Paradoxically, these were the same journalists who loved to point out the shortcomings of Fortune 500 companies who put too much emphasis on next quarter's earnings. Yet, in the case of Amazon.com, they were incapable of seeing, let alone lauding, the long-term plan CEO Jeff Bezos executed. In the case of the broker-dealer, you'd think the lessons of Amazon would guide it as well. Focusing on short-term,

---

*My favorites: A banned Pete Rose being snuck into Riverfront Stadium to see his son, Pete Rose Jr., given one start by the Reds in a quest to get a major league hit. John Kruk and his manager hatching a plan to give Kruk one final chance to leave baseball a .300 hitter. I even supported the Mets allowing José Reyes to bunt his way to a batting title and then remove himself from the game on the last day of the 2011 season, "after all he's done for the team," as his manager said afterward.

bottom-line profitability, when attaining market share is the only way to achieve the ambitious long-term goals of the organization, is foolish. By changing business plans at the nascent stage of their business model, due to a focus on a short-term metric, they run the real risk of permanently relegating themselves to a marginal position in the marketplace.

9. Another Bullpen Misuse

The Pirates came to the end of July 2011 with the potential for a magical season* but fell prey to exactly the same problem that bedeviled the Yankees in the first example: misuse of the team's assets as a result of managing personnel with an eye to the save metric. Managers and relievers (and their agents) are addicted to the save. To maximize the chances of winning ball games, a change in that way of thinking must take place, and it must come from the top of an organization. The best manager and motivator of people I have ever seen ran the NASDAQ trading desk at Lehman Brothers the first eight years I worked there. To say he had a presence is a vast understatement. *Mad Men's* Don Draper, who's nearly a spitting image of my first manager, wishes he had a presence like Matt Johnson's.

Matt juggled his lineup of traders as expertly as any major league manager. He understood that, just as a baseball team

---

*On the morning of July 26, nearly two-thirds of the way through the 2011 season, the Pirates—not the eventual division-champion Milwaukee Brewers and not the eventual world-champion St. Louis Cardinals—were in first place in the National League Central.

doesn't want a lineup full of singles-hitting base-stealers or nothing but high-slugging, low-on-base-percentage power hitters, he needed a trading desk filled with traders who possessed different skill sets. He was also a master motivator, possibly as a result of all the time he spent around football coaches, including his four years as a defensive lineman at Penn State, capped by its national-championship victory over heavily favored Miami in his last game. He knew that every member of an organization has to be focused on the same goal. When that's the case, no one will be tailoring their performance to the wrong metric. The team's goals must come before individual goals. Having observed him for years, I have no doubt he could get baseball players to buy into his system of "team first" as easily as a desk full of traders and salespeople. If he were the Yankees' manager, he'd get his relievers on board with one meeting—a meeting I imagine might go like this:

At the beginning of the season, Matt would sit Mariano Rivera down in his office and say, "Mo, I think you're the greatest relief pitcher in baseball. If some deranged fans in Boston had kidnapped me and my life depended on the Yankees getting the best hitter in the league out, there's only one pitcher I'd choose. If they told me I couldn't have you, I'd tell them, 'Just kill me now. Mo's my guy.'"

He'd have delivered that last line with his arms out wide, like he was ready to be crucified. He'd pause, and they'd both have a laugh at that. Then he'd lean forward and narrow his blue eyes as they intently focused on Rivera. "If my life depended on it, could you get any hitter in this league out?"

"Of course, Skip."

Matt would get animated now. "With the City of New York watching and the greatest fans in baseball screaming your name, if this organization's success, if your teammates' entire season depended on you, could you get ANY HITTER in this league out?"

By now he's chanting. He's fired up, appealing to Rivera's competitive nature. I wouldn't be surprised if Rivera shouted his next answer, because I know I would.

"Yes! I would get him out!"

Now there'd be a pause to let it sink in. "You know," Matt would continue calmly, pointing to the picture of former Yankees manager and legend Billy Martin that he'd have hung on the wall, "that crazy SOB used his closer, Sparky Lyle—the Cy Young Award winner that year—in the *fourth inning* of the ALCS against the Royals in 1977 even though he knew Mr. Steinbrenner would fire his ass if it didn't work."* Rivera almost certainly doesn't know this, so he sits rapt. Then, almost off-handedly, Johnson would add, "Getting that hitter out we

---

*Lyle pitched five and a third innings of scoreless relief in Game Four of the American League Championship Series—a best-of-five series at the time. The Yankees faced elimination, having lost two of the first three games. But that's not even close to the most interesting aspect of the game. According to Jonathan Mahler's *Ladies and Gentlemen, the Bronx Is Burning,* Yankees owner George Steinbrenner watched this game from a dorm room at the University of North Carolina, where his daughter was a student. That is so mind-boggling I can't even think of a joke.

talked about—it wouldn't bother you if it wasn't in the ninth inning, would it?"

There isn't anyone alive who hesitates in the presence of this master motivator. The answer is no.

"All right, Mo. I knew you had as much confidence in yourself as I had in you. Get out of here and have some fun today." And then would come the coup de grace, the last piece of motivation, the thing that makes him such an effective leader. "I'm so glad to hear you say that, because one of your teammates is in here every day telling me *he* can get out anyone, on any team, at any time."

When Mariano Rivera opened the door to the manager's office, right outside would be Rafael Soriano, completely clueless as to why an assistant coach had instructed him to wait outside the manager's door.

That's how you motivate an entire organization to focus on the right metric.

20

"Markets Can Remain Irrational . . ."

Vindication is too strong a word, but I'll admit that I had begun to take the fund's poor performance in June and July personally, so when the model delivered excellent results in August—without relying on a few wins in top-rated, and therefore heavily weighted, games—I couldn't help but feel satisfied. Not coincidentally, the Minnesota Twins went 7-21 in August, although gains betting against the Twins only accounted for a little more than a third of the overall gains for the month.

The Model's Results in August	
Total Return	+8.51 percent
Year-to-Date Return	+16.62 percent
Total Games Picked	357 (out of 420 played)
Record in Games Picked	187-170

For the fifth month in a row, the model found an edge in about 85 percent of the games played. Betting favorites, which had been a problem in three of the first four months, resulted in the best monthly performance of the year for that category.

Return by Category of Team Selected		
	Win-Loss Record	Return
Favorites	108-59	+8.89 percent
Underdogs	70-105	-1.64 percent
Pick-'Ems	9-6	+1.26 percent
Total	**187-170**	**+8.51 percent**

Return by Wager Size		
	Win-Loss Record	Return
2 percent bets	4-3	+1.1 percent
1.5 percent bets	2-3	-1.5 percent
1 percent bets	4-4	-0.35 percent
50-basis-point bets	12-4	+3.58 percent

Return by Wager Size		
	Win-Loss Record	Return
40-basis-point bets	37-21	+6.76 percent
20-basis-point bets	49-53	-0.9 percent
10-basis-point bets	79-82	-0.18 percent

True validation of the model's edge requires a consistent win percentage in the areas where the most games are bet—the sub-50-basis-point bet levels—and for the third month in a row the results were strong. Looking at the results by team, the gains were more pronounced in the category of teams bet against, revealing that the gains made by betting on the favorites came from identifying overrated teams, not underrated ones.

+/- 2 Percent Returns on Teams Bet On			
Atlanta Braves	9	2	+3.33 percent
Colorado Rockies	4	6	+2.18 percent
Milwaukee Brewers	9	3	+2.08 percent
	.		
	.		
	.		
	.		
NY Mets	9	9	-2.67 percent

+/- 2 Percent Returns on Teams Bet Against			
San Francisco Giants	12	8	+6.18 percent
Florida Marlins	17	6	+5.59 percent
Minnesota Twins	15	6	+3.15 percent
Baltimore Orioles	6	6	+2.30 percent
Chicago White Sox	7	7	+2.19 percent
		.	
		.	
		.	
		.	
LA Angels	11	13	-3.06 percent
LA Dodgers	7	11	-4.34 percent

As economist John Maynard Keynes famously remarked, "markets can remain irrational a lot longer than you and I can remain solvent." That's another variation on the need for proper risk management. After the Twins flummoxed the model for two months, a bit of rationality returned as Minnesota had their worst month of the year up to that point. With a gain, betting against Minnesota, of 3.15 percent in August, the model had gotten back some of the losses betting against Minnesota in June and July. The big gains were to come in September, however, demonstrating that, as is true in all areas of asset management, even when an investable edge exists, the profit stream is rarely smooth; in fact, it's almost always lumpy.

Proper risk management during the lean times allows for the harvesting of gains when they eventually emerge.

With the summer coming to an end, the model was hitting a high note—almost certain to finish the year winning money—and it put a little more spring in my step. More likely due to the passage of time and eight months of physical therapy than a winning model, by the end of August I could walk with just a mild limp. I figured if the model were up in September, I might be able to dunk a basketball by the World Series. At least half of that equation came true.

21

The Weighting Is the Hardest Part

If a baseball bettor had, at the beginning of a baseball season, the chance to peer into the future and obtain the exact end-of-year total of any traditional statistic (i.e., the ones found on the back of a baseball card) for one player on each major league team, which statistic should he choose? A fantasy baseball player would probably pick the best-known slugger from each team and ask for home runs. For fantasy purposes, that's logical. Since fantasy players, under traditional league rules, have to excel in five different offensive categories, home run totals give insight into RBIs and runs scored as well.

But what should a baseball bettor do? Would it really be helpful to know before the 2010 season started that José Bautista would hit a stunning fifty-four home runs? I suppose when the difference between performance and expectations is that extreme, knowing about it in advance might offer some insight into Toronto's final win total that oddsmakers wouldn't possess. That's an extreme example, however, and the bettor would have had to have known to ask, when picking a player on the Blue Jays, for Bautista's home run total. Just as unlikely as José Bautista hitting fifty-four home runs in 2010 would have been the crystal ball–using baseball bettor who would have asked for Bautista's season-ending total instead of that of several of his better-known Blue Jays teammates.

According to the Pythagorean theorem, by far the most important factor in determining a team's win-loss record, and therefore its chances to win a single game, is its season-ending run differential. Therefore, the most valuable piece of information a baseball bettor could hold before the season—really at any time of the season—is the season-ending ERA of any particular starter. Even though that information would be helpful only about thirty times a year, or about once every five games per team, it would be invaluable in those thirty games. Further, unlike the Bautista example, the bettor doesn't need to decide the best pitcher on each team; he needs only to pick a starter likely to make a full season's worth of starts. That's another beauty of betting baseball: The oddsmakers post a line on every game. It's emotionally satisfying to pick the winner of a high-profile game, but the money is still green when Bruce Chen faces off against Tyler Chatwood. In fact, the bettor might be better off *not* picking the ace on each team. Elite pitchers at a certain stage of their career become quite predictable. Telling me before the season that Cliff Lee would have an ERA in 2011 of 2.40 isn't that valuable; it's merely confirming. Sure, he'd outperform expectations by a mild amount in putting up a Cy Young–caliber year, but, honestly, I already knew Cliff Lee was a great pitcher, the projection systems knew it, and, most important, so did the oddsmakers. But if you tell me at the beginning of the year that Bronson Arroyo will have a 5.07 ERA, now you've told me something I can make money on!

Using Bronson Arroyo isn't cherry-picking data; it would have been very logical to ask for his ERA before the season started. At the beginning of 2011—or, really, any year he's been on the Reds—Arroyo stood the greatest chance of starting the most games and pitching the most innings for his team. Entering 2011, he was coming off consecutive seasons of sub-4.00 ERAs, having posted a 3.84 and 3.88 ERA in 2009 and 2010, respectively. For a high-scoring team like the 2010 Cincinnati Reds, 3.88 runs allowed every nine innings over two-hundred-plus innings is extremely predictive of a lot of wins in those games in which Arroyo started. Sure enough, the Reds went 20-13 in Arroyo's thirty-three starts, a winning percentage of .606, and suggested that, all things being equal, anytime the 2010 Reds went off as less than a -150 favorite (implied win percentage of .600) with Arroyo on the mound, they were a potential bargain.

However, Arroyo's 5.07 ERA in 2011 consigned the Reds to giving up a bunch more runs over a season of his starts—about thirty—materially and adversely impacting their win total. In 2011 the Reds went 15-17 in Arroyo's thirty-two starts. In retrospect, anytime Arroyo went off as a favorite in 2011, there was value in betting on the other team. Over the first two months of the season, he started eleven games. The Reds went 4-7 in those games, but they went off as a favorite in seven of those eleven games at an average of -140. That means the other team, or the underdog, could be bet at a price of +130, representing tremendous value vs. a pitcher known to allow 5.07 runs every nine innings in 2011. The runs allowed wouldn't be the same every game, of course, and there would be no way to determine exactly how much run support the Reds lineup would give Arroyo in his starts, but it's still a critical edge. Sure enough, the underdogs went 5-2 in those games. A $100 bet on each underdog, at an average of +130, would be up $450 (5 x $130 for the five wins, less 2 x $100 for the two losses) after those seven games.

If only there had been a way to know Arroyo would end up having a much higher ERA in 2011 than in 2010.

Welcome to SIERA, or skill-interactive earned run average, the most important sabermetric statistic in existence for baseball bettors.

The existence of SIERA would not have been possible at the turn of the century, and by turn of the century I mean the era of Billy Wagner, not Honus Wagner. By the year 2000, the sabermetrics industry was no longer relegated to remote outposts, followed by just a few statistics-obsessed baseball fans. Baseball Prospectus had existed for a few years, and Baseball-Reference.com had launched in early 2000. Baseball broadcasters and mainstream reporters were citing OPS (on-base percentage plus slugging). However, the most important discovery of the modern era of sabermetric research hadn't yet occurred.

In 2001, Vörös McCracken published a truly revolutionary article that became the talk of the baseball analytics world and, eventually, front offices across baseball. In the article, McCracken essentially advanced the theory that major league pitchers had control of only three things when they pitched: their strikeout rate, their walk rate, and their home run rate. Everything else was out of their control. By extension, that meant pitchers had no control over the outcome of an at-bat once the ball was hit into play. In other words, the ability to "induce weak contact" with the ball was a myth.

That sentence contradicted everything baseball fans thought they knew about pitching. It meant that Cy Young Award pitchers had no more control over a ball hit into the field of play than a journeyman starter. Understandably, this conclusion caused a lot of discussion, and others tested the theory rigorously. Years of subsequent research, with modest modifications (McCracken himself noted knuckleball hurlers were excluded) have confirmed McCracken's conclusions. Bill James himself wrote, "I feel stupid for not having realized this thirty years ago." Still, some fans can't wrap their mind around the findings, even in the face of overwhelming evidence. A look at the statistics of the Philadelphia Phillies staff, baseball's best in 2011, helps validate McCracken's findings:

Starter	K percent	BB percent	ERA	Record
Roy Halladay	23.6	3.8	2.35	19-6
Cliff Lee	25.9	4.6	2.40	17-8
Cole Hamels	22.8	5.2	2.79	14-9
Roy Oswalt	15.7	5.6	3.69	9-10
Vance Worley	21.5	8.3	3.01	11-3
Kyle Kendrick	12.3	6.3	3.22	8-6

If you ranked the Phillies starters in any of those categories, one thing you'd notice is that Kyle Kendrick would be ranked fifth or sixth in every category, surprising no one. In fact, it wouldn't be the least bit controversial to say that there is nothing Kyle Kendrick can do on a pitcher's mound better than Roy Halladay, Cliff Lee, Roy Oswalt, or Cole Hamels.

One additional statistic: hitters' batting average on balls hit into play (BABIP) vs. Phillies pitchers in 2011, ranked by effectiveness:

Starter	BABIP
Cole Hamels	.259
Kyle Kendrick	.265
Vance Worley	.290
Cliff Lee	.293
Roy Halladay	.305
Roy Oswalt	.321

All the things that can make a comparison between two pitchers in the BABIP category suspect are neutralized here. All the Phillies pitchers played in the same ballparks, against the same opponents, and in front of the same fielders. Prior to McCracken's research, it might seem that Kyle Kendrick had an above-average ability to "induce weak contact," but the truth is that BABIP is largely random around a mean just below .300. Can anyone truly believe that Roy Halladay is below league average in any skill-based pitching metric or that Kendrick is better than Lee or Halladay at controlling how a batter hits the ball?

This finding led to entirely new ways to evaluate pitchers. Tom Tango created a statistic called fielding-independent pitching, or FIP, that helped determine just how lucky or unlucky a pitcher was. Using a pitcher's strikeout rate, his walk rate, and his home run rate, FIP calculates an expected ERA. If the actual ERA is lower, it suggests that level of performance isn't sustainable and is therefore lucky. Conversely, if the actual ERA was higher, the pitcher was unlucky and probably more skilled than his ERA suggested.

FIP reflected a pitcher's skill set, not his results, so scouts and general managers could better evaluate a pitcher's talent and how he could be expected to perform going forward. In evaluating future performance, however, FIP had a major shortcoming. Two of the three inputs, strikeout rate and walk rate, are extremely stable for pitchers. In other words, they correlate strongly from year to year. However, home run rate does not. Enter xFIP. Credited to Dave Studeman, xFIP (the x stands for "expected") replaced actual home run rate with the league-average rate. Fans, analysts, and baseball GMs now had tools to evaluate pitchers on what did happen (FIP) and what was predicted to happen (xFIP). xFIP gained immediate acceptance in sabermetric and fantasy circles because analysts could easily determine that it predicted future ERA better than current ERA or FIP. As a predictor of future runs allowed, it has value to a baseball bettor as well.

The big research leap required one more refinement, and with a series of articles introducing SIERA, or skill-interactive ERA, Matt Swartz and Eric Seidman provided it. Subsequent research had yielded one major addition to McCracken's initial conclusions: Pitchers also had control of their ground-ball rates. Swartz and Seidman leveraged that knowledge and discovered interplays between the factors that pitchers could control. For instance, walk rate—obviously a negative factor for pitchers and, therefore, on the margin, additive to ERA—didn't hurt ground-ball pitchers quite as much as fly-ball pitchers. This makes sense; ground ball pitchers have a greater chance of erasing their mistake (the walk) by inducing a double play. A high fly-ball rate (and, therefore, home run rate), while always negative on the margin, isn't quite as damaging to a high-strikeout pitcher, because on average there are fewer runners on base when home runs are hit.

Essentially, Swartz and Seidman performed a multiple linear regression analysis and created a complex formula for predicting future ERAs. Some squabbling between sabermetric rocket scientists emerged, and while the original research is archived at baseballprospectus.com, Swartz and SIERA in its current form are at fangraphs.com.

As a baseball bettor, I didn't care about the complexity or other theoretical disagreements about the existence of squared terms and negative coefficients; I simply wanted the best ERA predictor possible. Running year-to-year root-mean-square error (RMSE) calculations of my own, instead of correlations, I found SIERA a superior tool. (That cat is now out of the bag, since subsequent work published at FanGraphs after the 2011 season came to the same conclusion.) Therefore, I incorporated SIERA into the model.

As the 2011 season progressed, each month I phased out the pre-season projection at a greater rate and replaced it with

SIERA until, by the end of August, I relied solely on in-season SIERA to evaluate starting pitchers. Given that the model had its strongest performance in September, weighting SIERA more heavily earlier is something I'm going to consider in future seasons.

Earned runs allowed, of course, are not the same as total runs allowed, which is really what matters to bettors. Therefore, I'd prefer if skill-interactive runs allowed, or SIRA, were published instead of SIERA. Swartz actually calculated the SIRA formula but has written that, although there is a slight tendency for ground-ball pitchers to give up more unearned runs than fly-ball pitchers (more errors are committed on ground balls than fly balls), the ranking of pitchers barely changes. So bettors are left with SIERA unless they want to recalculate SIRA separately—a complicated undertaking. I simply assume that each pitcher's total runs allowed will exceed his earned runs allowed by the league average of a little less than 9 percent.

Turning back to Arroyo's pre-season projection, SIERA predicted a 4.56 ERA for Arroyo in 2011, based on his 2010 performance. That is mildly above or worse than league average but still comfortably above replacement level, translating into a projected WAR a little below 2. Using that projection, the model consistently bet against Arroyo in the first two months of the season. After that, the oddsmakers adjusted their lines, and the opportunities disappeared. In fact, the oddsmakers probably overcompensated, because by August the model actually bet on Arroyo five times (winning four) and against him only three (winning two of those bets) over the last few weeks of the season.

Bronson Arroyo proved very profitable for the model in 2011. I'm convinced that's because SIERA provided the model with a better predictor of runs allowed in his starts than the oddsmakers were using. At the beginning of the year, oddsmakers relied too much on Arroyo's outwardly impressive 2009 and 2010 ERAs, and the model profited by finding value in his opponents. By the end of July, oddsmakers had overcompensated when Arroyo's ERA hit an unsightly 5.58. SIERA actually hadn't changed its mind on Arroyo all year and still pegged him as a mid-4 ERA pitcher at that point. His skills hadn't changed at all; Arroyo was just unlucky during the first two-thirds of 2011 to about the same extent he'd been lucky in 2010. Oddsmakers, though, started pricing the Reds as if Arroyo had minor league talent. When he improved the last two months, ultimately lowering his full-season ERA to 5.07, the model took advantage of the oddsmakers again, this time by backing Arroyo. It's why I regard SIERA as the most important saber-metric tool a baseball bettor possesses; it assesses repeatable skills, not random outcomes.

22

A Winning End to the Season

There are a lot of reasons to mock MLB commissioner Bud Selig. His dogged preservation of "the human element" has extended baseball's refusal to utilize anything but the barest minimum of available technology to ensure the umpires' calls on the field are correct. The industry's handling of the Steroids Era is rife with hypocrisy. Under Selig's watch, the length of an average major league game has increased to nearly three hours and stretches even longer in the playoffs—and when the Yankees and the Red Sox square off.* Finally, Selig himself regularly comes off as uncertain and uninformed, making him an easy target for mockery, epitomized by his look of helplessness

---

*If someone told me a Yankees–Red Sox game had taken only two hours and forty-five minutes to complete, my first thought would be that rain must have shortened the contest to six innings.

when declaring the 2002 All-Star game a tie because both teams had run out of players.

Because of that general perception, it's easy to overlook many of the forward-thinking advancements made by the industry during Selig's time as commissioner. Despite shunning technology at the ballpark, Major League Baseball has used technology to become a leader in enhancing the fan experience off the field. MLB.com is top-notch. MLB.tv is a fantastic product. On cable, the MLB Network is packed with compelling material year-round. The At Bat app is brilliant in design and execution. Topping it all off, at some point during 2010, when the league constructed the 2011 schedule, the commissioner's office struck gold with a seemingly meaningless change to one of baseball's long-standing traditions.

For my entire life, baseball's regular season has ended on a Sunday at the end of September or the beginning of October, forcing the season's final day to take a backseat to a full slate of pro football games. In the U.S. sports world, nothing sucks the air out of the room quite like the NFL. For the 2011 season, however, MLB announced that the regular season would end on Wednesday, September 28. That decision, seemingly devoid of significance when MLB released the 2011 schedule, might go down as the single best decision of the Selig era. The residue of that decision may have created new fans as well as years of goodwill and long-lasting memories for current fans and commentators.

When questioned about their in-game strategy, managers often retort, "Can you guarantee me things would have turned out differently?" That, of course, is irrelevant. The entire reason strategy exists is that there are no guarantees. The goal of any organization's management should be to put it in the best position to succeed at all times. MLB had no idea how the 2011 regular season would unfold, but it put its final games in the best position to be noticed and savored—there were no other professional or major college sports events competing for the spotlight—if something exciting or dramatic ensued.

Effectively, baseball's 2011 post-season began on the last night of the regular season.* Virtually every post-season seed had yet to be finalized, and there were four teams fighting for the last two wild-card berths. The Braves lost in dramatic fashion to the Phillies, capping off an epic September collapse that

---

*Even this starting point ignores the incredible drama that occurred on the season's penultimate evening. On the night of Tuesday, September 27, the Cardinals finally caught the Braves, the Rays turned a triple play against the Yankees to key a comeback, and the Red Sox desperately held on to a one-run lead to win against the Orioles and remain tied with the Rays. However, the most amazing event of the entire week—not a typo—occurred past midnight Eastern time, in Arizona. With two outs and nobody on base, the Diamondbacks trailed the Dodgers 6–1 in the tenth inning. Again, not a typo; the Dodgers scored five in the top of the tenth. Twenty minutes and six batters later, the Diamondbacks' Ryan Roberts saluted his manager, Kirk Gibson, with a slow-motion fist pump as he rounded second base during his walk-off grand slam. Coming back from five down with two outs and no one on had never happened before—hardballtimes.com estimated the odds were about 3 in 10,000—and Arizona's win mattered even more because it kept its hope for the number-two-seed and National League Division Series home-field advantage alive. Milwaukee, now needing a win in its last game to capture the number-two seed, rushed ace Zach Greinke to the mound on just three day's rest. That move compromised Milwaukee's rotation for the rest of the playoffs, badly damaging its chances of winning the pennant. I was holding a 25–1 ticket, bought for $1,000 in December of 2010, on the Brewers winning the National League pennant, and, yes, I'm still bitter.

allowed the eventual world-champion Cardinals into the play-offs. The Braves' collapse may ultimately receive little notice historically, however, thanks to the drama in the American League East. The Red Sox blew a game they had all but wrapped up, while the Tampa Bay Rays came from seven runs down with nine outs to go to beat the Yankees in extra innings, moments after the Red Sox's improbable and dramatic loss against the Orioles. Baseball had its own March Madness, and thanks to the foresight of Bud Selig's office, the MLB Network and ESPN captured it all and presented it to American sports fans, who weren't distracted by any competing events.

I have never seen a reaction to baseball games like the next day's. Everyone, it seemed, was talking about baseball. Bill Simmons, of Grantland.com, has long written about his Mom Test. When his mom is talking about an event, it has moved beyond the sports world and into the general population's consciousness. For me, it's the *Today* show test. When I get a call at work from my wife about some sports-related news item she saw on the *Today* show, it's the equivalent of Simmons's Mom Test. On the morning of September 29, my wife came to the kitchen table gushing about the Red Sox and the Braves.

As much as I love baseball, I don't resent the fact that the NFL sits atop the American sports landscape. It deserves to. March Madness annually enthralls offices and non-basketball fans in a way baseball rarely has. I noticed something this year after the last day of baseball's regular season, however. Unlike the drama of March Madness or the morning after a thrilling Sunday of NFL football, the talk after the last day of the 2011 regular season was solely about baseball. I didn't hear one person say that Evan Longoria's home run killed their fantasy team. No one lamented that the Braves busted their bracket or cursed the Orioles for a back-door cover. No, they were simply talking about baseball, and for that, Bud Selig deserves a huge amount of credit.

The Model's Results in September	
Total Return	+11.63 percent
Year-to-Date Return	+30.18 percent
Total Games Picked	351 (out of 396 played)
Record in Games Picked	194-157

The model posted its best results in September, as the fund closed at a high for the year on September 28, the last day of the regular season. Picking right up where August left off, favorites once again paid off handsomely.

Return by Category of Team Selected		
	Win-Loss Record	**Return**
Favorites	110-65	+14.88 percent
Underdogs	73-90	-5.00 percent
Pick-'Ems	11-2	+1.75 percent
Total	**194-157**	**+11.63 percent**

Return by Wager Size		
	Win-Loss Record	Return
2 percent bets	8-6	+4.3 percent
1.5 percent bets	5-1	+7.8 percent
1 percent bets	5-8	-2.15 percent
50-basis-point bets	8-9	-0.93 percent
40-basis-point bets	29-31	-1.76 percent
20-basis-point bets	61-49	+2.13 percent
10-basis-point bets	78-53	+2.24 percent

For the model, September was all about capitalizing on the collapse of the Minnesota Twins. The Twins went 6-20 in September, and the model bet against Minnesota in twenty-two of those games, cashing in seventeen times. The returns were enough to make betting against Minnesota a net winner for the year, despite large losses incurred in June and July.

+/- 2 Percent Returns on Teams Bet On			
Texas Rangers	11	2	+5.04 percent
Milwaukee Brewers	9	6	+3.30 percent
Detroit Tigers	11	4	+3.05 percent
Cleveland Indians	11	16	+2.95 percent
	.		
	.		

+/- 2 Percent Returns on Teams Bet On			
		.	
		.	
Seattle Mariners	3	7	-2.57 percent
Colorado Rockies	4	11	-2.79 percent
Atlanta Braves	6	9	-4.08 percent

+/- 2 Percent Returns on Teams Bet Against			
Minnesota Twins	17	5	+13.87 percent
Florida Marlins	13	7	+2.25 percent
NY Yankees	4	3	+2.17 percent
		.	
		.	
		.	
		.	
Kansas City Royals	2	4	-4.19 percent

For the entire season, the model made money on favorites, underdogs, and pick-'ems. Additionally, five of the seven categories of wager size made money. These were very satisfying results and provided strong evidence that the model had a sustainable edge. The regular-season results looked like this (due to compounding, the sum of the total returns will not equal the season results):

Return by Category of Team Selected		
	Win–Loss Record	**Return**
Favorites	626-443	+14.84 percent
Underdogs	400-516	+ 7.18 percent
Pick-'Ems	61-49	+6.79 percent
Total	**1,087-1,008**	**+28.81 percent**

Return by Wager Size		
	Win–Loss Record	**Return**
2 percent bets	26-13	+22.7 percent
1.5 percent bets	20-15	+3.95 percent
1 percent bets	38-34	+2.47 percent
50-basis-point bets	59-56	-4.06 percent
40-basis-point bets	189-164	+10.22 percent
20-basis-point bets	307-339	-12.05 percent
10-basis-point bets	448-387	+5.58 percent

With the regular season completed, the return on the preseason basket of futures was calculated as well.

Regular-Season Future Results				
Longs (1.25 Percent of Initial Capital)				
		Actual Wins	Bet Result	
Arizona Diamondbacks	Over 72½ Wins	94	Won	+1.25 percent
Baltimore Orioles	Over 76½ Wins	69	Lost	-1.375 percent
Kansas City Royals	Over 67½ Wins	71	Won	+1.25 percent
Seattle Mariners	Over 69½ Wins	67	Lost	-1.375 percent
Total				-0.25 percent
Shorts (1 Percent of Initial Capital)				
		Actual Wins	Bet Result	
Florida Marlins	Under 82½ Wins	72	Won	+1 percent
Houston Astros	Under 72½ Wins	56	Won	+1 percent
LA Angels	Under 83½ Wins	86	Lost	-1.1 percent
Minnesota Twins	Under 85½ Wins	63	Won	+1 percent
San Diego Padres	Under 75½ Wins	71	Won	+1 percent
Total				+2.9 percent

Total Return of Futures Positions: +2.65 percent

2011 Daily Return (Compounded Monthly):

30.18 percent

Final Regular-Season Portfolio Return: 32.83 percent

As trying as the June and July results were, as depressing as it was to collect from the few friends for whom I'd placed bets

during those two months, and as much as the doubts and criticism of some during that period stung, the final results were
even more satisfying. Even better was the observation of one
person who saw the results for the entire year and became an
indispensable advocate during the subsequent construction of
this book: "You built an airplane from scratch," he marveled,
"and it flew."

23

What Does Work in the Playoffs?

No Wall Street memoir seems to be complete without a review of the author's interview process. Describing (and often mocking) the personalities and actions of those on Wall Street who conduct interviews is a staple of the genre. From *Liar's Poker* to Jim Cramer's memoirs, it's clear that investment banking interviews make for some good stories.

The thinking from the interviewer's perspective is that by creating an uncomfortable environment for a would-be trader, the interviewer can assess a candidate's ability to function under stress. The trouble with that logic is this: I'm pretty certain I'd be unable to crack the ultra-confident demeanor of, say, Mike "The Situation" Sorrentino, of MTV's *Jersey Shore* by asking him to open a window that's been nailed shut. I'm certainly not going to be able to physically intimidate him. So while he might pass the "stress test" interview, I don't want him anywhere near, let alone in control of, any of my money—right down to my loose change.

I preferred to assess a candidate's capacity for critical reasoning. One of my favorite questions, especially if the candidate has listed poker as an interest on his résumé, is this: "You are taking a trip with Phil Ivey, widely regarded as the world's best poker player, and for the duration of the trip you are playing him heads-up for $50,000 in a poker game of your choice. Whoever has the most chips at the end of the trip takes the pot. What is the probability you win $50,000 off of Phil Ivey?"

The "correct" response is some variation of this: "How long is the trip? Because if we're taking a boat ride to Europe, there is no chance at all. An Acela train ride from NYC to D.C.? Also remote, but at least my chances of winning are non-zero. If it's a shuttle flight between New York and Boston, though, the odds might be as high as 10 percent."

This is relevant because the baseball playoffs are essentially a subway ride—on an express train—from Manhattan's City Hall to the Upper East Side.

In 2011, if every post-season series went the maximum number of games, a total of forty-one games would be played. That's four games fewer than are scheduled each Friday through Sunday over the season. Therefore, there should be no change to the model's capital allocation schedule just because there were fewer, higher-profile games to be played. Prudence still ruled the day, because, as Billy Beane put it in *Moneyball,* "My shit doesn't work in the playoffs."

I kept the model running for the post-season, fully expecting to find zero games to invest in. I couldn't imagine there would be an edge to be found. There would be no projections; I'd simply assume the teams taking the field would perform as they had over the previous 162 games. Since every oddsmaker and bettor had access to the same data, I expected nothing but minor differences between the model's game projections and the Vegas line.

For the most part, that did turn out to be the case, especially once the World Series rolled around and the model passed on three out of seven games, finding only modest edges in the other four. The model did find value in two series, however. The first was likely attributable to oddsmakers' overvaluing the popular New York Yankees, and the other suggested oddsmakers simply underrated the Texas Rangers' offense. That edge had disappeared by the time the World Series began, since oddsmakers eventually recognized the Rangers' firepower.

To get ready for the playoffs, I needed to update the model. I took the runs scored and runs allowed for the eight teams in the playoffs and, using the Pythagorean theorem, calculated their expected win-loss records. That resulted in a mildly different look for a couple of teams:

	Regular-Season Wins	Pythagorean Wins
Philadelphia Phillies	102	103
St. Louis Cardinals	90	88
Milwaukee Brewers	96	90
Arizona Diamondbacks	94	88
NY Yankees	97	101
Detroit Tigers	95	89
Texas Rangers	96	98
Tampa Bay Rays	91	91

While the six-game difference between the Brewers' and Diamondbacks' actual wins vs. their expected wins is notable, for the first round they canceled each other out, because Milwaukee and Arizona were facing each other. Only the apparent widening of the gap between the Yankees and Tigers looked significant. By this point I'd become a staunch adherent of the predictive qualities of "cluster luck" analysis. After all, Tampa Bay did score ninety-five fewer runs in 2011 than in 2010. It took eight amazing runs in the last three innings of its final game to just exceed my out-of-consensus prediction that the Rays would score one hundred fewer runs in 2011 than in 2010. I recalculated the Pythagorean wins based on the runs scored and runs allowed each team would have expected to have, absent cluster luck.

	Pythagorean Wins, Adjusted for Cluster Luck
Philadelphia Phillies	94
St. Louis Cardinals	90
Milwaukee Brewers	93
Arizona Diamondbacks	84
NY Yankees	94
Detroit Tigers	92
Texas Rangers	102
Tampa Bay Rays	91

Now I had something to work with. Suddenly the two teams considered prohibitive favorites to win their series, the Yankees and the Phillies, didn't look like overwhelming favorites anymore. On the other hand, the Brewers and Rangers looked underrated, albeit for different reasons. The Brewers looked like a strong favorite due to the apparently overachieving Arizona Diamondbacks, while Texas simply looked like the best team in baseball.

I still needed to make one more adjustment. I wasn't going to adjust for players who had played above or below expectations during the regular season. I had to assume that the best predictor of each player's production over the next week was the body of work he had put forth over the previous 162 games. However, with the Phillies, for example, the players responsible for putting together a 102-win season (adjusting down to ninety-four wins to account for cluster luck and the Pythagorean theorem does not change the logic) were not the same ones taking the field for the playoffs. The craptastic* duo of Brian Schneider and Dane Sardinha produced a batting line of .185/.287/.255 while starting forty-seven games at catcher in place of the vastly superior Carlos Ruiz (.283/.371/.383). Perennial All-Star and Silver Slugger Award winner Chase Utley started only one hundred games in 2011 due to an early-season injury and was replaced at second base by the somewhat serviceable Wilson Valdez and barely serviceable Pete Orr and Michael Martínez. Finally, mid-season acquisition Hunter Pence represented a vast upgrade over first-half right fielders Ben Francisco and Domonic Brown. Based solely on 2011 production, the Phillies team that took the field for Game One of the playoffs was sixty-five runs, or 6.5 wins, better than the one that collectively played during the regular season.

I ran this exercise for all eight teams and came up with a

Craptastic may not be a word, and it may not be fair. But I need to vent a little. Due to the extreme difference in projected production, virtually every time Schneider started for Ruiz, the model favored a bet against the Phillies. Oddsmakers simply ignored this lineup change, which I calculated to be the equivalent of at least three and maybe four wins. It turned out the Phillies went 26-3 in the first twenty-nine games Schneider started (27-8 on the season). So you're thinking, "Joe, your model missed on someone's production." Oh, it missed alright. It missed to the downside! Over 162 games, Schneider's 2011 production vs. Ruiz's would cost a team about seventy-five runs, or 7.5 wins. And yet the Phillies played nearly .900 ball for most of the season when Schneider started. By August I was sulking in front of the TV, convinced the model would be up 50 percent for the year without this misfortune, and while Schneider would be dragging his (.176/.246/.256) bat to the plate, Phillies announcer Chris Wheeler would prattle on and on about how the Phillies' record when Schneider started proved his value to the team. It's amazing I don't go through more TVs in a season.

final restatement showing the Rangers as the clear favorite to win the World Series.

	Pythagorean Wins, Adjusted for Cluster Luck and Lineup Changes
Philadelphia Phillies	101
St. Louis Cardinals	93
Milwaukee Brewers	99
Arizona Diamondbacks	84
NY Yankees	95
Detroit Tigers	90
Texas Rangers	106
Tampa Bay Rays	97

That restatement represented each team's Game One starting lineups as well as the 2011 contributions of each team's entire pitching staff. However, no team would be using its entire pitching staff in a five-game series. Every team would be dropping its fifth starter, with a possibility that even the fourth starter could lose a start to the staff ace pitching on short rest. Pitching staffs that receive a disproportionate amount of their overall production from one or two starters are dangerous teams in the playoffs. (There is no better recent example of this than Randy Johnson and Curt Schilling on the 2001 Diamondbacks.) When Justin Verlander takes the mound for the Tigers, the Yankees aren't facing a ninety-win team; they're facing a one-hundred-plus-win team. CC Sabathia improves the Yankees as well. Based on my calculations, however, the Tigers had the starting pitching edge in every game vs. the Yankees. I saw this series as a toss-up, with only the Yankees' home-field advantage enough to project them as a small favorite. I ran that calculation for all the series and came up with win probabilities. Here are the posted odds, implied win percentage of those odds, and the model's projection for each series (as a reminder, the amount by which each game's implied win percentage exceeds 100 percent represents oddsmakers' juice):

	Vegas Odds	Implied Win Percentage	Projected Win Percentage
Philadelphia Phillies	-300	75 percent	71 percent
St. Louis Cardinals	+260	27.8 percent	29 percent
Milwaukee Brewers	-175	63.6 percent	60 percent
Arizona Diamondbacks	+155	41.5 percent	40 percent
NY Yankees	-150	60 percent	51 percent
Detroit Tigers	+130	43.5 percent	49 percent
Texas Rangers	-170	63 percent	61 percent
Tampa Bay Rays	+150	40 percent	39 percent

Whether it's because the Yankees are a popular "retail" team and therefore carry premium pricing like a Hèrmes scarf or because analysts underrated either the Tigers' offense or their starting pitching advantage, I saw solid value in backing

Detroit for the series. I allocated 1 percent of the fund to Detroit +130. (St. Louis was the only other team with a projected win percentage greater than the implied win percentage, but with their edge at just 1.2 percent, I passed, deeming at least a 5 percent edge necessary for a bet on the series.)

In the second round of the playoffs, the Rangers (-130) were actually a smaller favorite vs. the Tigers than the Yankees were. According to my projections, which had Texas as the World Series favorite, that made no sense, since the Rangers had a >60 percent chance of winning the ALCS vs. Detroit. I made a 1 percent bet on Texas.

Those were the only two series all post-season that produced enough of an edge to place a bet on, but there were plenty of single game opportunities. The model may have found plenty of plays but with a much smaller difference vs. the oddsmakers' line in most of them, compared with that of the regular season, it resulted in modest-size bets.

The Model's Post-season Results	
Individual Game Returns	+3.87 percent
Series Pick Returns	+2.3 percent
Total Return	+6.17 percent
Year-to-Date Return	**+41.03 percent**
Total Games Picked	29 (out of 38 played)
Record in Games Picked	16-13

Return by Category of Team Selected		
	Win-Loss Record	**Return**
Favorites	7-3	+3.02 percent
Underdogs	9-10	+0.85 percent
Pick-'Ems	0-0	+0 percent
Total	**16-13**	**+3.87 percent**

Return by Wager Size		
	Win-Loss Record	**Return**
2 percent bets	0-0	+0 percent
1.5 percent bets	1-0	+1.58 percent
1 percent bets	0-0	+0 percent
50-basis-point bets	0-0	+0 percent
40-basis-point bets	5-1	+2.06 percent
20-basis-point bets	5-3	+0.62 percent
10-basis-point bets	5-9	-0.39 percent

The model found an edge on twenty-nine of the thirty-eight playoff games. That represented 76 percent of the games, down from 86 percent during the regular season. The increased synchronization with the oddsmakers also revealed itself in the perceived edge of the twenty-nine games the model selected. There was just one game with an edge in excess of 10 percent and only six others with an edge exceeding 6 percent. The rest were all small plays.

The last two bets the model made were small 10-basis-point wagers on the Rangers in games six and seven of the World Series. Both bets, as every baseball fan knows, lost. Game Six, with six different leads overcome in total by Texas and St. Louis, was as great and improbable a World Series game as any played since 1986's Game Six, when the Mets' miracle victory sentenced Red Sox fans to a dose of misery that wouldn't be erased for another eighteen years. It took twenty-five years for 1986's Game Six to be surpassed in drama, and it wouldn't surprise me if 2011's Game Six wore that mantle for just as long. I lost those last two bets, and, honestly, as the celebration unfolded on the field, it didn't bother me.

As I watched delirious Cardinals fans on TV and fielded texts from my Cardinals-obsessed fourteen-year-old godson, I thought about the celebration in San Francisco just the year before. One of the off-the-field story lines of the 2010 World Series, between Texas and San Francisco, was the Giants' attempt to win their first World Series since the franchise moved from New York, in 1957. The once-dominant Giants franchise (14 pennants, including five World Series titles in the fifty-two years before they moved from New York) had gone fifty-two years without a title in San Francisco.

Fox had a camera stationed at San Francisco's Civic Center, where thousands of fans watched the telecast on outdoor screens. Shortly after the final out of Game Five, which gave San Francisco its long-awaited championship, Fox replayed the scene at the Civic Center when the final out was made. Predictably, when Brian Wilson struck out Nelson Cruz to end the game, the crowd went crazy. Everyone in the frame was vibrant and young—after all, it was outdoors, nighttime, and no warmer than 50 degrees. All in all, it was a fairly standard crowd shot, interchangeable with any other city's celebration, except for the black-and-orange hats.

And then, seven minutes after the final pitch and no more than five seconds before Fox faded to the commercial break, *she* appeared on the screen. In a sea of leaping twenty-somethings, there was a woman I'd confidently put in her eighties. At least twice as old and maybe four times older than anyone else in the frame, she too was jumping up and down, as high as you'd expect someone her age to jump. She wore a frilly orange hat and an orange sweatshirt over a black shirt. On top of it all, she had a black vest adorned with dozens of pins, presumably collected over the years while attending games at Candlestick Park.* She looked exactly like the rapping grandma in *The Wedding Singer.* As she jumped as best as she could, I noticed her arms were raised—she was looking for someone to high-five! Finally, an Asian girl with orange hair—because how could this scene have been anymore perfect?—saw her as she danced through the crowd and gave her a high five. With that, the screen faded to a commercial.

---

*With a nod to the cold winds that swept through the stadium, the Giants used to award Croix de Candlestick pins to anyone who stayed for the duration of extra-inning games.

(It seems the Fox production team missed this iconic moment, one of the sweetest scenes I've ever witnessed. After the commercial break, the announcers were focused on interviews in the locker room, and I'm sure Joe Buck, also the network's lead football announcer, was already anticipating that weekend's Cowboys game.)*

In 2011, Texas fans watched, in two different innings, the Rangers come within one strike of winning their first World Series. I thought about how wrenching this World Series loss had to be for them. I'd seen what winning the city's first World Series did to San Francisco. For the next year, the bars were packed in the Marina during game days, teenage boys heckled me when I wore my Phillies hat, and twenty-something women all over the city overrode their fashion instincts and deemed it cool to wear orange. That's why I didn't mind losing a couple of model-based bets. I may have made an investment in the Texas Rangers in the form of a bet, but I wasn't *invested* in them.

Fans from Texas who follow every game every season understand the distinction.

After all, owing to the Rangers' move of their own, from Washington, D.C., in 1972, they almost certainly have an eighty-year-old fan who has been waiting her whole life to celebrate a world championship.

---

*My favorite tweet after the incredible Game Six in 2011 came from someone posing as Joe Buck on Twitter: "That game was so great, I'm thinking of becoming a baseball fan."

24

Launching a Fund

Hedge Funds Will Be Winners If Greek Bailout Arrives

Could Greece's next rescue payout go straight into the pockets of London hedge funds? That, more or less, is the bet that a growing number of investors are making now as they load up on Greek government securities that mature in March [2012]. . . .

This article ran in *The New York Times* on January 10, 2012, and described the buying spree—mostly embarked on by European hedge funds—of Greek debt due, at the time, in fewer than ninety days. Essentially, these investors were paying forty cents for every dollar worth of debt. If Greece ultimately secured a lifeline from the EU and/or the IMF, the debt would be paid in full. If, however, Greece defaulted on its debt, the purchased securities would be worth nothing.

Does this sound analogous to anything in this book? Not to put too fine a point on it, but what if I stated short-term Greek debt currently traded at +150?

As I tallied up the performance of the fund for 2011 and began to prepare projections for the 2012 season, I thought about the parallels between being a portfolio manager at a hedge fund and managing a baseball fund for investors. There are, it must be acknowledged, enormous differences between the underlying securities that either enterprise would invest in. Companies issuing financial securities, whether debt or equity, gain working capital to start or expand their business(es). The entities issuing the securities could be publicly traded corporations, private companies, or, as in the example above, sovereign nations. There is a very real benefit to society in an established mechanism that allows entities to tap the pool of investable capital looking for a home. However, after the initial sale of the securities, the issuer derives no benefit from any subsequent exchange of the security between investors. The issuer may have a fiduciary duty to a rotating cast of stockholders and/or creditors, but the issuer is, by and large, indifferent to the buying and selling of the securities in the marketplace.

This secondary trading of securities in the market does provide a less obvious but very real benefit to all issuers and to society at large. Without the existence of a secondary trading market, the initial investors would likely be less willing to buy the offered security. As such, issuing companies would be forced to incur higher costs, either through higher interest rates or cheaper stock, or wouldn't be able to access the capital market at all. For all the negative headlines the financial markets and their participants attract—often with good reason, in the case of, say, insider-trading scandals—the secondary trading market and the investors that risk their money in it are vital to the operation of a functioning economy.*

No one should be under any illusions when it comes to the motives of those who operate in the secondary market, however. When Warren Buffett buys stock, he is buying the business of the company, intending to hold it for a decade or more; he presumably has little intent to make use of the secondary market's liquidity. Most everyone else, especially hedge funds, buys paper evidence of ownership, in electronic form, with the sole incentive of selling it at a higher price at a later date—and that later date is often measured in days or even hours. What's the motivation for this trading? To make money, of course, and from a critical-reasoning standpoint it's an exercise in comparing an implied rate with an expected rate. The price of every single security implies a rate of return. In the case of stocks it's not so obvious, because it requires knowledge of a company's

---

*The existence of the financial markets has other benefits, too. During the fall of 2011, they briefly made camping outdoors in urban public spaces cool!

financials. But in the case of other securities, it's much easier to determine.

When an option, whether a put or a call, is trading with a volatility reading of 40, or "40 vol," it implies the underlying security on which the option is based will move 2.5 percent a day. A buyer of the put or call can secure a profit if the underlying security moves more than 2.5 percent daily. If it moves less, the value of the option will erode. For a seller, the profit-and-loss equation is equal and opposite. That's all a standard derivative is.* A bet on the volatility the buyer expects vs. the implied volatility of the option. Sometimes, as in the case of the short-term Greek debt above, a binary event (full payment or default) with an obvious implied price presents itself in exactly the same manner as a sports bet.

Not only are the funds themselves solely engaging in trades in the secondary market with the purpose of making short-term money through their analytical skills; their investors are demanding that they do so. Typically, hedge fund investors

---

*Many will object, citing the strike price or the direction of the move of the underlying security. For instance, a 4 percent move down kills a call buyer, but a 4 percent move up raises the value of the call. That is true, but only because, along with the call, the buyer also bought stock (and shorted a bond, creating leverage) synthetically. The buyer can simultaneously, if they choose, neutralize that part of the purchase. The only unique security that cannot be hedged (without a transaction in a different option) is the implied volatility in the option. That's why, if you ever talk to a professional options trader or a sophisticated investor, they never say things like "I'm long one hundred calls on Dell at a strike of $12.50." They always express their positions as either being "long-vol" or "short-vol." From a moral hazard standpoint, it's also why executives who have been granted massive amounts of options from their employers have a huge incentive to take the company down a risky path, by either pursuing high-risk/high-reward ventures or adding debt to the company's balance sheet and increasing its leverage, making their options more valuable by increasing volatility.

place no restrictions on how the PM invests their money. "Make money any way you can" is essentially the instruction of the hedge fund investor.

According to some accounts, Warren Buffett, while a Columbia University student, used to study public-company filings searching for companies that were trading for far less than their intrinsic value. Ken Griffin, the founder of Citadel, one of the world's largest hedge funds, reportedly enjoyed spectacular returns trading convertible bonds from his Harvard dorm. Convertible bonds are simply debt with a call option attached, and Griffin exploited the disparity between the value the market assigned to the combined security (debt and equity call value) and its actual value.

Isn't that exactly what model-based betting on baseball games represents?

There are two ways someone or some entity should take advantage of this. The easiest way would be to build a model, establish a Nevada-based LLC, and relocate there to manage it. Then, like a hedge fund, accept investments from outside investors. The instruments this type of fund would invest in are admittedly different from the instruments traditional hedge funds invest in, but I have a hard time distinguishing the motives of investors in either fund. The typical well-heeled individual or institutional investor invests in a hedge fund based on some variant of this logic: "I have excess capital but don't have the time to properly vet attractive investment opportunities" or "I am not as good at investing my money as I am at making it. Please do it for me, professional investment manager." In either case, it's just a classic element of capitalism, division of labor, based on specialization. I find it hard to believe that if a fund manager made money for his investors through careful analysis, while discovering and exploiting minor pricing inefficiencies, and provided an attractive rate of return, his investors would care if he'd found the inefficiencies in Greek bonds, shares of Google, or National League futures.

Perhaps the biggest difference between a traditional hedge fund and a baseball fund would be the enjoyability of the latter's quarterly report to investors: "Due to rising interest rates, a competitive marketplace, and the Brewers' inability to find anything resembling a closer who could protect a lead, the fund suffered a 3 percent drawdown...."

Of course, there would be logistical hurdles. Chiefly, would large investor inflows constrain the fund's ability, even at a maximum outlay of 2 percent a game once or twice a month, to place sufficiently sized bets? Would the sportsbooks be leery of a large-size gambler? Personally, I don't think a fund like this should operate in the dark. It should establish relationships with every major sportsbook in town, akin to hedge funds using multiple prime brokers to manage their transactions and move their money. Initially, all sportsbooks love high-volume, high-stakes bettors. There's a reason they send private jets to Japan to transport "whales" to and from Las Vegas. Additionally, just as virtually every hedge fund is officially located off-shore, there are vast outlets available outside the United States for baseball wagering. Event betting is legal across the Caribbean, in many European countries, and in addition to the wealth of bookmakers and betting shops in Paris and especially London, there are publicly traded companies based in England and Ireland that operate live and Internet-based gambling sites.

There is no doubt that casinos are not static objects. Were their sportsbooks to lose money repeatedly, they'd adjust, and to some degree an arms race would develop between the books and a model-based fund. However, their primary mandate is to balance flow. Evidenced by the apparent premium pricing on the Yankees during the playoffs, not only on the series price but especially the Game Five elimination game, there is often ample money on the other side of the trade. Sportsbooks shouldn't really care if the same entity is regularly on the winning side of their balanced books.

I'm also skeptical as to how fast the bookmakers would move. Consider the Arizona Diamondbacks' lines during the 2011 season. Before the season started, oddsmakers pegged Arizona, a team that had won sixty-five games in 2010, as an even bet to win 72½ games. My model projected them to win eighty games, so I jumped on the over. Not surprisingly, the model often saw value in betting on Arizona early in the season. After all, the model saw a nearly .500 team at work, while oddsmakers were presumably still working from their seventy-two- or seventy-three-win scenario, making Arizona a .445 or .450 team. In fact, for April, per the implied odds from each of Arizona's games, oddsmakers expected the Diamondbacks to win 11.84 games, or 45.5 percent of its twenty-six games. By the end of May, however, the Diamondbacks were playing .545 ball, a pace they would improve upon over the rest of a season in which they would finish with ninety-four wins, equivalent to a .580 winning percentage. Predictably, due to the differences in pre-season projections, the model cleaned up on Arizona through May. At this point the lines started moving up against Arizona—but very slowly. In fact, it took until August until the implied lines finally projected Arizona to be better than a .500 team going forward. By the end of the year, the total implied wins for all Arizona lines totaled 80.75—just under .500—even though Arizona won 58 percent of its games. The oddsmakers may have adjusted to Arizona's better-than-expected performance as the year went on, but they never caught up to it.

Of course, the model didn't stay static either. It realized at each quarter-post of the season that Arizona was even better than my above-consensus pre-season projection. As a result, Arizona ended up being the model's top moneymaker, posting monthly gains in every month but August. Evidence like this shows that a savvy bettor doesn't have to be overly concerned with oddsmakers getting in front of the model, even when they have access to the same information.

*　　*　　*

Which brings us to another application for a model like this one. Rather than fear a model that differs from the consensus line, the largest of the industry's bookmakers should embrace their own proprietary models. Do you know why, when the odds for a game are first posted, the lines, regardless of the sport, are identical in Europe, on offshore Internet sites, and in Las Vegas? Because every outlet takes its cues from Las Vegas Sports Consultants instead of doing its own work. Can you imagine the investment bankers at Goldman Sachs taking their cues on how to price an upcoming initial public offering from a group of industry consultants, let alone the same ones who advise Morgan Stanley?

There's a reason for this, of course. The first is outsourcing of work in the name of cutting expenses, America's latest innovation and number-one export of the past thirty years. The inefficiencies associated with bloated companies, especially the conglomerates that dominated the Fortune 500 in the early 1980s, are legendary. One only needs to read *Barbarians at the Gate,* Bryan Burrough and John Helyar's seminal account of the 1988 takeover of RJR Nabisco, to get a picture of the entire era. There's a reason Gordon Gekko's "Greed is good" speech in *Wall Street* became an inspirational guide instead of the narrow morality play Oliver Stone probably intended it to be: It railed against inefficient corporations. The problem with that philosophy is that companies often take it too far. Put a bunch of cost-cutting executives together at a pizza company and, eventually, one will suggest getting rid of the cheese.

The second reason is that oddsmakers rightfully worry about creating arbitrage opportunities (that is, opportunities to create riskless profits) for other parties if their lines differ from everyone else's. For instance, at the sportsbook at the Wynn (a beautiful sportsbook with lavish appointments, by the way—try the veal; you won't be disappointed), bookmakers would fear making the Angels a +130 underdog and the Rangers a -140 favorite if every other book on the Strip, having taken their cues from the consultants, had the Rangers a -120 favorite and the Angels a +110 dog. Someone could bet the Rangers at one sportsbook and the Angels at the Wynn and lock in a profit before the game started. However, if in running the Wynn the manager had conviction that Tyler Chatwood, that night's starting pitcher for the Los Angeles Angels, was, by a wide margin, the worst starting pitcher of any regular in a five-man rotation in the majors during 2011, and that +130 odds (implying an Angels expected win percentage of 43.5 percent) still gave the house a 10 percent edge because the true odds—thanks to Chatwood's consistent "skill" at allowing lots of runs—were closer to one in three, he shouldn't care a bit. The best market-makers, when they have an edge, should never be afraid to buy at a price above where others are selling. Or, in the parlance of *Wall Street* (both the movie and the industry), "Take it and bid it."

The sportsbook at the Wynn is a division in an enterprise—
Wynn Resorts, Limited—valued at about $10 billion. (Another
huge presence in the Las Vegas sportsbook industry is the Las
Vegas Sands Corp., a company with a market capitalization in
excess of $30 billion.) It should have no fear at all of commit-
ting capital if it has an edge. Of course, there would be some
volatility to this division's earnings, but it always comes down
to this: Is it the kind of corporation, are you the kind of manager, do you have the type of stockholders that would rather
make 15 percent lumpy than 12 percent smooth?

If you answered 15 percent lumpy, you're more unique than
you might think, and you're the perfect candidate for running
a trading desk on Wall Street, managing a well-capitalized
sportsbook, or searching for investments for Warren Buffett's
Berkshire Hathaway.

You're also perfectly suited for investing in a baseball fund.

25

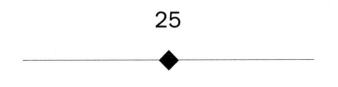

"Hey, Dad, Wanna Have a Catch?"

Aaron Sorkin writes brilliant dialogue. All of his characters, in movies or television shows, speak in compound sentences, are unfailingly witty, and are so adept at rapid-fire exchanges that it can be hard for the audience to keep pace. The first time I saw his cult-classic but short-lived TV series *Sports Night*, I thought, "Someone watched a lot of *Moonlighting* growing up."* Recently, Sorkin's sparkle has enlivened *The Social Network* and *Moneyball.*

---

*Moonlighting, along with *Late Night with David Letterman,* the movie *Fletch,* and the comic strip *Bloom County,* converged to form the four dominant influences on my life as a college student during the mid-1980s that essentially shaped my personality. That wasn't necessarily a good thing, since I would have liked to have had a girlfriend periodically. It's impossible to overstate how much I loved *Moonlighting* and Bruce Willis other than to say I spent my junior year in college drinking Seagram's Golden Wine Coolers and can still sing the commercial for them that Willis starred in. Well, that's an awkward disclosure. I should be going now.

At the end of *Moneyball*, Billy Beane, played by Brad Pitt, is shown the videotape of a minor league prospect in the Oakland A's system and says, "How can you not be romantic about baseball?" It's a curious line, because it's not in the book *Moneyball*, and Billy Beane never said it. Knowing that Sorkin crafts dialogue carefully, it's clear he put that line in the movie for effect; in fact, it's nearly the last line Pitt utters onscreen. My guess is that Sorkin put it in the movie as a counter to the common accusation that those who see the game of baseball only through statistics love their spreadsheets more than they love baseball. It's a cliché as common as the basement-dwelling baseball blogger.

After I graduated from college, I became friends with a guy who played center on the University of California basketball team in the mid-1980s. One of the nicest men you'll ever meet, David Butler was also a tremendous storyteller, precisely because he didn't seem to realize how great a storyteller he was. He had the unhurried delivery of a guy who grew up in a beach community, a knack for including the perfect details, and the requisite humility to regularly make himself the butt of the joke.

My favorite David Butler story took place in a Northern California Bay Area gym during one of the summers he was at Cal. One of the people he was playing with that day was his Cal teammate, point guard Kevin Johnson. Johnson would go on to several All-Star seasons in the NBA with the Phoenix Suns, and today he is the mayor of Sacramento, California, but at the time he and David were simply college teammates playing in a pickup game.

As David tells it there were two teams running a full-court game with another half-dozen or so sitting courtside that had "next." In the middle of the game, Johnson drove the lane as all five members of the other team converged on the basket. Johnson leapt toward the rim and, according to David, just kept rising until he threw down a thunderous dunk through all of the traffic. Effectively, David explained, he had just dunked on all five guys at the same time.

About a decade later, the six-foot-one-inch Johnson would drive the baseline in the NBA playoffs and dunk over the Houston Rockets center, seven-foot Hakeem Olajuwon, in a play so memorable it regularly appears on video montages of the greatest NBA dunks of all time. David says the one in the pickup game was better. Watching a highlight of the dunk over Olajuwon with a bunch of us during a televised Suns game in the late 1990s, David nonchalantly said, "That's not even his greatest dunk. Did I ever tell you guys about the time K.J. cleared out an entire gym with a dunk?" (Did I mention David had an unhurried delivery? This story was more than ten years old when he relayed it to us.) "So after he dunks on the entire team, pandemonium broke out. On the court, we started going crazy, falling

327

over each other and whooping it up. All the guys on the side of the gym waiting for 'next' though—they were even better. They just started shouting, 'WHOOOOOOOOOOOOOOOOAAAAA AAAAAAAAAAAA,' and then they picked up their gym bags and ran out of the gym, still screaming."

We asked him, "What do you mean, 'ran out of the gym'?"

"I mean exactly that. While the ball was still bouncing on the ground, they grabbed their stuff and ran out like there was nothing more to see here."

"What did you guys do?"

"We grabbed our bags and ran out of the gym, too. Seemed like a good idea. Didn't matter what the score was, that game was over."

In the top of the fifth inning of Game Five of the 2011 ALCS, Justin Verlander and the Detroit Tigers were in trouble, down three games to one and facing elimination if they lost again. Verlander had just allowed three straight batters to reach base on a walk and two hits. The second hit, by Josh Hamilton, plated Ian Kinsler, who had started the rally with a walk. This tied the game at two, and Texas had runners on first and third base with just one out. For Detroit, the situation was even worse than it looked, because the Tigers were without their two best relievers (due to their heavy workload the prior three days) and Verlander had already thrown nearly one hundred pitches. Detroit's season hinged on getting the next batter out without allowing a run.

Up to the plate for Texas came right-handed-hitting Michael Young. Young, a seven-time All-Star and former batting champ, was, at the time, a lifetime .304 hitter. By today's standards, he doesn't strike out much. Michael Young is a dangerous hitter, especially if your season hangs in the balance. Young got ahead in the count 1–0 and then 2–1, since Verlander couldn't quite spot his nearly hundred-mile-per-hour fastball. Verlander got a second strike to bring the count even to 2–2 on yet another fastball.

With the count 2–2 and the Tigers season hanging in the balance, Verlander threw the prettiest pitch I've ever seen. It was a curveball so devastating, it didn't just buckle Young's knees; it buckled his entire body. His knees, his torso, and his head all jerked, temporarily freezing Young as the ball crossed the *outside of the plate* for strike three. I've never seen a batter do a full-body twitch on a curveball that crossed over the outside of the plate. And this was Michael Young, an All-Star hitter who hit .338 in the regular season.

That wasn't a pitch; that was watching Van Gogh paint or Charlie Trotter cook.

By this point, I'd been watching baseball nearly nonstop for more than six months. I had created spreadsheets and downloaded data to the very limit of my non-engineering mind. I'd obsessed over my model and worked to convince my sports-gambling friends that the discoveries of the sabermetric community armed us with the tools to beat the oddsmakers.

The truth, however, is that baseball lay at the heart of my newest obsession, just like it did when completing the 1976 Topps set was the most important thing in my life. Just as it was when my brother and I vowed to replay the 1980 National League season with APBA. Just as it was when my heart broke as a fifteen-year-old when I didn't make the district all-star team. I started the 2011 baseball season watching games in a wheelchair, recently fired, separated from my family, racked with pain, and unable to sleep at night. The spreadsheets and the critical reasoning provided me with a perfect outlet to engage my mind, but numbers didn't drive my passion for baseball.

You don't need numbers to appreciate baseball, you don't have to be statistics-obsessed, and on the afternoon of October 13, during the top of the fifth inning of the ALCS, you didn't have to be rooting for the Tigers or Rangers, you didn't need to have a bet on the game, and, in fact, you didn't even need to be a baseball fan. When Justin Verlander struck out Michael Young, you only had to be a sports fan to do what I did: put your hand over your mouth, make some unintelligible sound, and then look for someone else to share it with as you pointed at the screen.

I wish I'd been in a sports bar with baseball fans and non–baseball fans alike that afternoon. If somehow we'd have been lucky enough to have David Butler with us, in honor of K.J. we would have certainly picked up our beers and run out of the bar.

So, despite the transparent purpose of Sorkin's line, as I watched *Moneyball* it still made me smile, because I get romantic about baseball. I'm not a purist who deplores the wild card and claims to hear the heartbeat of America every time Tony La Russa makes a double switch while surveying the emerald chessboard. As a spectator, I've been part of and embraced the changing sports scene in America as much as anyone. I love March Madness, I think fantasy baseball is more likely to save the game than hurt it, and I accept that the NFL is king among American sports fans. Casual sports fans don't plan their schedule around the World Series anymore. I get it, and it doesn't bother me.

I also understand that the era of immigrants coming to this country and adopting baseball as a way of being "American" is past. Today, if I overhear a son ask his dad, "Where are we watching the game this week?" I'm sure he's talking about a football game. If he calls on the phone and asks, "Did you see that game last night?" that question could be referring to a lot of things, but I'm realistic, and in this day and age there's a better chance it was a basketball game in March or a bowl game in January or an NFL game in November than anything else. But I'm just romantic enough about baseball that if you tell me the son said, "Hey, Dad, wanna have a catch?" I picture him wearing a glove, not holding a football.

And just maybe, the next time I hear a sports-obsessed friend of mine come to work on a Monday morning in September, announcing that he crushed the sportsbook yesterday, it won't be because he won a couple of football games but because he swept a slate of baseball games. After all, I'm even romantic about betting on baseball.

◆

A SUMMER IN VEGAS

My parents love to tell a story about my first exposure to televised baseball games: As a two-year-old, I was so familiar with the sound of a Phillies game filling our apartment that I had memorized the jingles of many Don Draper–era ads. In particular, beer commercials.

After putting me to bed, my mother would linger for a while before quietly easing out of my bedroom, assuming I had finally fallen asleep. She would then return to the adjacent room to watch television with my father. Generally, the evening passed without incident unless two events conspired to disrupt their peace—the Phillies were on TV and between innings a Schaefer beer commercial aired. The opening notes of a Schaefer commercial would cause me to jump up in my crib, grab the wooden slats, and sing, "Schaefer is the one beer to have, when you're having more than one."*

The description my parents give their grandchildren of sprinting across the room to silence the television whenever a beer commercial aired (there were no remote controls and thus no mute buttons in those days) never fails to send my daughters into giggling fits. Years later, I didn't remember the tune of the Schaefer jingle that enthralled me as a toddler, but I do remember one commercial that stuck with me from the countless hours of Phillies games I watched as a teenager. The late 1970s were marked by corporate CEOs taking to the airwaves to personally pitch their company and its products. Lee Iacocca, Orville Redenbacher, and Dave Thomas each successfully vouched for the quality of his company's offerings—in very different ways. Into this CEO-as-pitchman setting stepped Steve Wynn and, in the process, he ushered in an era of comedic irony.

When Resorts International opened the first U.S. casino outside of Nevada in Atlantic City in 1978, it brought a gaming destination within a short drive of the Philadelphia (and New York City) metropolitan area. Its success led to a building boom in Atlantic City and by the 1980s there were a half dozen dif-

---

*I found this one-minute-long commercial on YouTube and it is priceless in its ability to define an era. As if the slogan isn't great enough, when it appears on screen, "When You're Having More Than One" is italicized! On top of that, one of the verses urges drinkers to keep drinking Schaefer because "Schaefer pleasure doesn't fade, even when your thirst is done." Who is this target market? Binge drinkers and alcoholics? I'd love to hear the "one for the road" verse that got rejected.

ferent hotel-casinos in Atlantic City vying for the attention of the residents of the Philadelphia area. Steve Wynn, CEO of the Golden Nugget, starred in commercials in which he personally vouched for the high quality of his hotel. During one commercial, as Wynn, with noticeable pride, showed the viewer sweeping grand views of the lobby and hotel suites, Frank Sinatra entered the hotel. Wynn smoothly welcomed Sinatra and introduced himself: "I run this place." Sinatra, an Academy Award winner, had the look of a man exhausted from travel and resigned to yet another intrusion on his privacy. With a sigh he reached into his pocket, slipped a bill into Wynn's hand and told him, "You see I get enough towels."

It's hard to understand now how unexpected and hilarious the comeuppance of a CEO during a television commercial was at the time. Consider this: David Letterman, who elevated irony to an art form, didn't debut his talk show until 1982—a full year after Wynn's commercials. It's not a stretch to say that the wildly successful, nearly two-decade run of the "This is SportsCenter" commercial series traces its comedic roots to Steve Wynn's Golden Nugget ad with Frank Sinatra.

I saw this commercial so many times during Phillies broadcasts that, as a sixteen-year-old, I decided I wanted to work for Steve Wynn. While that never happened, in the summer of 2012, I attempted to become one of his bigger customers.

After I submitted the manuscript for *Trading Bases*, I received a call from my editor. "Joe," he said, "the response here has been strong. We wondered if you would consider going to Las Vegas during the season, perhaps with our marketing budget for the book, and betting on baseball games?"

He may as well have asked a Kardashian if she would consider making a sex tape.

Over the next few months I talked it over with my wife, sat down with some lawyers, and decided that after the 2012 All-Star Game, I'd go out to Las Vegas for two or three months and give it a trial run.* With an expansive, legalized bookmaking industry at my disposal, I'd have the necessary infrastructure in place to run a sizable baseball-centric hedge fund. I notified a small group of friends and family members of my plans and invited them, if interested, to invest in the fund. After spending fifteen years on Wall Street trading desks, I knew I'd have a number of friends interested in getting in on the action, in large part so they could get in on "the action." So I expected many of them to have interest in a baseball fund. What I didn't expect were the questions—or more accurately the type of questions—I subsequently received.

I was prepared to explain the model. How did I pick teams to bet on? What baseball statistics did I use in making selections? Who did I think was going to make the playoffs? Instead

---

*While I went to the city where time stands still thanks to the absence of windows and clocks, my wife and daughters spent part of their summer at Plymouth Plantation to study the pilgrims and on a Little House on the Prairie road trip through the Midwest, essentially going back in time. When our schedules realigned in October, I believe our friends and family were amazed we were still married in the year 2012.

I got questions like this: Can you send me the daily percentage changes in the fund's NAV since inception? What is the fund's turnover? Does it have a Sharpe Ratio? Are the historical returns leverage-free? One friend, a veteran of the venture-capital industry gave me what he called a "starter check" and summed up what a number of different investors were thinking when he said, "You may have found the holy grail of uncorrelated returns." Uncorrelated returns refer to the idea that it's extremely hard to find new investments that aren't linked, or correlated, to the factors that will influence the success of one's existing investments. The idea that one of Silicon Valley's savviest professional investors would consider an investment in a baseball-handicapping model a suitable alternative investment should make the industry of bookmaking in Las Vegas take notice and think about their future differently.

In July 2012, backed by friends and family members, I set off for Las Vegas to explore the feasibility of operating a baseball-focused hedge fund, to discover how large a scale such a fund could operate, and to see if the bookmaking industry could support an expansion to include investment funds. After three months of betting on baseball every day, hotel living, and struggling through one-hundred-degree heat that turned my arms and legs the color of bock beer, I'm convinced there is a huge opportunity to develop this industry, but only if the Las Vegas hotels and casinos change their operating philosophies.

The business of bookmaking in a modern casino reminds

me a lot of NASDAQ trading in the early 1990s. It's a clubby, extremely fragmented business, suspicious of every customer who walks in the door, and barely tolerated, let alone respected, among the other lines of business on the same premises. In both cases, the customer is eyed warily rather than embraced and the lack of customer service results in a missed opportunity. The same consolidation that came to NASDAQ market making twenty years ago is coming to the Las Vegas strip today, and if the casinos adopt the same customer-friendly advances that NASDAQ market makers did in the mid-1990s, a similar explosion in revenue and profits may follow as well.

For all of their well-documented faults, one of the things Wall Street investment banks do really well is understand the philosophies, goals, and motivations of its stock-trading customers. Within each firm on Wall Street this mandate is referred to as Know Your Customer, or KYC. Salesmen and -women covering a customer make it their job to know how much money the customer has under management, how many different PMs make portfolio decisions, whether or not the customer shorts stock, etc. They know who relies on technical indicators or if the customer adheres to a certain discipline such as value, momentum, or growth investing. Knowing this allows the salesperson to proactively offer trade ideas or shop the other side of different customer's orders and effortlessly increase business while *lowering* risk, when they're able to match two customers against each other. Contrast that to the stark reality of my experience: Over a three-month period, I made bets every single day in a number of different casinos (totaling nearly $3 million) introduced myself to the heads of operations via e-mail, learned the names of managers, filled out W-9 forms at multiple locations, and required management approval for transactions almost daily. Not once did anyone proactively ask me a single question about my intentions or what they could do to get me to do more business at their establishment. In what industry does an organization not want to find out how they can better service their big customers? To be clear, I'm not talking about nightclub passes or free meals; I wanted a sportsbook to know my style so I could do more business with them when it was beneficial for both of us. Paying close attention to the customer also benefits the bookmaker in another way. Knowing which customer wins, or in Wall Street parlance "has alpha," allows a bookmaker to interact far more intelligently in the marketplace.

Here's another problem I had: I felt vulnerable constantly walking around with enough money to get boxer Floyd Mayweather and his entourage bottle service at any club in town. Can you imagine the stock-trading customers of Wall Street's investment banks running all over downtown Manhattan from broker to broker, paying and collecting cash every time they bought or sold a share of stock? That's exactly what I had to do in Las Vegas. If casinos adopted Wall Street's prime brokerage model, that logistical nightmare could be eliminated. Prime brokers act as the custodian of money and securities; casinos could provide that same custodial service, and make money, because it's a recurring, fee-based business. In other words, it's grafting a 12 percent smooth business to a 15 percent lumpy one.

America's tolerance of gambling, along with state governments' need for new sources of revenue, has increased tremendously in the last couple of decades. Thirty years ago, only Nevada and New Jersey had casinos in its states. Today, more than two-thirds of the states in America have casinos. Sports betting shows every sign of following that trend. In 2012, New Jersey Governor Chris Christie—a Republican with apparent presidential aspirations, no less—brazenly challenged a federal law when he announced sports betting would be allowed in licensed New Jersey establishments. While bets have yet to be legally placed in New Jersey, the resulting legal battles will lay the groundwork for eventual legalization. Based on subsequent bills in the state legislatures of New York and California, other states are keenly watching this development.

Poker exploded in popularity a little more than a decade ago and, judging from the huge increases in floor space devoted to poker rooms, became a new profit center and area of revenue growth for casinos. The surge in poker's popularity is commonly attributed to the emergence of the "hole cam," a camera installed at every seat on a poker table which allowed televisions viewers to see a player's facedown, or "hole" cards. However, the hole cam isn't the reason tens of thousands of people took up poker worldwide, some of them moving to Las Vegas full-time. The hole cam may have been the *catalyst*, but the *reason* for the surge of interest in poker was that viewers were captivated by the idea that they could make money through critical reasoning. Sportsbooks, and the casinos that run them across Las Vegas, should take note—especially the fact that in poker the casino doesn't even compete against the customer, it merely facilitates the action—and do everything in their power to transform the bookmaking business to leverage that appeal of critical reasoning. They are sitting on a potentially huge new line of revenue; they just need to look to Wall Street for the practices that will let them best capitalize on the opportunity.

The model got off to a tremendous start in 2012, and the previews I wrote for every team paid off in terms of season-long futures bets (eight out of twelve winners)* and a consistent run of daily winnings the first three months of the year. The second half of the year was a different story as July turned out to be the worst month the model ever had, and while August was profitable, September saw a return of those profits as well. Although the path of results for 2012 weren't satisfying given the

*All 2012 team previews are at http://tradingbases.squarespace.com and the futures bets at http://tradingbases.squarespace.com/blog/2012/4/4/2012-preview-final-projected-standings.html.

move to Vegas in July, overall the model had a nice year and held up very well relative to its peers as evidenced by the results of an online season-long competition.

WagerMinds.com, a sports handicapping website that allows users to prove their handicapping skills among a community of amateur and professional handicappers, ran a season-long contest during the 2012 regular season. During that time, I submitted nearly nine hundred of the model's picks under the Springsteen-inspired username Magic Rat and finished 12th overall out of more than two thousand contestants.[*]

Here are the monthly results for the 2012 season, including futures and playoffs:

April	6.38 percent
May	13.60 percent
June	3.21 percent
July	-12.64 percent
August	2.77 percent
September	-3.45 percent
Total regular season results, compounded monthly	+8.12 percent
Futures positions	+3.60 percent
Postseason results	+2.05 percent
Total 2012 season return	+14.01 percent (Regular season [+11.72 percent] compounded with postseason)

[*]http://www.wagerminds.com/Contests/2012-MLB-Picks-Contest

From April to October, the 2012 baseball season provided great stories for baseball fans in many different cities. The Baltimore Orioles (who the model never embraced) and the Oakland A's (who, by mid-season, the model insisted would overtake the Rangers to win the AL West) shocked even their own fans with post-season berths. Miguel Cabrera of the Detroit Tigers became the first Triple Crown winner in forty-five years while Los Angeles Angels rookie Mike Trout's talents electrified fans and invoked memories of Mickey Mantle. Together they helped ignite one of the most intense arguments ever between traditional journalists and sabermetric analysts over who should have been named the AL MVP, which was ultimately awarded to Miguel Cabrera. And, of course, I got to watch firsthand as the fans in San Francisco celebrated the Giants' second world championship in three years.

I watched even more baseball in 2012 than in 2011, spent so much time in buffet lines in Las Vegas that I began to muse about things like "if someone invented mimosa-flavored toothpaste, I'd totally buy that." After three months, I had become so inured to the Vegas lifestyle that by the time I got back to San Francisco after the regular season ended, I kept thinking people were trying to pass me counterfeit money if it didn't have glitter on it. As the baseball playoffs started, I was surprised and thrilled to find out my oldest daughter, age 8, was interested in the post-season fate of the San Francisco Giants. Eager to further her interest, I chose my words carefully when providing in-game play-by-play. This is a girl who was inconsolable when Gryffindor lost a Quidditch match to Hufflepuff during Harry Potter's third year at Hogwarts. I didn't want to snuff out her budding interest in baseball by exposing her too soon to the unique disappointment being a baseball fan can bring.

Then again, it's experiencing that pain that can make someone a fan for life.

From 1985 to 1994, I lived in the Washington, D.C., area and became familiar with a specific banner perpetually hung at RFK Stadium. The first time I remember seeing it was at a Bruce Springsteen concert in the summer of 1985. While introducing "Glory Days," Bruce paid homage to legendary pitcher Tom Seaver who had won his three hundredth game the day before and acknowledged a banner hanging from a railing that read, BASEBALL IN '87. As the years passed, and the organization working to bring an MLB franchise to the D.C. area made little progress, the wording changed to "Baseball in '88" then "'89" and so on until the organizers realized it was simpler (and less embarrassing) to settle on "Baseball in D.C." For the next few years, no matter if you were at a concert, a Redskins game, or a World Cup match at RFK Stadium, the sign was always on display.*

The movement to get an MLB franchise back to Washing-

---

*Tony Kornheiser, a *Washington Post* sports columnist at the time, summed up its ubiquity perfectly when he wrote, after attending a World Cup match between Mexico and Norway, that even though he couldn't understand the foreign-language signs of the fans from Mexico, he was "pretty sure...there was one in Spanish that said 'Baseball in D.C.'"

ton for the first time since the Senators relocated to Texas in 1972 suffered a major setback when MLB awarded new franchises to Miami and Colorado for the 1993 season, and a seemingly fatal blow when Tampa and Arizona were the choices for baseball's last expansion in 1998. Potential ownership groups in Washington persisted however, and after years of torturous negotiations with the owners of the Florida Marlins, the Boston Red Sox, the Baltimore Orioles, and the City Council of the District of Columbia, the Montreal Expos relocated to Washington after the 2004 season ended. On April 4, 2005, nearly twenty years after I recall seeing the first public display of ambition, "Baseball in D.C." became a reality.

Seven and a half years later, shortly after midnight on Friday, October 12, 2012, I thought to myself, "Be careful what you wish for."

The Washington Nationals had the best record in baseball during the 2012 season, winning ninety-eight games while losing just sixty-four. That marked the first time the franchise had had a winning record since relocating from Montreal, and during the year, attendance at Nationals' home games increased more than 20 percent. After management launched a marketing campaign during spring training around their recently coined word for the team's combination of youthful talent and confidence, "Natitude" became a constant presence on Twitter and impossible to avoid during a Nationals' telecast. As a Phillies fan, I found this utterly annoying. Entering the 2012 season, the Phillies were the five-time defending champions of the NL East, and other than some classless comments directed at the Philadelphia organization from its former right fielder and current Nationals outfielder, Jayson Werth, to Phillies fans the Nationals were most notable for one thing: It was easier for many Philadelphia-area fans to get tickets to a Phillies game when they played the Nationals in Washington than it was to get tickets to a home game at Citizens Bank Park. For the last few years, it seemed a healthy chunk of Washington's attendance was made up of Phillies backers. Therefore, I didn't think there were many true baseball fans in the D.C. area.

Although, or perhaps because the spring training bravado turned out to be spot-on, the Nationals' success on the field in 2012 irked me all season. Moments after the Nationals were eliminated from the playoffs in the early morning of October 13, Matt Swartz summed up the feeling of Phillies fans everywhere when he tweeted, "Our long Nationals nightmare is over!"

I laughed, considered retweeting the comment, but ultimately embraced that sentiment for no more than a minute or two. Then I looked back at the television screen and considered what had just happened on the field. The St. Louis Cardinals, down 6–0 after three innings, had completed yet another improbable post-season comeback by scoring four runs in the top of the ninth inning despite being down to their last strike five different times during the inning. With no warning at all, the

team with the best record in baseball had gone from a seemingly assured place in the National League Championship Series to elimination. Nationals Park looked like a funeral home
complete with vacant stares, a lifeless procession, and, yes,
even tears. Instantly, I had empathy for the entire fan base. Although all season I accused the locals of noticing the Nationals
only once the team started winning, as they filed out of Nationals Park I thought, there is no such thing as a fair-weather
fan of the Washington Nationals right now. Maybe many in the
crowd *had* got caught up in the local excitement of the 2012
season and attended their first games this season, heck, maybe
someone on a date attended their first game that night, but even
if they came to baseball this year with a detached coolness,
they're in love now.

It's the kind of love that springs from the ashes of pain and,
to my mind, is unique to being a baseball fan. Nationals fans
now know what it's *really* like to be a baseball fan. They know
what it's like to have been a Cubs fan in 2003, a Red Sox fan in
1986 and 2003, a Phillies fan in 1993, a Rangers fan in 2011, and
so on.* They'll be despondent for the near future, many won't
watch another minute of the post-season, and they'll wonder
how they let themselves get so caught up in the fortunes of the
local *baseball* team. Those fans who are parents of eight-, nine-,
and ten-year-olds might be spending a lot of time consoling

---

*To capitalize on the hottest trend in publishing, I thought about naming this book, *50
Shades of Shea, the Exquisitely Tortured History of the New York Mets Fan Base.*

their children the next day, explaining disappointment, while noting to themselves that this type of emotional devastation never seems to accompany a Redskins loss.

As baseball fans who have suffered excruciating defeats know, at some point, though, as the winter wears on, the crushing disappointment subsides, and even if they swore, shortly after the devastating loss that they'd never let themselves get *that* caught up in the fortunes of a baseball team, they'll start thinking about spring training. They'll start thinking about Bryce Harper and Stephen Strasburg, and they'll realize they don't hate themselves for falling in love with the Nationals. No, they hate Pete "Bleeping" Kozma for his opposite field, two-strike hit. And they'll think, "You know what, there's no reason the Nationals can't win a hundred games this year." And they'll start talking to their kids about what games they want to attend in 2013, and in the end what really happened on the night of October 12 wasn't that the St. Louis Cardinals once again came back from near-playoff elimination, it's that an entire generation of lifelong baseball fans were formed in the Washington, D.C., area.

From one lifelong baseball fan to another, I say "Welcome aboard. We have a lot to talk about."

ACKNOWLEDGMENTS

After having gotten to the playoffs by going 21–8 down the stretch to overcome a ten-game deficit in the Wild Card standings, after winning playoff series against the two teams in the National League with the best records during the regular season, and then after twice overcoming a two-run deficit in its last at bat during Game 6 of the World Series, the St. Louis Cardinals won Game 7 of the 2011 World Series on a Friday night in late October. That same week, I learned that the rights to this book had been purchased by a major U.S. publisher.

There was no doubt in my mind which was the more improbable event.

Four months earlier, without advanced notice, I dropped two sample chapters onto the desk of my wife, a former magazine editor. Realizing that I was trying to write something far more ambitious than the family Christmas letter I annually needed help constructing, she recommended that I get professional help from an expert in the field of nonfiction writing. She suggested I take an online course at Media Bistro. It was a brilliant suggestion because the instructor of my nonfiction book writing course, Leslie Sharpe, a professor of nonfiction writing at Columbia University, not only tirelessly aided me as the concept for this book took shape but she also happened to be a rabid baseball fan with roots dating back to the Shibe Park–era Phillies. She helped me get over my embarrassment of being a baseball nerd and encouraged me instead to let the reader see my passion for both the sport and the numbers behind it.

I also took a nonfiction book proposal course from Mollie Glick, where I not only learned how to properly construct and target a book proposal, but where I also learned an enormous amount about the publishing industry. More than one industry professional told me my proposal did not look like the work of a first-time author. For that I have Mollie to thank.

By the time Labor Day 2011 arrived I had completed both my courses, had a finished book proposal, and thanks to eight months of physical therapy, walked with just a mild limp. I figured it was time to get back into the workplace and was about to start looking for a job in finance when another improbable twist of fate took place.

During a weekend get-together in Las Vegas with two friends from New York, I disclosed that I had an idea for a book and showed them the first chapter from the proposal. When asked what my next step was, I told them I needed to find a literary agent. Deric Senne then floored me when he said, "My former next-door neighbor is an agent. Do you want me to show her the proposal?"

Deric has been a good friend of mine for fifteen years; he would help me in any situation as he is a tremendously loyal friend. That said, there is no one in New York City I would have suspected less of knowing a literary agent. Not to put too fine a point on it but he has an arcade in his penthouse apartment. It turns out Deric not only knew an agent, his former neighbor was Laura Dail, who runs the literary agency that bears her name. Nothing could have been more fortuitous, for Laura instantly championed my proposal. During our first phone call when I told her my plans for the book were to try to market it to a niche publisher of arcane baseball material, she instructed me to aim much higher. Laura saw the potential for a mass market book and she has expertly guided me every step of the way to publication. I can't thank her enough for the chance she took on a complete novice.

From the first time Stephen Morrow interviewed me on the phone and told me Dutton had an interest in the manuscript, I hoped Dutton would win the rights to the book, he'd be my editor, and I'd become a Penguin Group author. Over the next year, I never questioned that initial instinct as Stephen could not have been a better editor for a first-time author. Every suggestion he made resulted in a better book, and most assuredly made me look like a better writer.

I knew Jared Dillian and Shilpi Somaya Gowda as a former coworker and classmate respectively, which served as yet another fortuitous development because each of them had recently published their first books. They were both very helpful in advising me what to look for in an agent, a publisher, and an editor.

As if my wife, Caitlin Sims, doesn't bring enough to the table that is our marriage, she also has provided me with the greatest in-laws any spouse could ever hope to have. Not only have Crystal and Dick Sims never questioned why their son-in-law hasn't had a job in two years, watches endless baseball, and spends far too much time in Las Vegas, they facilitated my completion of the book by allowing me to use their house in the mountains as a two-week retreat when my submission deadline approached.

Caitlin and my brother, Doug Peta, used their professional editing and writing skills, respectively, to polish many versions of the manuscript before it ever made it to the publisher. They improved so many areas of my writing through corrections and suggestions that I cringe at what the reception for the manuscript would have been at Dutton if Caitlin and Doug hadn't protected me from myself.

Dave Houser, Scott Shimamoto, and Tim Ranzetta, all longtime friends who I've bonded with over baseball games, read early versions of this book's initial chapters and enthusiastically encouraged me to keep writing. Dave, in particular, had a great ear for tone and helped me find the right voice early in the process.

Before my wife ever saw the first chapters I dropped on her desk, I showed them to my best friend since college, Matt Lugar. Matt's review was crucial because as he's told me innumerable times over the years, "I'm not a baseball guy." If my numbers-heavy passages fell flat with him, I may have lost the nerve to keep writing. I knew his support would be unwavering, but when he told me he went to the standings during the 2011 season to find out how many runs Tampa Bay was scoring, he unwittingly provided me with all the encouragement I needed.

Far too many times during the writing of this book, my daughters, Lily and Calista, had to endure the bewildering, unsolicited reply of "I'm working" when they'd wander into our family room to find me in front of the computer with the television tuned to a baseball game. One of the little joys in my life is when they shout down my "root, root, root for the Phillies" during a seventh-inning stretch and replace my lyrics with support for their hometown Giants. Along with Caitlin, they provided me with the inspiration to see this project to its completion.

It's important to note that none of my ideas pertaining to

building a sabermetric-based model would have been remotely possible without the decades of research and work done by the pioneers in the baseball analytics industry—work that they have largely disseminated into the public domain. Throughout the book, I attempted to name as many individuals as possible responsible for specific areas of research. Broadly, however, there are three writers whose work and writing skills I admire so much I never fail to read every word they publish. Aaron Schatz may write about football, but he's never hesitated to cite the pioneers of baseball research as his inspiration. In turn, his critical reasoning has inspired me to apply some of the principles of his football research back to baseball. Matt Swartz never fails to captivate me with his economics-based logic when writing about baseball, and he's a Phillies fan to boot. Joe Sheehan is, for my money, the best baseball writer in America. Before I ever started writing the first chapters of this book, Joe tweeted a link to an essay I wrote about taking my youngest daughter to her first baseball game. The response to the essay was so positive that it gave me the idea to possibly merge the gambling-related e-mails I was sending to my friends with that essay and use it as the basis for something larger.

Caitlin supported me in this endeavor beyond any reasonable measure—from nursing me back to health, to raising our daughters alone while I was in New York, Las Vegas, or sequestered in the mountains of California. I can never thank her enough or repay her properly.

Finally, my mother bought me my first pack of baseball cards when I was six, she drove me to countless games and practices over the years, and endured endless father-son-brother discussions about the Phillies at the dinner table. My father not only fulfilled the American ideal of father-son bonding by playing catch with me but also hit me fungoes into the dying light of many summer nights so that I could pretend I was the Phillies center fielder. Martha Joan and Erminio Joseph Peta instilled the proper appreciation for baseball in me at an early age and without their guidance this book never happens.

INDEX